CAMILLA
— And —
CHARLES

CAROLINE GRAHAM

CAMILLA
~ And ~
CHARLES

THE LOVE STORY

JOHN BLAKE

Published by John Blake Publishing Ltd,
3, Bramber Court, 2 Bramber Road,
London W14 9PB, England

www.blake.co.uk

First published in hardback in 2005

ISBN 1 84454 167 3

British Library Cataloguing-in-Publication Data:

A catalogue record for this book is available from the British Library.

Design by www.envydesign.co.uk

Printed in Great Britain by Creative Print and Design

1 3 5 7 9 10 8 6 4 2

© Text copyright Caroline Graham

Papers used by John Blake Publishing are natural, recyclable products
made from wood grown in sustainable forests. The manufacturing
processes conform to the environmental regulations of the country of
origin.

Every attempt has been made to contact the relevant copyright-
holders, but some were unobtainable. We would be grateful if the
appropriate people could contact us.

For mutti and Daddy

Acknowledgements

When I was first 'introduced' to Camilla Parker Bowles more than ten years ago, her friends asked me to 'set the record straight' about the real woman behind the public image. At the time, precious little was known about Camilla. Diana had just co-operated with Andrew Morton on his devastating exposé about the royal marriage and I was commissioned to write the true story about the woman Diana famously branded 'the Rottweiler'. Of course, at the time, I had no idea how much her life – or mine – would change in the intervening years.

At the start, Camilla's friends were defensive and protective. They felt hurt by the way 'Diana's camp', as they called supporters of the late Princess of Wales, had portrayed Camilla as a vindictive and cruel woman who had purposely set out to destroy the 'fairytale' wedding of the century. In their minds, the marriage of Charles and Diana was never the dream it was portrayed as being. And Camilla was never the evil villainess ruthlessly painted in the press.

As time went on, those within Camilla's closest circle began to truly open up about the real woman behind the lurid headlines. What emerged was a picture of a woman who had been misrepresented and yet who, to this day, has never spoken publicly to say a word in her own defence. Instead, it was left to her friends to give her version of events; to tell the real story of the love affair which began so inconspicuously on a muddy polo field in 1971 and which has endured to this day.

Today, Camilla's role in the life of Charles, Prince of Wales, is beyond doubt. She has stood loyally by his side as his confidante, lover and best friend for more than three decades. The stunning announcement that he is to make her his bride would have been unthinkable all those years ago when, in a series of furtive meetings, I first met those closest to her. For obvious reasons, many of those people spoke to me only on condition of anonymity. They know who they are and to them, for their loyalty and help over all these years, I say a heartfelt 'thank you'.

I am also grateful to Stuart Higgins for providing invaluable help and assistance. Without him, this book would never have been written. Thanks must also go to my editor, Peter Wright, for his support in allowing me to work on this project. I am also indebted to Kelvin MacKenzie for coming up with the idea for the book.

John Blake, my publisher, and his terrific team, including Rosie Ries and Michelle Signore, have been with me on this journey since the beginning. They have worked tirelessly to bring Camilla's story into the public arena, a story which for many years remained untold.

The relationship between Camilla Parker Bowles and Prince Charles has not been the easiest one to tell, or, at times, to understand. In the beginning, being the lone voice supporting Camilla against Diana's slick publicity machine was a daunting, and often uncomfortable, position to be in. When the engagement announcement was released, it was extraordinary to read the tidal wave of support from around the globe. Such encouragement would have been unthinkable a few years ago to everyone, not least Camilla!

Hers has been a love affair which has endured, against all odds, for more than three decades. For years, Camilla was content to live in the shadows, preferring to take the insults and unfair criticism of her role in the Prince's life rather than defend herself and risk damaging the institution of the monarchy she so admires and the man she so truly loves.

She is someone who knows full well how harshly she has been judged, as the love triangle between Charles, Camilla and Diana unfolded in such a dramatic fashion, often in a manner beyond her control. But now she has emerged on to the world stage as a woman rightfully entitled to stand proudly beside the man she loves, and has always loved. As she becomes Prince Charles's wife, she has finally accepted the role in life destiny always had in store for her.

This is her story.

Caroline Graham
Los Angeles, March 2005

Contents

Introduction

Prince Charles got down on one knee. In his pocket, nestled in a satin-lined box, sat the priceless ten-carat diamond and platinum engagement ring that had once belonged to his beloved grandmother. His heart was filled with anticipation, excitement but not, he later told friends, 'one moment of doubt', as he was about to propose to the only woman he had ever loved; a woman he describes as 'my rock, my life' – Camilla Parker Bowles.

Twenty-four years earlier, Charles had proposed to a very different young woman, the blushing Diana Spencer. Then he had been filled with fear and trepidation. In his head, he believed he was doing the 'right thing' for his family and his country, but his heart told him otherwise. Despite the fanfare that greeted that announcement, Charles had grave reservations. The young Diana Spencer appeared 'perfect' for him. But he was filled with nagging doubts and wondered if he could ever love this young girl as deeply as he cared for his first true love.

Time, and the course of history, would take a deadly

toll. The 'fairytale' marriage of Charles and Diana would disintegrate in the full glare of the harsh public spotlight. Both Charles and Camilla would be vilified for their role in destroying the fairytale. Diana would meet her own sad, lonely end in a Paris tunnel sitting by the side of her playboy lover, going to her grave believing that her husband had never truly loved her.

The tragic love triangle of Charles, Camilla and Diana has been one played out on the world's stage for more than two decades. It is a story so full of Shakespearean drama and tragedy that few have ever known the truth behind the headlines.

But, as Charles proposed at his estate in Birkhall, Scotland, on a grey and windswept day in January 2005, he knew, for the first time in his life, that he was doing the right thing.

As he looked up into the eyes of the woman he had adored, mostly in secret, for so long, he knew the final chapter of one of history's greatest love stories was about to be written.

As he whispered the words 'Will you marry me?' to his great love, he never had a doubt what the answer would be. As she replied: 'Of course, my darling,' he gently slipped the ring on to her finger. It was a moment he had longed for over the years. Finally, he would get the chance to walk side-by-side in life with the woman he truly loved.

For Camilla, the proposal marked the end of a life lived in the shadows. From the moment of their first meeting in 1971, she had always known she and Charles were destined to be together. What she could not have been aware of at the time was how their love would change history and how she would be forever known as 'the King's mistress'.

For both, the engagement was the end of a long story of

heartbreak. But it also signified a new beginning; the start of their 'official' life together, as husband and wife.

When the stunning news of their engagement was released to the press on 10 February 2005, the woman whose name was once greeted with howls of protest, instead, was greeted with acceptance, and, in most cases, genuine affection. The reason for this was that, once being famously branded by Diana as 'the Rottweiler' and 'the third person in my marriage', Camilla had, above all, stayed true to her dream of one day being married to the man she loved; a man who just happened to be the future King of England.

For Camilla Parker Bowles, a girl born to obscurity, it was a remarkable day. She would later describe the proposal as 'the happiest moment of my life'.

Yet despite the headlines and the lurid stories, very little is known about the woman whose love almost destroyed a dynasty and who brought the House of Windsor to its knees. Camilla has rarely spoken about her life or her love for Prince Charles, which has spanned three decades.

This is her story, the story of a remarkable woman who risked, and nearly lost, all for the man she loved. Above all, this is a saga of how true love finally won through.

The Wife He Always Wanted

The official announcement was simple and took the world by surprise: 'It is with great pleasure that the marriage of HRH the Prince of Wales and Mrs Camilla Parker Bowles is announced. It will take place on Friday, 8 April 2005, at Windsor Castle. [The venue was, of course, subsequently changed to the Guildhall in Windsor, as it was felt that licensing the Castle would cause too much disruption]. The Prince of Wales has said, "Mrs Parker Bowles and I are absolutely delighted. It will be a very special day for us and our families." Mrs Parker Bowles will use the title HRH the Duchess of Cornwall after marriage. It is intended that Mrs Parker Bowles should use the title the Princess Consort when the Prince accedes to the throne. The wedding will be a largely private occasion for family and friends. There will be a civil ceremony at Windsor Castle. There will subsequently be a service of prayer and dedication in St George's Chapel at which the Archbishop of Canterbury will preside.'

Almost simultaneously, statements were released from both the Queen and Prince William and Prince Harry. Buckingham Palace issued a statement from the Queen saying: 'The Duke of Edinburgh and I are very happy that the Prince of Wales and Mrs Parker Bowles are to marry.' The announcement from the boys said: 'We are both very happy for our father and Camilla and we wish them all the luck in the future.'

Later that night, at a reception at Windsor Castle, a radiant Charles and Camilla stepped in front of the cameras for the first time as a betrothed couple. Wearing an ankle-length fuchsia dress by Jean Muir, Camilla admitted: 'I am very happy. I'm only just coming back down to earth.' Her beaming groom-to-be said: 'I'm very happy and very excited.'

What wasn't evident from the couple's composed, but clearly ecstatic, first appearance together were the months of behind-the-scenes machinations and careful negotiations which led to the historic announcement.

In fact, the engagement story began with a blazing row some three months earlier, days before the wedding of Charles's godson, Edward Van Cutsem to Lady Tamara Grosvenor, the Duke of Westminster's daughter. Charles had insisted on sitting next to Camilla during the ceremony in Chester Cathedral, but when he was told protocol forbade that from happening, he was not happy.

His private secretary Sir Michael Peat told the Prince that appearing beside his mistress at such a formal royal occasion would be 'unacceptable'. The comment provoked a tirade from Charles.

'The Prince just exploded,' said a former royal aide. 'At that point, Diana had been dead for seven years, and Charles and Camilla had been together, living as man and wife. For Charles, it was the straw that broke the camel's back. In private, Camilla could be by his side, but she was to be publicly humiliated by being seated far from him at this wedding, at the back of the church. Charles responded by saying neither he nor Camilla would attend the wedding if those were the ground rules. But that was what finally spurred the Queen into action.

'She is 79 and is planning a series of events to celebrate her 80th birthday in 2006. The situation between Charles and Camilla was something that had to be resolved. For the first time, the question of marriage was formally raised within the court and with high-ranking government ministers. The Queen saw the situation as one which needed to be resolved. She is in good health, but she is not getting any younger. Her idea of a nightmare would be if she died and Charles still had Camilla as a mistress. That would provoke a constitutional crisis. It was the Queen who called a meeting and demanded that the situation be formalised. It was madness for it to continue as it was.'

Throughout January 2005, meetings were discreetly held between Charles and those who had to be 'sounded' out about a marriage, including Prime Minister Tony Blair and the Archbishop of Canterbury, Dr Rowan Williams. The raw grief of the public over Diana's death had waned and both men gave their complete approval for the union. But there was still the question of Camilla's 'royal' role: she could not assume the title of Princess of Wales, which would be forever associated with Diana.

A courtier said: 'Charles has always been the one pushing for marriage. Camilla was actually content for the situation to remain as it always was, with her on the sidelines supporting the man she loves. But Charles was determined she should have a proper title and a proper role. He wants her by his side, both now while he is Prince of Wales and also when he assumes the throne.

The negotiations took months and became quite heated. Charles was determined Camilla should be given the title of "Her Royal Highness", a title which was stripped from Diana when she divorced. Only immediate members of the royal family can be given the HRH title, but Charles was insistent that Camilla should be afforded that honour.

'It was obvious to everyone close to the negotiations that a new title had to be brought in which would give Camilla the position afforded the wife of the future king, but one which would not antagonise the public, particularly that section of the public who still blamed Camilla for Diana's unhappiness and, ultimately, her demise. That is why the title of Duchess of Cornwall was chosen. It is an ancient title and one which Diana never used, but it is the title Camilla will use after the wedding. When Charles accedes to the throne, she will be the Princess Consort, never the Queen. Diana once famously said she never thought she would ever be Queen but Camilla has equally never sought to be Queen. As Princess Consort, she will have all the entitlements of a queen but she will not be crowned as such.'

Lord St John of Fawsley, a friend of the couple said: 'The marriage does not present any constitutional problems. Once the Queen gave her permission, the Prince of Wales, as a widower, was free to marry who he wished. There is nothing in the constitution which forbids the Prince marrying a divorced person. The title the Duchess of Cornwall is appropriate. To most of us, the Princess of Wales will always be Diana. Hostile feeling would have been raised had Camilla been called that. But nomenclature is not of primary importance – it is the fact that Prince Charles needs a supportive wife and a publicly recognised one to assist him in discharging his public duties. Divorce that was shocking in the days of Edward and Mrs Simpson simply does not register today. Things have moved on considerably. Rather than undermining the monarchy, this wedding could make it more relevant because Prince Charles and Camilla are in the same situation as many of the people over whom they will one day rule.'

Friends of the couple say Camilla never wanted the title of 'Queen'. One woman who has known her since childhood said: 'Camilla never pushed to be Queen; in fact, she never pushed to be married. Of course, marriage was something she always longed for, for the reason that she wanted to be formally recognised as Charles's partner in life. But titles mean little to her. She simply wants his happiness. One day – and that day may be a long time coming – the Queen will die and he will ascend to the throne. She will be there for him and she would always be there for him. Being married will simply make his position easier and that is something she wishes for. You are not going to see Camilla suddenly emerging big-time onto the world stage. She has never wanted fame and glory in the way Diana craved it. She just wants to be by Charles's side and if this is what he wants, and a marriage makes it easier for both of them to live their lives together, then that is what she wants.'

The acceptance of Prince William and Prince Harry were of 'paramount' importance to Charles. When Diana died, both were still young. But, in the intervening years, both children have seen how Camilla has supported their father. While there has been speculation that Harry has found it more difficult to come to terms with the role Camilla plays in their father's life, friends say that is simply not the case.

Said one friend: 'William and Harry both adore their

5

father. They have both spent a lot of time in Camilla's company. You have to understand that William and Harry are both now grown men and leading their own full lives and their main wish is for their father to be happy and fulfilled. Camilla gives him happiness and joy. William actively supported the marriage plans. Harry is still young and headstrong but even he gave the marriage his full approval when he first heard about it. They have met Camilla on numerous occasions and they are very fond of her. She is a stabilising influence on Charles's life and they see how happy she makes him. Neither one of them raised a single objection when he told them he wanted to marry Camilla. They both knew this was on the cards and they both gave their full approval. Camilla had a private luncheon with both boys when she asked them if they supported the marriage plans. They both immediately said "Yes". They are much closer to Camilla than people think. When Harry got into trouble with drugs, Camilla was one of the first people who called him. She had her own experience of drugs because her son Tom was caught with cocaine, so she knows the problems young people have being surrounded by this sort of thing. Harry truly loved her and he loves her because she has always been there for him and his father.'

The Queen also gave her 'unequivocal' support for the marriage. After spurring Charles on into formalising the relationship, she took the unprecedented step of inviting Camilla to Sandringham during the royal family's Christmas celebrations.

'It was kept quiet, but Camilla was there and she was accepted as part of the family,' one source said. 'The Queen is a pragmatist and she, more than anyone, wanted to clear the decks and have this relationship set on an even keel. Where once she might have been dismissive or disapproving of Camilla, she has formed a close bond with her over the years. Camilla has always played by the rules and has never said or done anything to embarrass the family. The Queen respects that.

'One of the biggest signs of her approval was the engagement ring. It was a ring the Queen Mother wore constantly. It was given to the Queen Mother in 1926 by her husband King George VI to celebrate the birth of the Queen. When the Queen Mother died, the ring was returned to the royal collection. It was the Queen's to give and it was she who suggested to Charles that this priceless family heirloom be given to Camilla. When Charles became engaged to Diana, he purchased her sapphire engagement ring from Asprey's. But when he told his mother he was going to propose to Camilla, she thought it would be a unifying gesture for Camilla to receive one of the family's heirlooms. The simple fact she gave her mother's ring to Camilla speaks volumes about the esteem she has for her. The Queen knows this marriage is for keeps.'

For Camilla, the news of her engagement was far less complicated to handle. She telephoned her father Major Bruce Shand, who immediately approved. He would later tell the press: 'Being Prince Charles's father-in-law will be fine. I am looking forward to the wedding.'

Her children Tom and Laura were equally delighted. Tom, a food writer, said he was 'thrilled' by her announcement. Laura told a friend: 'I just want my mother to be happy. This is good for everyone.'

Camilla's final call was to her ex-husband Andrew, who was on holiday with his new wife in the Caribbean. 'Good luck, old bean' was his response.

Finally, Charles and Camilla were to get their dream wedding. Unlike the wedding of Charles and Diana which was seen by millions around the world, the 8 April affair would be far more low-key: a civil ceremony at the Guildhall in Windsor, followed by a simple blessing in St George's Chapel in the castle grounds. There would be little pomp or circumstance. Just a union of two people, desperately in love, who would take their vows and before 200 close friends and family.

For Camilla, it was all a long way from her simple beginnings.

Growing Up

It all began, quite inconspicuously, at seven o'clock on a perfect English morning, 17 July 1947.

Inside a primrose-coloured maternity room in the private wing of King's College Hospital, London, as the first rays of morning sunlight glinted through the window, a child was welcomed into the world. It had all the hallmarks of a blue-blooded birth. A simple bunch of wild country flowers sat on the table. The congratulations cards carried gold-embossed messages from the finest addresses in Mayfair, Park Lane and the Home Counties.

As the child's mother, the Honourable Rosalind Shand, rested in her bed, she could never have imagined just what life held in store for the beautiful baby girl, her face framed by a mop of golden curls, who lay in her arms that July morning.

Nothing seemed more certain on Camilla Rosemary Shand's birth day than her future. Like the members of the generations before her, she would be educated in the ways of nobility, groomed in the joys of huntin' and fishin' – and then she would land herself a rich husband.

Yet fate had other plans: within fifty years, Camilla would become one of the most notorious women in history.

As Camilla Parker Bowles, she would scandalize a nation by having an affair with the future King of England, take centre stage as the most famous marriage of its day crumbled – and bring the monarchy to its knees.

Camilla was a child born with not just one silver spoon in her mouth – she had a whole canteen of silver cutlery. Her credentials for being a society lady were impeccable, her breeding awe-inspiring.

Her mother, the Honourable Rosalind, was the daughter of the fourth Lord Ashcombe, whose forefather, Thomas Cubitt, founded the powerful Cubitt construction company, which built the bulk of Mayfair and Belgravia.

Her father, Bruce Shand, was the partner in a Mayfair wine merchants and had been a major in the 12th Royal Lancers. Twice decorated with the Military Cross for bravery in the Second World War, he spent two years as a German prisoner of war. He was a Master of Fox Hounds and once held the position of Vice Lord Lieutenant of East Sussex.

They were, as one of Camilla's closest friends says, 'the most suitable people. They were not titled, but they were as close to the aristocracy as they could be without having a title of their own. To be blunt, Camilla's parents were "the right sort". In the landed upper classes, Camilla certainly came from fine stock.'

Perhaps the most quirky twist of fate was that Camilla's maternal great-grandmother, Alice Keppel, had been the long-time mistress of Prince Charles's great-great-grandfather Edward VII in the 1870s.

More than a century separates the lives of Alice Keppel and Camilla Parker Bowles. Wars and revolutions have come and gone. Men have explored the outer reaches of space and walked on the moon.

But in the high-society world into which Alice and Camilla were born, little has changed.

Camilla's notorious link with the royals is something she was not only proud of, but something in which she would positively revel.

One friend says: 'Camilla would often go on endlessly about Alice. She would sit on her mother's knee and beg Rosalind to tell her all about her famous ancestor.

'Camilla never tired about hearing about Alice. While most children are content to be entertained with fairy tales, Camilla would beg her mother to "tell me about granny Alice" again and again and again.

'Camilla's eyes would light up as her mother spoke in her soft tones about Alice, the scarlet woman who was Edward VII's secret lover.

'Her favourite anecdote was the family story of Alice's famous saying: "My job is to curtsy first . . . and then jump into bed." Camilla would smile every time she heard that line.

'Camilla was captivated. She wanted to know how Alice walked and talked. She begged to see crinkled old photographs of Alice.'

Another schoolchum says: 'From the moment Camilla arrived at school, she would regale us with stories about Alice. She told us how Alice would go to Biarritz in Switzerland every year with the King. Camilla would say: "Down there, Alice was as much the Queen of England as the real one."

'She was particularly fond of telling the story that when King Edward VII was dying, Alice's position as his mistress was so widely acknowledged that the King's wife, Queen Alexandra, sent for Alice Keppel to join her at the King's bedside as he passed away.

'Camilla was always saying: "My great-grandmother was practically royal, you know. She may not have been Queen, but she had the ear of the King. That made her jolly powerful"'.

In her child's mind, Camilla could have had no idea how prophetic those words would be.

Indeed, on the very first occasion when flirtatious Camilla met the young Prince Charles in 1970, she uttered the immortal line: 'My great-grandmother was your great-great-grandfather's mistress. How about it?'

Camilla's early years were traditional and happy. She was raised at The Laines, a five-bedroomed Tudor country home in Plumpton, Sussex – the perfect upbringing for a girl of her class and social bearing, in a sprawling home full of dogs, love and laughter.

Camilla remembers her childhood with fondness. She told a friend only recently: 'If people think I am strong, then it is all thanks to my family. I had so much love and security growing up, I never doubted my family would be there for me in times of crisis. Whatever happened, I knew I was wanted and loved. To give that to a child is the greatest gift of all. I had the best start one could wish for. As I have matured, I have realized the solid foundation I had as a child gave me the stability to face any upset. And there have been a few upsets along the way.'

Two years after Camilla's birth, the family was joined by another daughter, Annabel. Eighteen months later, a brother, Mark, was born.

A dashing man with a shock of blond hair, he was to be the adventurer of the family; a man who would pursue a life of exploration, earning his living writing brilliant accounts of his travels around the world.

The family all rode and hunted. Camilla's father would open the grounds of his house once a year for a Conservative Party fête.

A former neighbour says: 'They were classic gentry. They had nannies and held croquet parties on the lawn in the summer. It was pretty idyllic, really. They were a highly respectable family. Camilla would always be impeccably dressed on Sundays when the whole family would go to church. During the rest of the week, she was a tomboy. While the other girls were happy to sit and read and play with their dolls, Camilla was always the one who sided with the boys. She had a rough-cropped short bob hairstyle and, with her muddy face and grazed knees, she could easily have passed for a young boy. She was always shimmying up trees. She was a fine athlete. She had a stocky, powerful figure and was quite fearless.

'Camilla was always as brave as a lion. If there was a tree-climbing contest between the local children, Camilla would be the one to scale the highest bough.

'When the children swam in the local stream during hot summer days, Camilla would be the one leading the way. She was always supremely confident in her own abilities. If her brother Mark could do something, Camilla wanted to do it too – or do it better.

'She was fearless. She was born with a self-confidence rare in women of her generation.'

With her long, golden curls, pert nose and translucent 'English Rose' complexion, Camilla was judged to be a 'pretty' if not stunning-looking young girl, but it was her character which set her apart from the other well-bred young 'gels'.

At five years old, she was sent to her first school, Dumbrells in the village of Ditching, three miles from the family home. The school cost the princely sum of £10 a year and was populated by the daughters of the local gentry.

Spartan and tough, Dumbrells was run along lines similar to those of Gordonstoun, the rigid Scottish boarding school where Prince Charles spent his formative years.

But while Charles was a sensitive child who loathed the rough and tumble of his school, Camilla positively blossomed at Dumbrells.

In the winter, she would be driven to school by her mother, but in the summer, Camilla would happily walk the three miles to and from school, accompanied only by the family nanny. She excelled at hockey, a game played in the winter months, and in 'stoolball', a traditional Sussex game similar to cricket, in the summer.

A fellow pupil recalls how the classrooms were unheated during even the most bitter winter's day: 'We would dress up in thick socks and boots and wear about seven layers of jumpers, coats and scarves to stay warm in the classroom. If you took off your gloves to remove the lid of a pen, your fingers would turn blue. It was bitter in there.

'A school inspector came one day and was dumbstruck. He never knew such a place could exist. The school was so harsh that I used to say if you could survive Dumbrells, you could survive anything. It was like something from a different century. It was a classic upper-class school. The most important thing was to learn how to suffer and endure in silence.

'We would have games lessons on a Wednesday afternoon. The showers were freezing cold. If you dared complain, you would be punished. It was all about teaching the children to survive. It was tough on discipline. From the age of five, children would be punished with a lash of the cane to the bare buttocks for any misdemeanour.

'Camilla was a good pupil, quick-witted and bright. My only memory of her getting into trouble was for being a real chatterbox. She was a bundle of energy who found it hard to be quiet, even for a few moments. She was always getting told off for talking.

'But she had such strength of character, nothing would upset her. That's what I remember most about her – she never allowed anything to get her down.

'Once, she was caned for talking in class. She must have been about six or seven years old. She came back into the classroom and when she sat down you could tell she was wincing in pain. But she did not hang her head in shame and she absolutely refused to cry. The tears were in her eyes and her bottom lip was quivering. But she bit her lip and sat there with her back straight and her face full ahead, looking at the teacher defiantly. She was a tough one, that Camilla, a real tough cookie.'

The Shands had a home in London and when Camilla was ten years old, she was sent to the fashionable Queen's Gate School for young ladies in South Kensington. It was a school proud of its unofficial function of 'providing wives for half the Foreign Office and most of the nobility'.

Lynn Ripley, a classmate, said in one interview: 'We called her "Milla", that was her nickname. She was a Sloane Ranger before Sloane Rangers were invented.

'She was looked up to by the other girls. She had an

inner strength. There was no question that she might do badly, with or without A levels. That didn't matter. She would live the life she wanted – that's what she exuded.

'She wasn't a beautiful girl, but she had a certain aura. What she lacked in looks, she made up for in confidence. She had the same hairstyle then as she does today.

'She was always a hoity-toity little madam. I used to wear way-out clothes, but Milla was always in twinsets, tweed suits and pearls. We didn't get on very well because she was into hunting and shooting. We used to have mammoth rows about that because I was totally against it. But she had a magnetism and a confidence I envied like anything.

'She was one of those people who know what they want and know that they will be a success in life. She was only fifteen-and-a-half years old, but I knew even then that the world was going to hear a lot more of Milla Shand.'

Another friend said: 'Camilla fitted in beautifully with the school. She was smart, but not outstanding; she was keen at sport, but not overly so. Milla was always going to do "the right thing" with her life. She was never brash or rude. She was no pushover, but she wasn't a rebel either. She was just a good, solid, dependable type, lots of fun and popular.'

Actress Lynn Redgrave, who was in the year above Camilla, hated the school. She said: 'I remember the place with nothing but disdain. I was the only girl who had a working mother. My mother was an actress. The idea was for us to leave as marriageable young ladies. The girls didn't think they had to learn much because all they had in mind was going to parties. Being a debutante and landing a rich husband was top of the agenda. There would be endless classes teaching us to be good wives and mothers. I was the odd one out because I wanted to have a career – and a career on the stage at that. My dreams were made fun of. Camilla, on the other hand, revelled in the whole concept of the school. She wanted to have fun, but she also wanted to marry well because that would be the best fun of all in her mind.'

As author Penelope Fitzgerald, who gave Camilla French lessons, told top royal author Nigel Dempster in his 1993 best-selling book Behind Palace Doors: 'Queen's Gate was changing slightly by the time Milla got there. It had been a place where girls were taught how to write cheques and play bridge. Slowly, it was trying to bring itself into the twentieth century.

'Our girls were so beautiful. Many of them came from old country families where in each generation the man would have married a beautiful young wife. So, of course, many of our girls were quite lovely to look at. Those who were less lovely were allowed to wear a little make-up in a discreet fashion.'

Camilla was one of the girls allowed to wear a little make-up.

Neighbours in Sussex recall that both Camilla and her brother Mark took to the opposite sex early on.

One says: 'They were down-to-earth, wholesomely sexual. She didn't have film-star good looks, but she was one of the first girls to start taking an interest in boys. She was always far more interested in men than she was in women.

'Mark, of course, was devastatingly handsome. He could have had any girl he wanted. He and Camilla were extremely close. She watched over him, and he protected her. They were brother and sister, but it was an extremely close relationship. They were true friends, they would protect one another,'

Carolyn Benson, who was at school with Camilla and

remains one of her closest friends to this day, says: 'Camilla was funny and bright; boys loved her. Even when she was too young for them to have a sexual interest in her, Camilla always had lots of boy friends. She could talk to boys about things which interested them. She was never a girl's girl. She was always a boy's girl.

'She wasn't particularly clothes-conscious; nothing's changed there. But she always exuded a sexy confidence over men. She was quite a flirt, she liked men. She still does. Camilla was always the one who made friends with boys first. She was able to talk to them then.'

After school, Camilla spent six months at finishing schools in Switzerland and Paris before returning to London for her grand entry into society.

Her time abroad helped broaden Camilla's horizons.

One girl who knew her well said: 'When Camilla came back from Europe, she was even more confident. She had learned French and knew how to cook. But more than anything, she had adopted the European attitude towards sex. She was still a virgin at this stage, but she would talk quite openly about how she kissed the son of one of her mother's friends. She said it was "quite deliciously wonderful". There was a new gleam in her eye. She had clearly discovered sex. When she went off to finishing school she was still rather pudgy and plump. When she returned to London she'd got rid of her puppy fat. Her cheekbones were more prominent. She was quite the young lady about town, with the added sophistication of having spent the summer abroad. She was quite grown up. Camilla never had any hang-ups about the opposite sex. While most of us would giggle and get nervous around boys, Camilla was always confident and secure around them. And that made her very attractive to the chaps. She always had plenty of suitors.'

In 1965, like the rest of her classmates, Camilla became a debutante and threw herself into 'The Season'.

A fellow debutante says: 'Camilla was never going to be Deb of the Year, but she was determined to have the best fun she could. Her parents didn't have the fabulous wealth of some of the other girls. In fact, several of Camilla's dresses were off-the-peg numbers, not designer gowns like those of some of the wealthier girls. But Camilla carried herself with such aplomb.

'Even as a teenager, she could walk into a room and you felt her presence there. She was no beauty, she did not have a perfect figure, she did not have a title or even particularly great connections. But she had something. She oozed confidence and sensuality. She always held her head high. She had a great sense of humour. She was a very sexy girl. She never spent much time on her hair or her nails. That's one of the things I remember about Camilla, she never painted her nails. They were always rather stubbly and bitten and dirty. Her hair was always unkempt and she had these rosy cheeks from being out in the sun so much. She was a natural-looking girl. If I had to use one word to describe Camilla, it would have to be "earthy".

'But she filled a room when she entered it. Camilla was, quite simply, fascinating. She was born with raw sex appeal.'

'The Season' was a four-month period between the end of March and July when the most socially desirable girls would enjoy endless rounds of parties, dinners, dances and 'top' social functions like Royal Ascot and Henley – in the hope of meeting equally socially acceptable men to marry.

Camilla's 'Season' opened on 25 March 1965, with a cocktail party thrown by her mother at 30 Pavilion Road, Knightsbridge. A partygoer recalls: 'Camilla's London home was not big enough or grand enough to hold a coming-out party at. Pavilion Road was a place you hired if you didn't have a sufficiently grand London address. It was a fairly raucous affair. Most of the coming-out cocktail parties were rather stiff and dull. But Camilla's was fun. She wore a lovely white dress and was the life and soul of the party. Everyone had such fun, the cocktails stretched on until eleven at night. Everyone got tipsy and Camilla was at the centre of it, throwing her head back telling bawdy jokes. She must have danced and flirted with every man in the room. But she was not a girl the other girls felt threatened by. She wasn't pretty enough for one thing. No, Camilla was fun, and that's what everyone loved about her.

'From that moment on, she was one of the stars of the Season. If you wanted a party to go with a swing, you invited Camilla. With Camilla around, you could guarantee the evening would never be dull.'

Two days after her coming-out bash, Camilla went to bed with her first lover.

She told one of her girl friends: 'I may as well find out what all the fuss is about. Who knows, I might enjoy it.'

The friend says: 'It was the Swinging Sixties and she wanted to play a part in it all. She didn't actually proposition the chap in question, but she gave him the very clear signal that if he would like to enjoy her favours, she wasn't going to put up a fight.'

Princess Diana, later her rival in love, was just four years old the night Camilla finally became a woman. Prince Charles, the man Camilla was to captivate for a quarter of a century, was still a fresh-faced virgin schoolboy in his last year at Gordonstoun.

Camilla's first love was Kevin Burke. She was eighteen, he a year older. An Old Etonian, Kevin was the son of aviation pioneer Sir Aubrey Burke, the chairman of Hawker Siddeley.

He recalls: 'She was terrific fun, enormously popular, and although she wasn't a classic beauty she was attractive and sexy. She was never tongue-tied or shy and she always had something amusing to say.

'She was always mentioning Alice Keppel. It was constantly on her mind. It was almost like a talisman, something she wanted to equal, if not better.

'Every night we went to two or three cocktail parties and then a dance. All you needed was enough petrol for the car and to pay for your cleaning and the rest was provided. It was the best time and I had the best partner you could wish for. Camilla was always at the centre of things. She was never bad-tempered. She knew how to have fun, I remained with Camilla all that year.

'I suppose we were in love . . . as much in love as anyone can be at that age . . . Then she ditched me.'

Camilla had met her future husband, Andrew Parker Bowles.

At this time, Camilla was sharing a two-bedroomed, ground-floor flat at No. 1 Stack House in Ebury Street, Chelsea with Virginia Carrington, daughter of Mrs Thatcher's onetime Foreign Secretary Lord Carrington. Camilla was working part-time as a secretary.

A girlfriend who visited Camilla's home said: 'It was typically Camilla. Her bedroom looked like a bomb had hit it. Virginia was fairly tidy and organized and Camilla drove her nuts, in the nicest possible way. Virginia once said to me: "You know, Camilla has this inability to hang anything up on a hanger. And she has an aversion to cleaning fluids of any description. You should see the state of the bathroom when she's been in it!"

'But she was so sweet, it was impossible to be angry with her. She was like a big, boisterous puppy.'

An army friend of Andrew Parker Bowles recalls the first time Camilla met the man she would end up marrying. 'Andrew was a dashing man about town. He was an officer in the Blues and Royals, much more sophisticated than the men she'd known and, of course, very, very handsome.

'She was besotted. I remember the first time she saw him. He walked into the room at one of the endless parties and Camilla nudged me and asked me who he was. I told her his name was Andrew and he was terribly eligible. She said: "Introduce me to him now."

'We walked across and Camilla started talking to him. They were inseparable for the rest of the evening. They left to go off for dinner with each other later that night. She touched his arm as they left the party. I remember thinking she was rather too plain for Andrew, not his type at all. He was so handsome, he had his pick of the most gorgeous girls in London. But he appeared enchanted by Camilla.

'She intrigued him. She wasn't as stunning as his other girlfriends but she had a certain earthiness which he found charming. Camilla could always match his bawdy jokes one for one. It was clear there was something special there from the start.'

Andrew also had the right connections to make him a suitable beau for Camilla. His father, Derek Parker Bowles, was a close friend of the Queen Mother – she was a frequent guest at Donnington House, the Parker Bowleses' family home on a 1,000-acre shooting estate near Newbury in Berkshire.

A Household Cavalry officer, Andrew Parker Bowles was a ladies' man and, according to friends, he and Camilla embarked on 'a very hot affair indeed' in 1967. According to another lady who had enjoyed the advances of Andrew, 'his greatest gift to women was the knowledge that sexuality was healthy – something to be explored. That openness about sex was his gift to Camilla. She was very innocent when they met, but they spent many, many nights together. He schooled her in the ways of the world.'

Lady Caroline Percy, another of the 'in crowd', says: 'Andrew behaved abominably to Camilla, but she was desperate to marry him. They saw each other on and off for three years, but he was always messing around with other women. Camilla was too smart not to know the truth, of course. She tolerated it for a while, then she got fed up.'

But Andrew's bachelor pad in Portobello Road in Notting Hill was where Camilla spent most of her time. A friend says: 'You would go around there on a Saturday morning and Andrew would be up and about cooking breakfast and making coffee. Around eleven, Camilla would stagger downstairs, looking bleary-eyed and a little dishevelled. She would walk around wearing one of his big shirts. She was very open about their relationship, which was unusual for ladies of her class even in the sixties. She would sit on Andrew's knee and tease his hair. Very often, they would disappear upstairs together in the middle of the afternoon and one would hear giggles and moans coming from the bedroom. They clearly had a very lusty, healthy life together.

'But Andrew found it impossible to be faithful. When

Camilla wasn't there, he'd pick up some leggy Sloane Ranger type at a party and bring her home. Camilla knew Andrew had a roving eye.

'One morning she turned up unexpectedly. Andrew opened the door dressed just in his underpants. For once he totally lost his cool. Camilla asked to be allowed in and Andrew started fumbling around for excuses.

'Camilla was livid. She said to him: "Who the hell have you got in there? Which tart was it last night?"

'Andrew went very red-cheeked, but Camilla refused to back down. She wasn't the type to burst into tears and run away. She pretty much pushed the door down and barged in. As she walked into his bedroom there was a pretty girl scurrying out of the bathroom, hastily fastening her bra and trying to pull her dress over her head at the same time.

'Camilla just looked at her, then looked at Andrew, then looked back at the girl and said to Andrew: "Rather plain, old man. Couldn't you do better than that? What's wrong with you? Happy to have someone else's shop-soiled goods, are you?"

'Then she turned on her heel and walked out, leaving the other girl in tears.

'That was when Camilla decided that if she couldn't beat him, she would join him. But being such a competitive soul, Camilla decided to go for a big catch. In the back of her mind, I think she wanted to find someone who would make Andrew green with jealousy. She looked around for a while and then she found the biggest catch of all . . .'

Love at First Sight

The meeting which was to change the course of history took place on a typical English summer's day. The rain lashed down and gusting winds whipped across the polo fields at Windsor Great Park.

Prince Charles, his hair slicked down by rain, was standing beside one of his beloved polo ponies, stroking the animal's damp mane. Suddenly, a lone figure dressed in green wellington boots, brown corduroy trousers and a dripping wet green Barbour jacket appeared by his side.

'That's a fine animal, Sir,' said the woman.

Turning around, Charles found himself looking at the woman who was to dominate his life for the next quarter of a century.

With a relaxed smile, she said: 'My name is Camilla Shand. Very pleased to meet you.'

It was a simple sentence, but it began an affair that was to span more than a quarter of a century; an affair which was to lead Charles to tell a close friend: 'You know, Camilla is simply my best friend in the whole wide world.'

An onlooker who witnessed that very first exchange of words in June 1970 recalls: 'Camilla looked pretty awful that day, we all did. It was chucking it down and most people were feeling pretty dejected because the match was postponed due to the rain.

'Camilla saw the Prince standing alone on the other side of the field. Cool as you like, she walked across and started talking to him. To be honest, no-one thought it surprising or strange. She was part of the inner circle. She'd been at social functions with the royal family before. We all had powerful and influential friends. Most of our families had connections with the royals. There was nothing peculiar about Camilla going over to talk to the Prince.'

Charles was just twenty-two years old, fresh from Cambridge University. Camilla was twenty-three, and already wise in the ways of the world. The couple chatted animatedly for more than an hour.

The Argentinian polo player Luis Basualdo, who played for the same team as the Prince at the time, says: 'If he wasn't precisely a virgin, he was certainly still wet behind the ears. For the Prince, real life began with Camilla.'

Charles was, at this time, an unhappy and troubled young man. A childhood starved of affection and an upbringing in a harsh boarding school he hated had left him lonely and aloof.

But Camilla was a breath of fresh air.

Another friend recalls: 'Charles was smitten with Camilla from that very first day. When she started talking to him, she wasn't affected in the slightest. I think she was the first girl who'd spoken to Charles directly. You have to remember he'd met very few girls before. He'd only met the suitable girls who had been invited to the Palace. Any other girls he met at university were awed by his stature.

'But Camilla was fearless. She knew she was his equal. She spoke to him quite naturally. And he found that refreshing.

'He could talk to Camilla then, as he does now, in an open way he can't talk to anyone else. He feels safe with Camilla.

'She was, and is, frankly not the most pristine of women. You're not sure whether they're today's knickers she's got on. I don't think she ever went to the hairdresser.

'But he loved her from the start. She wasn't intimidated by him. She was his equal. She still is. Even on that first day, Camilla had him throwing his head back in laughter. She always had a dry wit, a great turn of phrase. She was a girl who could make a joke about anything. She never had a cruel sense of humour, it was either a dry observation about something totally absurd or it was making a joke at her own expense. That wit is what first attracted Charles to her. They say the couple that laughs together stays together. I believe that is very true in the case of Camilla and Charles. Even in his darkest depths of depression, Camilla could always make him laugh; see the lighter side of life. That's what made her special back then, that's what made her special through the years.'

The pair shared a love of 'The Goon Show'. It was back then in 1970 that Charles christened Camilla 'Gladys', his favourite character from a Spike Milligan sketch, and she dubbed him 'Fred', a favourite 'Goon Show' name. They would use these names at the end of the regular love notes they began sending to each other, but they were nicknames which were to come back to haunt them both in the turbulent years to come.

Back in the heady summer of 1970, Charles and Camilla were simply young – and in love. Within a matter of weeks they were inseparable.

A friend remembers: 'Camilla offered something he'd never had before. She was worldly-wise and fun. He could let down his guard in front of her. When she was around, there was a lightness in him that had been missing in his life for a very long time.

'She became his ideal, his prototype woman.

'From her point of view, Prince Charles was perfect. She didn't set out to fall in love with him, that happened later. No, when they met, she was still hurt from the way she had been treated by Andrew Parker Bowles. Camilla was madly in love with Andrew but she knew he wasn't being faithful to her. She'd pretty much given up any hope that Andrew would marry her.

'She genuinely liked Prince Charles, but he didn't set her pulse racing. What he did do was create a perfect way of getting even with Andrew. Within a few weeks, the whole of London was buzzing with talk about the Prince and his new lady.

'It was only a matter of time before Andrew heard about Camilla's growing relationship with Charles. And she knew it.'

Camilla was soon spotted regularly by her Prince's side at top London nightclubs like Annabels.

The relationship stunned London society.

One of Camilla's friends of the time says: 'People were amazed by how quickly the relationship blossomed. At first, everyone just smiled inwardly that Camilla had taken up with the rather naïve and innocent Charles. But within a few short months it became clear they were closely involved and very attached to one another There was a genuine love and friendship there. It was clear to anyone who saw them together.

'Camilla was very discreet about her friendship with the Prince. If one mentioned or teased her about it she would giggle. She would never give anything away. She was always terribly discreet, even back then.

'It was a different time back then. There was no press keeping an eye on the royals, but no-one said a word outside the immediate circle of friends. Why should we? Camilla was one of us. There was no reason to cause a scandal.

'Anyway, they were both single and free to enjoy their romance without hurting anyone.

'When one saw them together, it was clear they were having a physical relationship. I remember one night at Annabels. The Prince rarely drank at that time and almost never danced. But that night he let his hair down. He was drinking champagne and Camilla kept dragging him on to the floor. At one stage, he put his hand around her waist and then allowed it to slip down on to her bottom. It was an extraordinarily intimate thing for him to do in public with a girlfriend.

'But Camilla was clearly very special to him. When you looked at them talking together, his eyes would light up and he was relaxed. They were always laughing in each other's company.

'It was extraordinary to see Prince Charles, at that age, so intimately involved with a real woman like Camilla. One just knew they were having a great time in bed together.'

Indeed, Camilla's sexual hold over Prince Charles is something widely discussed by their closest circle of friends even today.

29

One pal who has known Camilla for twenty-five years says: 'It's widely known that Camilla is great in the bedroom. She's a woman who knows what she wants and who is an expert in satisfying a man. She's supposed to be mind-bogglingly good at it. If you talk to any of her old boyfriends, that's one of the things they remember most. Back in the sixties, it was unusual for a girl to be so forward in the bedroom. And it was certainly unusual for a girl of Camilla's class to be so adventurous and uninhibited.

'To a young Charles, she must have been a real eye-opener. He was very inexperienced when they met. She was the first woman he had a long-term sexual relationship with. That early sexual relationship has given them an intimacy through the years that no-one can take away. They say you never forget your first love – well, Charles never did.

'But it was always more than sex with Charles and Camilla. It was intimacy. They just bonded, It was like you were talking to one person when, in fact, there were two people there. They just clicked. They shared the same interests, both were very out-doorsy types and sporty and they laughed at the same things. They made a lovely couple.'

As well as his own deep feelings for Camilla, there was another very important reason why Charles felt so relaxed and comfortable with her: his closest ally, his uncle Lord Louis Mountbatten, gave the burgeoning friendship his seal of approval.

Mountbatten's former private secretary John Barratt said: 'Charles was always closer to Mountbatten than he was to his own father. Charles and Prince Philip always had a difficult relationship. But Lord Mountbatten took Charles under his wing. He always spent time with

Charles, both as a boy and a young man. Charles considered him a father figure.

'When Uncle Dickie approved of Camilla, that was the final seal of approval as far as Charles was concerned.'

Mountbatten had a master scheme. His granddaughter, Lady Amanda Knatchbull, would make a perfect bride for the future king. But she was only fourteen years old at the time Charles began dating Camilla. Mountbatten knew Charles needed female company until Amanda could assume her place at Charles's side. Barratt said: 'Mountbatten knew Camilla would make a perfect mistress for Charles until Amanda was of marriageable age. So he gave the blossoming love affair his full blessing. He encouraged Charles to sow his wild oats while he could. He advised his nephew not to marry until he was thirty. He told Charles that Camilla was "excellent" mistress material.'

Mountbatten invited the young lovers to spend weekends at his magnificent Broadlands estate in Hampshire. He told his loyal manservant: 'Charles needs some privacy. From now on, he can come here for a bit of privacy and not even his own family need know.'

To keep up appearances, Camilla was always given the Portico Room, the same room where the Queen and Prince Philip had consummated their marriage on their honeymoon in 1950.

Charles was assigned the Lady Louis Suite next door. The two rooms had an inner oak door connecting them. That door was discreetly left unlocked.

Barratt recalled: 'Of course everyone knew Charles and Camilla were sleeping together, but things like that were never discussed, they were just expected to happen and no-one batted an eyelid.

'Staff members would go into their suites in the

morning and it was obvious only one bed had been slept in. But there was nothing shocking about it. Charles and Camilla were both young and single. Everyone above and below stairs adored Camilla.

'She is someone who is equally charming to everyone. She's not a snob. I remember meeting her on many, many occasions and she always had a cheery smile and a friendly word. She was completely unpretentious. She was sleeping with the future King of England, but she never once tried to pull rank. She was just a tremendously nice, down-to-earth girl who was in love.

'Mountbatten greatly admired Camilla. She was witty, intelligent and very funny. She had this racy sense of humour which appealed to both Charles and his uncle. They both loved her dearly. She had lived, she'd had worldly experiences. Mountbatten loved her character and her strength. He knew Camilla was "the right sort".

'During their weekends at Broadlands, Charles and Camilla were inseparable. They were like any couple in love – holding hands, laughing and joking together. They would go fishing together, go out riding or simply go for long walks around the estate.

'I have never seen him so relaxed with a woman. She made him feel special – the same way her great-grandmother Alice Keppel had made Edward VII feel when she was his mistress.

'Lord Mountbatten once told me how much Camilla resembled Alice. He said the physical likeness and her mannerisms were "extraordinarily" close. He gave a silent nod as if to say that those qualities in Alice had obviously been passed on down. Secretly, he was also rather pleased that Charles was involved in a sexual relationship with Camilla. He thought it was healthy and good for him.'

Throughout 1971, Charles and Camilla were 'an item'. He regularly visited her parents' home in Sussex at weekends, always discreetly and anonymously.

According to a friend of the family, Charles and Camilla's father Major Bruce Shand 'got on famously'. The friend said: 'Bruce Shand was everything Charles admired in a man. He was a decorated war hero, a pillar of the local community. But he wasn't stuffy in the slightest. He was a raconteur who immediately accepted Charles as part of the family. Those weekends with the Shands down in Sussex became very precious to Charles. It gave him the chance to experience a normal, happy, intimate family group. He was truly happy in their company. And, of course, he was with the woman he loved.

'Camilla and Charles would often be seen walking the local lanes on a Sunday before lunch. They would stroll along, talking and laughing the whole time. No-one paid Charles much attention. They just looked like any other young couple enjoying each other's company.'

But despite her obvious love for Charles, Camilla was still secretly nursing a broken heart over Andrew Parker Bowles.

Andrew had been sent to Germany with his regiment. At the time Camilla was embroiled in her affair with Charles, she sadly told a friend: 'I love Charles very much, but I simply cannot forget Andrew. I often wonder where he is and what he is doing. I think of him all the time. Is it possible to love two men at the same time?'

Despite Mountbatten's full seal of approval for her affair with Charles, Camilla knew she would never marry her Prince.

Carolyn Benson, who knew them both well, says: 'He was younger, simply a nice boy – Camilla was conscious of her select status but she never wanted to be Queen. He would more than likely have married her – but that's not what she wanted.'

Another friend said: 'Camilla would laugh if the subject of marriage was even mentioned. She had grown up around the royal family, she knew what becoming the Princess of Wales would entail. And she didn't like the idea one bit. Camilla wanted a quiet life. She was always destined to marry well and have a family. Becoming Queen wasn't something she ever wanted.'

In September 1971, Charles enrolled at Dartmouth Naval College, part of the 'master plan' to prepare him for kingship. It would mean long periods away at sea.

He and Camilla bade farewell to each other in his private rooms at Buckingham Palace. A friend of Camilla's said: 'There were tears on both sides, but mostly from Charles. Camilla was the one who had to comfort him. He had been excited about the prospect of going to sea, but when the time came, he was mortified at leaving Camilla. He was more in love with her than she was with him. It was the first great love of his life. And as time has shown, Camilla was *the* great love of his life.

'Charles knew he had to do his duty and go to sea, and he knew he had to give up Camilla, the woman he loved. What he did not realize was that this would not be the first time in his life he would have to give up Camilla in the name of duty to the Crown and the country.'

While Charles was at Dartmouth, the couple wrote to each other on an almost daily basis. A friend says: 'Charles would write these long, passionate letters telling Camilla how much he missed her. She would write back, telling him it was only a matter of time before they would see each other again. His letters were terribly sweet and naïve. Camilla never parted with any of them. She still treasures them to this day.'

In October 1971, Andrew Parker Bowles returned from abroad and quickly re-established contact with Camilla.

A friend says: 'When Andrew came back home he was flattered to discover his Camilla had been having her own fling with the Prince. After all, they were all part of the same social circle and, to be frank, within that social circle, having one's girlfriend bonking the Prince of Wales gave Andrew a certain elevated status.

'He was rather proud of her achievement. It was also a manly challenge to him. He knew Camilla was still in love with him; it was like waving a red rag at a bull. Andrew was hugely competitive. He got a secret kick out of Camilla sleeping with the Prince, but he was determined to win her back.'

Andrew's younger brother Simon says: 'He was flattered that Camilla had caught the Prince's eye. Basically, Andrew and Camilla had known each other for years and it was always Camilla who made the running to marry Andrew.'

As Charles and Camilla drifted apart, Andrew re-entered Camilla's life. A friend says: 'When Andrew came back from Germany he was even more dashing and desirable than when he went away. Camilla was still nursing a deep love for him. The fact that he'd cheated on her numerous times only appealed to her competitive nature. She still wanted him – but now she was determined that if Andrew wanted her, he would have to do the decent thing and marry her.

'She played a delicate juggling game. She continued to write to Charles and saw him during his weekends off from training at Dartmouth, but during the week, she would go out with Andrew.

'Camilla was never certain about her feelings for Charles. She loved him deeply, but she knew early on that she did not want to marry him. At that stage, she loved him but she wasn't in love with him. Camilla is a deeply private woman; the idea of living her life in the public eye did not appeal to her one bit. She used to laugh off the idea of her marrying Charles by throwing her head back and saying: "Why on earth would I want to live my life in a fishbowl? No thank you very much!"'

But Charles was determined to make one last-ditch attempt at happiness.

On one of his visits home, in January 1972, Charles invited Camilla to spend the weekend with him at Broadlands.

John Barratt said: 'Camilla was perfect for Charles. Many of us had expected the proposal for months. It took place in his bedroom at Broadlands. Charles clasped her hand and whispered: "Will you marry me?" Camilla told Charles that she loved him, but could not marry him.'

Devastated, Charles sought advice from Lord Mountbatten. He was shocked when his nephew confessed he had proposed – and relieved that Camilla had given the 'right' answer.

Barratt said: 'Charles always turned to Mountbatten for advice on affairs of the heart. But when Charles told him about the proposal, Mountbatten's first advice was that he should talk to his family. Mountbatten told Charles it was impossible for him to marry Camilla. As a future king, he had to take a virgin bride – and Camilla was not a virgin.'

Barratt added: 'At first Charles had been obsessed about marrying a virgin. He was a great fan of the novelist Barbara Cartland, who was to become his step-grandmother when he married Diana. He based himself on her romantic heroes. Every time he came to Broadlands, his bags would be packed full of her books.

'Prince Philip thought he should be macho and militaristic, but Charles had different ideas about being a man. He was a romantic.

'But he forgot all about marrying a virgin when he met Camilla. He liked the fact she had slept with other men. That was a trait he inherited from Mountbatten, who liked experienced, usually married women. Camilla had experience.

'But the royal family insisted Charles should marry a virgin. They were worried about a scandal breaking if he took a girl like Camilla as his queen. They feared a girl like Camilla might have skeletons in her cupboard which would embarrass the family if she were placed on such a pedestal.

'Charles was told that Camilla could still remain his mistress but he would have to keep looking around for a more suitable bride.'

Shocked by the intensity of his young nephew's feelings for Camilla, Lord Mountbatten encouraged Charles to sow his wild oats. He told him: 'Go out and sow them while you may. Be a moving target as far as girls are concerned. For goodness' sakes, you are in the most enviable position in Britain – you can fuck any girl you want!'

Charles took his uncle's advice to heart. He embarked on a string of affairs with hand-picked girls from the upper classes.

He enjoyed flings with Georgina Russell, the daughter of Britain's ambassador to Spain; Lady Jane Wellesley, daughter of the eighth Duke of Wellington; Jane Ward, the assistant manager at the Guards Polo Club; and heiress Sabrina Guinness.

As one woman who enjoyed a brief fling with Charles in the mid-seventies says: 'Who would turn down the invitation for an intimate dinner with the Prince of Wales at Buckingham Palace? My dear, the very thought is enough to make most girls go weak at the knees. I knew several girls who went there and who ended staying the night. But they all agreed Charles wasn't the best lover in the world. He was rather naïve, the sort who liked to get on top and get the job done, preferably with the lights out. Nevertheless, there was a certain honour in being laid by the Prince of Wales; it was like becoming a member of a rather exclusive club.'

In February 1973, Charles set sail for the West Indies on a six-month stint at sea aboard his ship HMS *Minerva*.

His affair with Camilla had been brought to an abrupt end. But although his heart was broken, the name of Camilla Shand and the extent of the future king's love for her was unknown to all but their most intimate circle of friends.

One says: 'It's ironic that Charles and Camilla had this torrid affair and no-one in the press even knew her name. How that would all change as the years went on . . .'

Just four weeks after Charles set sail, Camilla announced her engagement to Andrew Parker Bowles in the society column of the *Times*.

According to a shipmate, Charles reacted by locking himself in his cabin – emerging three hours later with red-rimmed eyes to join his fellow officers for dinner.

The Perfect Wedding

It was the society wedding of the year. On 4 July 1973, Camilla Rosemary Shand, resplendent in an antique lace gown with diamonds in her hair, walked down the aisle as a new bride. As the bells of the Guards Chapel rang out in celebration, the Queen Mother, sitting in the front row, smiled at the happy couple. Next to her, Princess Anne nodded her head in approval.

The guest list at the glittering reception at the St James Club afterwards read like the *Who's Who* of the British aristocracy.

Princess Margaret raised a glass of chilled champagne to toast the newly-weds. Lord Fermoy, Earl Alexander of Tunis, Lady Jane Wellesley and Lord Charles Spencer Churchill were all there. The Duke of Marlborough's niece, Mary Muir, was chief bridesmaid. One of the pageboys was Maurice Roache, now Lord Fermoy and Princess Diana's first cousin.

Camilla looked stunning in a £2,000 dress designed by the Queen's dressmaker Belville Sassoon; a ten-foot-long white veil flowed down from her upswept hair.

As Mr and Mrs Parker Bowles left in a vintage Rolls-Royce for their new home, the magnificent Tudor mansion, Bolehyde Manor in Wiltshire, everyone agreed it had, indeed, been a perfect day. But there was one conspicuous absentee, Prince Charles, the blushing bride's former lover. He was 3,000 miles away at sea.

One guest says: 'Charles's absence was mentioned, but only in the most hushed of tones and well out of earshot of the newly-weds. Everyone thought it rather odd he was not there. He sent a telegram and used the excuse that he was aboard ship. But no-one bought it. He is the Prince of Wales, for goodness' sakes; had he wanted to be there, it could easily have been arranged. It would have been no problem for him to have disembarked and taken a Queen's Flight home.

'But everyone knew the real reason. He simply could not face watching Camilla walk down the aisle. He was truly cut up when he heard she was marrying Andrew.

'He refused to discuss Camilla for at least six weeks after her engagement was announced. He really took it badly. He locked himself away in his cabin and rarely came out. For the first time in his life, he'd lost out on something and that was the woman he loved. For years, he would go on about how he should have grabbed the chance and nabbed Camilla when she was available.

'That was always Charles's problem. He is a ditherer. He simply cannot make up his mind on anything. He's become better as he's grown older, but back then he was terrified of upsetting his family, of doing anything to upset the status quo. He desperately wanted to marry Camilla, but he was afraid it would cause a scandal. His family adored her, but she had been around the block a few times, so to speak. Even his grandmother, the Queen Mother, told him: "Camilla's a lovely girl, darling, but she's not marriage material."

'Back in the early seventies, Charles was still expected to take a virgin bride. It's not like today when Prince Edward can live with a girl before marriage to test the waters. Charles is the future king, he is expected to do things by the rule book And everyone wanted and expected a fairy-tale princess. Camilla was many things, but she was no fairy-tale princess. Everyone in the circle knew she'd been sexually active for years.

'Charles regretted going against his gut right from the start. As soon as he heard he had lost Camilla to another, he wanted her more than ever. He realized then he should have married her. As the years went on, that belief became even more firmly ingrained in his mind.

'His love for her never died. It just sat there deep inside of him, slowly eating him up. Once she married Andrew, his honour prevented him from pursuing her. At least during the first years of her marriage, it did.'

Camilla quickly settled into married life. But from the onset, the Parker Bowleses did not enjoy a conventional marriage.

After a brief honeymoon in Cap d'Ail in the south of France, Andrew, by now promoted to the rank of major, returned to his regiment in London, travelling down to the barracks from Wiltshire on Sunday night and returning the following Friday. Camilla was happy staying at Bolehyde near Chippenham.

A fellow officer's wife recalls: 'Camilla never liked the bitchy world of life among the officers' wives. She would make an appearance at certain dinners and functions, but only when she absolutely had to. When she did appear, she never dressed up. Her clothes were always more Top Shop or Oxfam than *haute couture*. When you met Camilla, she always looked like she'd been dragged through a hedge.

'She much preferred to remain at home. She spent the first few months of the marriage sorting out Bolehyde. It was a magnificent, very comfortable home. Camilla never fretted much for modern design. Bolehyde was kitted out in furniture they'd acquired from both sides of the family. It was "shabby-grand" if there is such a thing.

'The place had a few ugly antiques and the carpet looked like it had seen better days. But Camilla loved that house. She was in her element in the country. She was much happier at home surrounded by her dogs, working in the garden in her smelliest clothes. She's always been a country girl at heart.

'The extraordinary thing was that she refused to talk about Charles. Everyone knew they had been friends, but if his name ever came up, Camilla would quickly change the subject. Her eyes would cloud over and she would look away. It was clear she still nursed deep feelings for him.'

By December 1973, Charles decided to break the ice with his old friend and again started writing her long letters.

A friend says: 'He decided that if he could not have her as a lover and a wife then he would at least have her as a friend and confidante. Charles always trusted her more than anyone else in his life. He had confided his innermost thoughts to her. She could read him like a book.

'Camilla never judges Charles. She can be firm with him, but her judgements are always fair and most of the time she's spot on. He knows she is totally selfless. She will always give him the best advice she can. She's not out to score any points off him. She simply knows and understands the man behind the mask. And Charles knows that. When things bothered him, he always wrote or called Camilla. She was the one person who would always tell him the truth.'

It may seem astonishing to those outside aristocratic circles, but Andrew Parker Bowles fully accepted his wife's continuing friendship with the Prince.

A friend says: 'Not only did Andrew accept it, he positively encouraged it. He knew all about Camilla's affair with Charles and it didn't bother him one jot if she wished to continue her special friendship after her marriage. He knew Camilla would never leave him. He knew his marriage was solid.

'When Andrew and Camilla married, Andrew did not give up a single one of his friends. Most of them were mutual friends of he and his wife anyway so why should he force his new wife to break ties with her friend? And anyway, what harm could come of having a pal as influential and powerful as the future king?

'Andrew and Charles got on well. They are very different types. Andrew is outgoing and racy while Charles is more deep-thinking and rather stuffy in Andrew's eyes. But both share a love of horses and country life. They both have this deep-rooted sense of duty. And, of course, they both love Camilla.'

On 18 December 1974, Camilla gave birth to her first child, a son, christened Thomas Henry Charles.

She asked Charles to be the boy's godfather and he willingly agreed. When Tom was christened in the same Guards Chapel at Wellington Barracks where Andrew and Camilla had exchanged their wedding vows, Charles looked on, smiling as he apparently shared the couple's joy

But inside, he was devastated.

A former naval officer who served with the Prince on HMS Minerva said: 'Seeing Tom finally brought home to him that Camilla had a family and a life of her own. He spent several years after that totally lost and bewildered. You know, it was extraordinary, he kept a photograph of Camilla on the mantel in his cabin. It struck us all as extremely peculiar that he would keep a picture of another man's wife on display.'

Four years later, Camilla's daughter Laura Rose was born.

The following year, on 27 August 1979, Lord Louis Mountbatten was killed by the IRA. The tragedy sent Charles running back to Camilla. Indeed, Prince Charles made a second marriage proposal to Camilla just days after Lord Louis was murdered.

A friend of Camilla's says: 'Camilla was the one he turned to to get him through those darkest days shortly after Dickie Mountbatten was murdered. Camilla hardly left his side. The loss of his uncle left Charles devastated. He was at a loss to know what to do. His grief was so overwhelming, he sank into a deep despair.

'Mountbatten was a father-figure to the Prince. Charles and his own father had never enjoyed a close relationship. Philip thought Charles was too romantic, too weak – and Charles thought his father too tough and regimented. They never did anything together. Charles never had enough affection from his own father. But Mountbatten plugged the gap. He was Charles's friend, father, older brother, confidant, adviser. When he died in such a tragic and horrifying way, the Prince was heartbroken. He once said it felt as if the IRA had killed a piece of him too.

'Camilla was the one who pulled him through. She helped him prepare to face the world for the funeral, she was the one who comforted him when he broke down weeping. She was the only one who could console him.

'Charles proposed again to Camilla that summer. He wanted her to leave her husband and marry him. Camilla again turned him down. It was Camilla who pointed out that the scandal would be disastrous for Charles and the monarchy. She knew the country would never accept him marrying a divorcee and that he would be forced to renounce the throne, Camilla rejected him outright. She stressed to him that she would always be there for him, but they could never marry. It was Camilla all the way through who was encouraging him to find a suitable wife.

With no chance of winning Camilla's hand, Charles consoled himself by throwing himself into a series of spectacularly unsuccessful love affairs.

Stephen Barry, his former equerry who was later to die of AIDS, said: 'He seemed reluctant to fall in love again so, quite frankly, he treated a lot of the girls like shit.

'There was no shortage of prospective bedmates, of course, and Charles threw himself into the task of sowing as many wild oats as he could.

'The girls would be invited over for supper, but it was expected that they would spend the night. In the morning, a car would take them back home. The prince never wanted the girls to stay, he never really wanted to give too much of himself. He was using women and he knew it.

'I was always finding ladies' underwear beneath his four-poster bed. I would discreetly send the panties to be laundered and would then return them by messenger to their rightful owners wrapped in brown paper.'

One of Charles's girlfriends at the time was Lady Sarah Spencer, the elder sister of Princess Diana.

Flame-haired Sarah was a fiery girl with a strong

personality She was later to tell her friends that her relationship with Charles was 'a disaster'.

Sarah's affair with the Prince ended when she told a reporter: 'I will not marry the Prince of Wales. I do not love him. I couldn't marry anyone I didn't love if he was a dustbinman or the future King of England.'

Her impertinence at speaking so frankly to the press shocked Charles. He instantly ended their friendship.

Luis Basualdo, the rakish Argentinian polo player who played on the same team as Charles, told royal author Nigel Dempster how he introduced Charles to another lover, the beautiful Venezuelan socialite Cristabel Barria-Borgia, at a ball when Sarah Spencer was the Prince's official escort.

Basualdo told Dempster: 'Charles danced with Cristabel for hours and Sarah wasn't very happy.'

Later, Charles insisted on driving Cristabel home to London in his Aston Martin. She sat in the front passenger seat beside him; Sarah and his detective were scrunched together in the back seat.

A few days later, Charles met Cristabel at a private party. He asked Basualdo to lend him his car.

Basualdo told Dempster: 'He said Cristabel was feeling tired. The next morning she told me that as they were getting into bed, she asked the Prince: "What shall I call you, Sir or Charles?"

'And as he started making love to her, he replied: "Call me Arthur."'

Sarah Spencer, struggling with anorexia, quickly disappeared off the scene. 'Too flighty,' according to the Prince.

He then took up with Anna Wallace, a rich, very attractive daughter of a Scottish landowner. Anna, nicknamed 'Whiplash' because of her prowess on the hunting field and in the bedroom, had a blazing row with Charles at a polo ball at the home of Lord Vestey in 1980. His official guest, she stood bored and glowing with rage as Charles danced the night away – with Camilla Parker Bowles. Anna ended up borrowing her host's BMW and driving off at speed into the night.

The following morning, Charles telephoned Anna. As he offered his apologies, she listened to him for a full five minutes before hanging up.

'He asked for it. I'd never been so embarrassed in my life,' Anna later told friends. Within six weeks she had married Johnny Hesketh, the younger brother of Lord Hesketh.

Anna, like all of Charles's 'inner circle', was now certain that Charles's obsession with his great love had never died.

A friend who was there that night says: 'It became painfully clear as the night went on that Charles only had eyes for Camilla. The second he saw her, his eyes lit up and he went across to talk to her. Then they danced close together all night. It was obvious to anyone with two brain cells to rub together that he was still madly in love with her.'

Another member of the inner circle says: 'He would call her constantly, he would ask her advice. They weren't sleeping together during this time, but they remained firm friends. They were always bumping into each other at polo matches and other social functions. The love never died between them, it was merely put on hold. It was like they were both waiting for the time to be right so they could resume their affair.'

That time came at the end of 1980 when Andrew Parker Bowles, now holding the rank of lieutenant-colonel, travelled to Rhodesia to work closely with Christopher Soames, the newly-appointed Governor as the country made the bumpy transition from Rhodesia to Zimbabwe.

Camilla chose to stay at home with her children. At the time, she told a friend: 'I have no desire to uproot my family and go all that way. I much prefer to stay at home. It's better for the children and it's better for me. Andrew can do his thing; I'll do mine.'

At the same time, Charles was in the process of buying his country estate at Highgrove, Gloucestershire, the former home of Prime Minister Harold Macmillan's son Maurice – just a fifteen-minute drive away from Camilla's home Bolehyde Manor. In fact, Camilla had helped Charles choose Highgrove. The pair had spoken at length about finding 'the right place' for the future king to reside. Highgrove was 'perfect'.

Gossips soon began commenting on how often the Prince's gleaming Aston Martin Volante was seen parked outside the Parker Bowleses' home – often arriving on a Friday evening and remaining in the same spot until Sunday afternoon.

A source close to Camilla says: 'It was Charles who made all the running. Camilla was married, but her husband was on the other side of the world, so Charles felt he had an "in".

'He missed the intimacy he had shared with Camilla for too long. It started off innocently enough. But within a short period of time, they were sleeping together again.

'This time, it was an even safer and more secure relationship for Charles. Camilla was married; there was no chance at all – if there had ever been one in the first place – that she would want to marry him. She had turned him down twice.

'They spent a hell of a lot of time together while

Andrew was in Rhodesia. Everyone knew. Charles wasn't that discreet. He would telephone Camilla the whole time. He was so smitten, he would call her from the car as he left London to drive down to the country and would stay on the phone talking to her all the way right up until he drew up at her front door. It was an open secret that Camilla and Charles were "on" again.'

Indeed, at the end of 1980, Camilla was the cause of a minor royal 'scandal'. She was staying at Balmoral as a guest of the Prince when she suddenly went down with a bad dose of the mumps. She immediately went home to Wiltshire but the Prince, unmarried and childless, was subjected to a rigorous battery of medical tests.

A courtier says: 'At the time it was a real crisis. Everyone knows mumps can affect a man's fertility and the idea of the Prince becoming barren before he married and produced an heir was intolerable. Even the Queen was alarmed. Luckily, he passed all the tests with flying colours. But everyone was seriously worried, for we all knew the extent of Charles's intimacy with Camilla.'

Meanwhile, Andrew Parker Bowles was enjoying a few new friendships of his own.

In Rhodesia he had met Charlotte Hambro, the beautiful daughter of his boss, Lord Soames. She was estranged from her husband, Richard Hambro and, according to pals, the couple became close in Harare.

According to one close friend: 'Charlotte was crazy about Andrew and he was very keen about her. But he kept messing her about. He simply wouldn't make the decision to leave his wife and commit to Charlotte, so in the end it went nowhere.'

A few months later Charlotte met and married the Yorkshire landowner Earl Peel. Andrew then began a relationship with a blonde photographer. This friendship led to a 'very embarrassing' moment, according to a friend of the photographer's.

Prince Charles was due in Rhodesia in April 1980 to preside over the independence ceremonies, but just two weeks before Charles's arrival, Andrew Parker Bowles made headlines of his own.

The *Daily Telegraph* reported that, in anticipation of the Prince's coming, Parker Bowles decided to 'test-drive' a buffalo. He attempted to ride the beast bareback – a feat which was to be copied by Charles if the experiment was successful in order to give the media a dramatic photo opportunity. Unfortunately, on the first 'test-drive', Andrew was thrown from the rampaging beast and badly gored – an accident which required him to have sixteen stitches put in his leg and groin.

Gallantly, Andrew rose to the occasion, telling reporters: 'It was damn near the end of a dynasty.'

Upon his arrival in Rhodesia, Prince Charles was invited to dine at Government House with Lord and Lady Soames, Andrew Parker Bowles and his photographer friend. But three days before the dinner, Camilla phoned from England and said she would be arriving in Rhodesia the following day.

A staff member inside Government House said: 'The table settings had to be hastily rearranged. The gossip mill was working overtime. No-one knew if Mrs Parker Bowles was coming to see her husband or Prince Charles. As it was, the whole evening passed without mishap. The Prince and Mr and Mrs Parker Bowles all sat there and seemed to have a splendid time together. It was as if their friendship overrode any other underlying feelings. It was a quite extraordinary scene to anyone who knew what was going on. But at that level of society, musical beds is a common pastime. They didn't think it was at all strange.'

Andrew Parker Bowles has often been portrayed as the spurned husband, loyally 'laying down his wife' for the sake of King, country and duty.

In fact, he is a devastatingly handsome man, and certainly no wimp. Even during his courtship of Camilla, he had a torrid affair with Princess Anne.

A Catholic, educated at Ampleforth College, Andrew had his own impressive pedigree. His father, Derek Parker Bowles, was a close friend of the Queen Mother and she was a frequent visitor to Donnington Castle House, the Parker Bowleses' family estate near Newbury in Berkshire. He is related to the Earls of Derby and Cadogan and the Duke of Marlborough. He was a pageboy at the 1953 Coronation of the Queen.

From an early age, Andrew was used to mixing with the royal family. A close family member says: 'Andrew was brought up around the royals. He treated the Queen and the Queen Mother with respect, but they were part of his extended family. He knew Charles, Andrew and Anne from the time they were all kids together. They'd meet at friends' birthday parties and at horsy events with their parents. He knew them all very well; you must never underestimate Andrew's position.

'He knew the Prince of Wales long before Camilla came along. He and Charles were riding to hounds together from the age of sixteen or seventeen.'

Andrew first began dating Princess Anne in 1965. A close friend of his says: 'They shared a love of horses; Andrew was a fine amateur jump jockey. He went out with Anne for about a year. Just a few months before his wedding, when he knew Camilla was sleeping with Charles, he went with Anne to the Ascot races. He was her guest in the royal box. He was always one of her favourite boyfriends. Anne had plenty of boyfriends before she married Mark Phillips. But Andrew was special. Of course, Andrew being a Catholic meant they could never marry. Anne would have had to renounce her claim to the throne. Anne wasn't particularly bothered about the claim to the throne, it was highly unlikely even back then that she would ever be in a position to succeed. But her marrying a Catholic would have been a real problem for the Queen in terms of the constitutional issues it would raise and the waves of negative publicity it would inevitably create.

'Anyway, the affair finally burned itself out.

'When her marriage to Mark Phillips hit the rocks, Andrew was the one she turned to to help her pick up the pieces. They started going out for dinner together and Anne would visit Andrew in London while Camilla stayed in the country, Only when Tim Laurence came along did the relationship cool. But Anne and Andrew are still great friends to this day.'

A friend said: 'Andrew always loved a challenge. He has a certain type he has always gone for. He prefers them blonde, rich and preferably titled. He messed around on Camilla right up to their wedding.

'He was never a cuckolded husband. He just enjoyed having an open marriage. If he wasn't with Camilla, he knew exactly who she was with. So that gave him the freedom to pursue his own dalliances. There's nothing surprising in that among the upper classes. It's been going on for centuries. A long as they stick to sleeping around within their own circle, it's acceptable. What causes gossip, talk and scandal is when people have affairs beneath them. That is considered very bad form indeed.'

John Barratt, Lord Mountbatten's former aide, said: 'Camilla and Andrew carried on being invited for shooting weekends at Broadlands even after the death of

Mountbatten. It was an extraordinary arrangement. Camilla would arrive with her husband but would spend all her time with the Prince. Everyone knew what was going on, but Andrew Parker Bowles accepted it, so far be it for any of us to judge.

'The Prince would arrive alone and he would telephone Camilla. They would go out for long walks together in the grounds, just like they did before she married. Then, in the evening, Camilla and her husband would leave together and Charles would go upstairs a few minutes later. Camilla would then bypass her own bedroom and go into the Prince's. Nothing was ever said. The next morning, there they would all be at breakfast – Camilla, the Prince and Andrew.

'I often wondered how Andrew coped with it, knowing his wife was sleeping with another man while they were all under the same roof together.'

How Andrew coped was to carry on leading his own active social life.

Indeed, in June 1993, Andrew was photographed leaving the London home of Camilla's best friend Carolyn Benson in the small hours of the morning. Both Andrew and Carolyn strongly denied that anything improper had taken place.

A friend of Camilla's says: 'Camilla saw the pictures. She was back home in Wiltshire. But what could she say? The marriage had been an open one for years. The sight of Andrew leaving Carolyn's house in the wee hours would have sent any other wife into spasms of jealousy. But not Camilla. She knew and understood her husband's needs. She is a woman who knows men better than anyone I've ever met.

'Their marriage was bizarre, but it was solid. The fact is, Andrew knew about Camilla's affair with Charles from the start. Camilla knew about all of his peccadilloes. The only one she was slightly concerned about was Charlotte Hambro. They appeared to be getting very close at one stage. But she was hardly in a position to complain.

'It's an arrangement they followed for years. Both Andrew and Camilla were perfectly happy with it. If the world did not understand, they did not care. To them, it was perfectly normal. The freedom of their marriage did not diminish the love they had for one another.'

Back in the summer of 1980, Camilla was still happily involved in her 'discreet' affair with Charles. But she, like the rest of the inner royal circle, knew pressure was mounting for him to take a bride. As in the past, it was to Camilla that Charles turned to ask advice about a prospective wife.

A friend says: 'Camilla always gave Charles advice on his girlfriends. She thought Anna Wallace a little too flighty. Camilla knew how easily Charles fell in love. She would draw up mental scorecards in her head to give his girlfriends marks out of ten. She looked at them all with detached realism, rather than any romantic notions.

'Camilla always told Charles he should find himself a younger woman, one who hadn't had time to develop too many of her own opinions. Her favourite saying was that Charles should find himself a wife who "wouldn't be too much bother".

'Camilla knew the way the royal family worked. And she understood that, at thirty-two years old, Charles was running short of potential suitors. I remember her saying: "How can it be so difficult to find a virgin from the right background? Surely, there must be one virgin out there?"'

Camilla was also increasingly concerned by conversations she was having with staff close to Charles.

Privately, many courtiers confided in her that they feared Charles was becoming a little too similar to his great-uncle, Edward VIII, the late Duke of Windsor.

Edward, like Charles, dithered for years about taking a bride. When he did fall in love it was with Wallis Simpson, an American divorcee who prompted the biggest constitutional crisis of the twentieth century when Edward abdicated to marry 'the woman I love'.

The spectre of Camilla haunted those within royal circles. They could not afford another scandal. And the last thing Camilla wanted was to become embroiled in the headlines. She preferred her affair to remain quiet and discreet.

In fact, it was Camilla who finally came up with the ideal solution. One night, Camilla and Charles were discussing the growing pressure for him to marry. Camilla told Charles he should look more closely at young Diana Spencer, saying to him: 'She could be perfect for what you are looking for . . .'

Love is Blind

Lady Diana Spencer was, indeed, 'quite perfect' for Prince Charles, according to everyone. Everyone, that is, apart from the worried Prince himself.

From the moment her name was first pushed into the frame as a serious potential bride for him, in the summer of 1980, he expressed his 'gravest reservations'.

The couple had first met on a muddy field at Althorp, the Spencer family's magnificent 1,000-acre estate in Northamptonshire in November 1977.

Diana was just 16 years old at the time, with mousy blonde hair and puppy fat. She was on a weekend break from West Heath boarding school in Kent and the pair did not exchange a single word.

Painfully shy, Diana watched her future husband walking forlornly across the ploughed field. As she later recalled: 'My only thought was, "What a sad man." He had such a forlorn expression. I felt quite sorry for him.'

At the time, Charles was having an on-off fling with Diana's older and infinitely more glamorous sister Sarah.

Diana said: 'I kept out of the way. Sarah was enthusiastic in her attentions to the Prince. All I remember about that weekend was that I was the podgy one. I wore no make-up, I was the unsmart lady. But I made a lot of noise and he seemed to like that.'

During an interview shortly after their engagement, Charles said: 'I remember her as a lot of fun. She was very jolly and amusing.'

In November 1978, the Queen Mother, already keeping a wily eye out for potential brides for her grandson, suggested Charles invite the young Diana to his thirtieth birthday party at Buckingham Palace. It was the finest party in London that season.

As shy Di sat at her table, watching the assembled heads of state from around Europe and the *crème de la crème* of British aristocracy, she hardly noticed the older woman with the tousled blonde hair who sat at a neighbouring table. Ironically, Diana had caught her first glimpse of Camilla Parker Bowles, the woman she would grow to despise and whom she would one day accuse of destroying her marriage.

That night, Camilla was escorted by her husband. Their second child, daughter Laura Rose, had been born the previous spring.

A friend of Diana's said: 'Diana was just thrilled to be invited. It was like Cinderella had finally been invited to the ball. It never even remotely entered her head that Charles might be interested in her and, indeed, he ignored her totally. She just sat there and watched what was going on around her. She wasn't asked to dance all night. Not once, not by anyone.

As the Prince's favourite pop group The Three Degrees

entertained guests, Charles ignored the blushing Diana – and danced the night away with Camilla. It was a chilling foretaste of what fate held in store for Diana – a life destined to be spent sitting on the sidelines while the Prince devoted his attentions to Camilla.

The Queen Mother was instrumental, with her good friend Lady Ruth Fermoy, Diana's grandmother, in promoting Diana's charms to the Prince. 'She is so sweet, so terribly quiet, so very innocent,' she would tell her favourite grandson a few days later.

'Yes, but she is so young,' said an uninterested Charles.

'But she would be perfect for you,' replied the Queen Mother.

Diana Spencer, indeed, had the perfect credentials as a future queen.

She was born the Honourable Diana Frances Spencer on 1 July 1961 in Park House on the Queen's Sandringham estate.

Growing up at Althorp she was surrounded by beauty and grandeur but, as her brother Charles would later reveal to Andrew Morton in his devastating book Diana: Her True Story, she was a lonely and troubled young girl.

Her unhappiness began when she was just seven years old: her father Johnnie, the eighth Earl Spencer, split from her mother Frances. Diana was deeply affected by the split. Her father sank into a deep depression and locked himself away for weeks on end in his bedroom, refusing to speak to anyone, including his own children.

Diana was later to tell a friend: 'It was the worst time ever. It made me decide that when I married, it would be for ever. I would never, ever get divorced.'

A member of staff at the Althorp estate said: 'It was a bleak and lonely time for Diana. She was so young and vulnerable and the split left her devastated. She adored her mother, but her mother was the one who moved out. Diana felt torn between her two parents. On one occasion, she had to attend a wedding. He father bought her a lovely new blue dress to wear. Her mother bought her a frilly green dress. Diana was in agony for days, knowing that she would offend one of her parents whichever dress she decided to wear. She was having to make decisions like that at a tender age. And it profoundly affected her.

'Her schoolwork suffered. Diana always had a brain, but she found it hard to concentrate on school when there were so many other issues to think about. In later life, that manifested itself in her belief that she was stupid. She was always putting herself down by making comments like "Brain the size of a pea, that's what I've got" and "I'm as thick as a plank of wood". In fact, she was a very bright child. She just wasn't academic.

'But right from an early age, she was perfect in social situations. She was, by nature, shy and retiring. But she could make people open up to her in a way no-one else could. When one watches her now talking to the elderly and AIDS patients, she has a flawless charm. It is a gift she was born with. As a child, she developed that motherly, nurturing side at school. Diana was always the one who comforted other girls when they were down or miserable. She knew what it felt like to feel alone, abandoned and afraid. And it was in her gut instinct to help other people going through those same, sad emotions. Her charms exceed anything you could learn from a book.'

When Diana's father remarried, to Raine, the former Countess of Dartmouth and the daughter of the romantic novelist Barbara Cartland, Diana was thrown into even deeper turmoil. She was sixteen years old when her father married his new wife quietly at Caxton Hall register office in July 1977.

She loathed her stepmother from the start. After Raine arrived at Althorp, Diana wrote a not so cryptic entry in her childhood diary: 'Raine stops play.'

According to family friends, Diana and her brother Charles were relentless in their hatred of their stepmother.

But Diana did enjoy her time at West Heath School. A schoolfriend remembers: 'She took to boarding school like a duck to water. She was one of the few girls who never cried on the first day at school. Diana would be the one who cried as the time approached to go home at the end of term. School was a welcome relief for Diana from the turmoil of her home life. She was a very sweet child, she was always a bit of a mother hen with the younger girls. But she also had a will of iron. Diana always knew what she wanted. She wasn't academic, but she had a wise head on those young shoulders. If she was determined to do something, she usually would.'

After leaving school with no qualifications, she spent six months at finishing school in Switzerland. When she returned home, her younger brother Charles, now the ninth Earl Spencer, remembers: 'She had developed high cheekbones and a new-found confidence. The ugly duckling was beginning to blossom into a swan.'

In September 1978, Diana had a premonition. She was staying at the home of an old schoolfriend, Caroline Harbord-Hammond, the daughter of Lord Suffield. A fellow guest asked about her father's health and Diana replied: 'I feel he is going to drop down in some way. If he dies, he will die immediately or otherwise he will survive.'

The following morning, the phone rang. Earl Spencer had collapsed with a massive cerebral haemorrhage in the courtyard of Althorp. Diana immediately threw her things into a bag and rushed to her father's side at Northampton General Hospital.

For days, Diana and her brother and sisters waited at the hospital. It was during this period that the bitter feud with stepmother Raine plummeted to new depths. Raine tried to stop the children visiting their critically ill father, who hovered between life and death for three months in a coma. She even instructed the nurses to prevent the children entering his private room. Diana was later to tell friends that, on several occasions, she and her sister Sarah would have vicious shouting matches with Raine in the hospital corridor.

In 1979, Diana moved to London and was given a three-bedroomed flat at No. 60 Coleherne Court, Pimlico, as a corning-of-age present from her father. The flat cost £50,000. She immediately landed a job at the Young England kindergarten. She made extra money for a while working as a weekend 'char lady' for her sister Sarah who lived nearby.

A friend says: 'Diana wasn't embarrassed to do the washing up, dusting and hoovering. In fact, she was never happier than when she was cleaning Sarah's place. She was simply young, naïve and happy to be living in London. She never really had a care in the world in those days. Diana was never a girl who lived the high life. She would spend free times going to dinner parties at the homes of her Sloane Ranger friends or making up the numbers at bridge. She had no thought for the future. She loved children and she just naturally assumed that, when the time was right, she'd find a suitable chap who would have a nice place in the country and life would take its natural course. Diana knew nothing about sex or men. She would flirt with a few of the chaps, but she never had a serious boyfriend, to anyone's knowledge. I would be surprised if Diana had ever even kissed a boy at that stage. She was always aloof, somehow detached from the rest of the crowd. She was fun-loving, but underneath, she never gave too much away. She was just plodding along in her own little world. She was a girl who always knew that, somehow, her future would be mapped out for her.'

By the summer of 1980, the search for a bride for Charles had become frenetic.

Most importantly for Charles, the two women he trusted more than anyone in the entire world, his grandmother and his mistress, were both putting forward the same name as a prospective bride – Diana Spencer.

The Queen Mother invited him to lunch at Clarence House in May 1980. She said: 'Don't dismiss Diana Spencer. She may be a shy little ugly duckling now, but she could be turned into a beautiful swan. She is unspoilt, Charles. Trust me; I know she will be good for you.'

Charles responded by maintaining a discreet silence.

His former valet Stephen Barry said: 'The Prince was pretty firm about the fact that Diana was a young girl and he was a man of the world. He could not see how on earth any relationship could possibly work out. And, of course, time proved his initial feelings were correct.

'But he knew the pressure was on for him to find a bride. He let out a huge sigh one day and said: "You know, if I had my way, I would happily stay single. But it's always duty, duty, duty. My only fear is that in my position, divorce is out of the question. If only one could live with a girl beforehand to test the waters. But I can't even do that."'

Two weeks later, Charles spent the weekend with Camilla in Wiltshire. Her husband remained in London 'on business'.

At this time, the Parker Bowleses, by all accounts, had reached an amicable agreement in their marriage. When they were together, they enjoyed a happy and fulfilling partnership, both devoted to their young family. But when apart, they both pursued their 'outside' interests, no questions asked, no recriminations later.

Camilla said: 'I have spoken to several people about Diana and they all concur she is a sweet young thing. She does not have a great mind, but she is kind and caring and good with children. She could be moulded into something good. And she is from the right stock.'

Finally, Charles's resolve began to weaken. What harm could possibly come of meeting this girl his mistress so thoroughly approved of? After all, if it didn't work out, he would still have the loving arms of the woman he adored to escape to.

He told Camilla he would agree to meet Diana again.

The meeting was arranged for early July 1980 at a party at the Sussex home of Prince Philip's polo-playing friend Commander Robert de Pass.

A fellow guest recalls: 'On the Saturday, we returned from polo at Cowdray Park and Diana was talking to HRH. She was sitting on a bale of hay; he was towering above her. She was wearing one of those stripy blouses and a pair of dungarees. It flashed through a few people's minds that perhaps Diana would be a good match for HRH but we all dismissed it as too implausible. Charles was a man of the world, he'd been sexually involved with Camilla for years. He still was. The idea that this shy little wallflower might interest him in the slightest was absurd. She was a little girl. He was a man. He was used to Camilla's earthy sensuality. Diana was totally un-sexual. She was pretty enough, but she was a girl just like any number of other girls from the right background you would meet fresh out of school. She had very little finesse, she had no sex appeal. All that, of course, would appear in the future. Anyone who looked at Diana back in those

those days would have filed her away under the category of "Must come back later; has potential".'

In fact, Diana *did*, surprisingly, captivate the Prince for the first time as she sat there chattering away on the hay bale. After the usual exchanges, she changed the tone of the conversation to a new level. Staring deep into his eyes, she talked about the death of his beloved Uncle 'Dickie' Mountbatten and his funeral at Westminster Abbey the year before.

She said: 'You looked so sad when you walked up the aisle at the funeral. It was the most tragic thing I'd ever seen. My heart bled for you when I watched it. I thought, "It is wrong. You are lonely, you should be with somebody to look after you."'

Her words struck deep into Charles's heart – and he looked at her with new eyes. Perhaps Camilla and his grandmother were right. There might be more to this girl than he had assumed at first.

A former member of the royal household says: 'At this point he was not in love with Diana, but he was certainly feeling something for her. The Prince is a complete idealist, sensitive and rather protective of his feelings. In his judgement, he was starting to believe a union with Diana could work. She seemed to agree with everything he wanted. He said she understood how he *felt*. For someone as "feeling" as Charles, that was an important plus in favour of Diana.'

A few days after the weekend in Sussex, Charles invited Diana and her grandmother Ruth, Lady Fermoy, to the Royal Albert Hall for a performance of Verdi's *Requiem* followed by a private dinner at Buckingham Palace.

After that dinner, his first thought was to call Camilla. No sooner had Lady Fermoy's Daimler glided through the gates of the Palace to drop Diana back off home at her bachelor flat in Coleherne Court than he was on the phone to his mistress.

Charles explained he had spent the evening with Diana and that she had been rather reserved and shy.

Camilla replied: 'Perfect. She's quite perfect. Quiet as a mouse. No bother there.'

With Camilla's wholehearted approval, Charles invited Diana to join him on the royal yacht *Britannia* during Cowes Week on the Isle of Wight.

A fellow guest on board says: 'Diana was still completely in his awe. He would call her Diana and she would call him "Sir". It was like a young girl talking to her mentor or even her teacher. She was clearly thrilled to be there, but she hardly said a word. She was pretty intimidated by everyone. She was a pretty enough little thing, though, and several of us wondered whether there was more to her and Charles than met the eye. They'd clearly not exchanged more than a few conversations at that stage. But he was quite kind towards her. He smiled in her direction once or twice. Of course, he spent hours every evening on the phone to Camilla.'

Diana was later to recall: 'It just seemed natural to call him "Sir" during those early days. It was obviously right to do so because I was never corrected.

In early September, Diana travelled to Balmoral to spend the weekend of the Highland Games with Charles and the rest of the royal family. Again, she was surprised to find that Camilla Parker Bowles was there.

It was during that weekend that the *Sun* photographer Arthur Edwards first spotted 'Shy Di' on a riverbank waiting patiently as Charles indulged his passion for fishing in the River Dee. In his best-selling book, *I'll Tell the Jokes, Arthur*, the top photographer remembers: 'I saw a boyish figure hidden in an old green Barbour jacket, wellington boots and peaked cap. When she heard our car arrive, she ran and hid behind a tree. Then she started to climb a hill away from the river without once turning her head to look back. In a minute or so, she had taken cover in the car.

'In fact, no-one pictured them together until the day of their engagement nearly six months later.

'But I knew something was up. I'd taken a picture of Diana at a polo match five weeks earlier. I took the picture on a hunch. She was just standing there watching the game, but I just felt she was watching it with a special type of interest. I just had a gut feeling about that girl.

'After seeing her at Balmoral, something twigged. It was like warning bells went off in my head. I rang the office and told them I just knew that Lady Diana Spencer was "The One".

'I'd been hearing her name mentioned by my royal sources for several weeks as the girl who was being groomed for greater things.

'We decided to go with the story.'

The following morning, the first story about Di and Charles appeared in the *Sun* under the headline: HE'S IN LOVE AGAIN . . . LADY DI IS THE NEW GIRL FOR CHARLES.

From the moment the first edition left the presses, the rest of Fleet Street were in hot pursuit. Reporters and photographers camped outside Diana's flat and she was caught in the glare of the public spotlight which was soon to become such an enormous part of her life.

Later that month, the now famous picture of Diana standing holding two children in the grounds of the Young England nursery school in Pimlico where she worked part-time appeared on the front pages – and captured the heart of the nation. Wearing just a flimsy summer dress with her back to the sun, Diana's lovely long legs could be clearly seen. Naively, she had forgotten to wear a petticoat. As the sun shone through the dress, Lady Diana Spencer's undoubted charms were on display for all to see.

Charles would later remark: 'I knew you had good legs, but did you really have to show them off to the entire world?' It was a comment which Diana said wounded her greatly.

But the Prince's half-hearted courtship continued. In October 1980, Diana was invited down to Highgrove, Charles's eight-bedroomed mansion on a 395-acre Gloucestershire estate, which was in the process of being renovated. She was to spend the weekend with Charles at nearby Bolehyde Manor as guests of Andrew and Camilla Parker Bowles.

She later told a friend: 'I was young and naïve, but I was beginning to feel this was not the normal way one conducted a romance. Camilla Parker Bowles was always there.'

That first Saturday morning, Andrew and Charles went shooting, leaving Diana alone with Camilla As the two women walked through the gardens of the seventeenth century manor house, Camilla quizzed Diana about her plans.

'Do you hunt?' she asked.

Diana replied that she was terrified of horses after breaking her arm as a child in a fall. Camilla smiled, knowing she would always be able to meet her Prince in the safety of the hunting field.

The two women never enjoyed any kind of friendship.

In earlier accounts of the 'wooing' of Diana Spencer by her Prince, it was suggested that the marriage proposal took place in the cabbage patch at Camilla's home. This is untrue. In fact, the Prince did have a long conversation with Diana about marriage in the cabbage patch at Bolehyde Manor.

A close friend of the Prince says: 'He didn't propose, he didn't even make a declaration. But they did speak for well over an hour about their feelings on marriage. Diana said all the right things about wanting children and believing a woman's place was in the home, supporting her husband. She was very frank with him that, if he were to propose, she fully understood what she was getting into. He was pleasantly surprised by that conversation. He felt Diana had shown a maturity beyond her years.'

A few days later, Camilla accompanied Diana to Ludlow Races. The Prince, a keen amateur jockey. was to ride his horse Allibar in the Clun Handicap steeplechase. While Camilla looked relaxed and smiling, Diana appeared tense and on edge. The two women were photographed leaning over a fence, watching the Prince's every move absorbed in their own individual and separate loves for the same man.

Diana later told a friend: 'I felt so vulnerable. It was clear that I was the outsider in that friendship. Charles was much keener to talk to Camilla than to me. He practically ignored me. I felt that, throughout that whole time, Camilla was simply sizing me up. When Charles finished racing, it was Camilla he ran towards and started talking to. He all but ignored me. You could tell by the way they were looking at each other that something was going on.'

The friend added: 'She was beginning to feel like a lamb going to the slaughter.'

A friend of Camilla's says: 'In those early days, Camilla was a king-pin in the budding relationship, but Diana never realized it. Diana was so naïve, she thought the Prince was pursuing her because he was madly in love with her. Charles was fond of the girl, of course, but his main reason for continuing the relationship was that

Camilla was so positive about Diana. Diana failed to realize how strong an ally Camilla would be if she became friends with her. Diana was scared of Camilla; to be honest, she always has been.

'Diana knew from very early on that Camilla had a relationship with Charles on a deeper level of intimacy than she could ever hope to achieve.

'Camilla knew everything. She tried to be friendly to Diana, but Diana always saw her as a threat. The problem with that girl was that she wasn't clever enough to play the game. If Diana had seen Camilla as an ally, as someone who knew the Prince so well she could have offered invaluable advice to Diana on how to handle him, things might have worked out very differently.

'But Diana always thought that once she'd bagged her man, Camilla would simply disappear out of the picture. Of course, that was never going to happen.

'For her part, Camilla thought Diana sweet enough, but rather dense and stupid.'

But Diana was not so stupid that the terrible reality of Charles's ongoing infatuation for Camilla did not dawn on her. When Diana, living under siege from the press in Coleherne Court, sought sympathy from Charles, he responded: 'Yes, yes dear. But Mrs Parker Bowles is going through precisely the same thing. Just hold your head up, smile bravely and say nothing. Camilla's going through it too, you know. You mustn't feel too sorry for yourself. It will soon be over.'

Diana, in an uncharacteristic outburst, told a friend: 'Why does he care more about her than he does about me? I'm the one he's supposed to be marrying, for God's sake.'

But what infuriated Diana more was that Camilla knew even the most intimate details of her romance with Charles, down to their most private conversations. Diana told a friend in exasperation: 'I feel like Camilla is watching over my shoulder, even when Charles and I are having dinner in private – which doesn't happen very often.'

In later years, Diana was to say: 'I remember I asked him once why he spent so much time with Camilla, a married woman. He just shrugged his shoulders and said: "Because she is safe."

'At the time, I thought the friendship was what he was talking about; that it was safe for them to be friends because she was married and no-one would gossip. What I quickly came to realize was that he meant Camilla was safe because he could carry on sleeping with her and no-one would suspect a thing, presumably, least of all, me.

'What really infuriated me was that the next time I saw Camilla, she patted me on the shoulder and told me "not to worry" about her.

'I thought about it later and it was obvious Charles had told her I was worried about her. He told that woman everything. I didn't just marry Charles, I married his mistress too. There was nothing that went on in my marriage she didn't know about.'

But the event which almost prompted Di to end the romance with Charles took place in November 1980. The *Sunday Mirror* ran a front-page story claiming that, on 5 November, Diana had enjoyed a secret romantic rendezvous with her lover aboard the royal train in a siding in Holt, Wiltshire.

Diana, who had been at home in her flat that night nursing a hangover from Princess Margaret's fiftieth birthday party the night before, knew the mystery blonde woman spotted slipping on to the train could not possibly have been her.

The Palace issued an instant denial. However, the story had been fundamentally correct. The Prince had enjoyed a late-night rendezvous with his blonde lover – but it had been Camilla, not Diana, who had slipped aboard the train that night.

The train's telephone log revealed Charles had made a late-night call to Camilla's home, Bolehyde Manor – less than fifteen miles away.

Only three people knew the truth – Diana, Charles and Camilla.

Camilla and Charles were never going to reveal the truth – and Diana chose to ignore it. She was close to realizing her main ambition in life, winning the Prince's hand in marriage, and she was not prepared to jeopardize it at this stage.

By January 1981 speculation was at fever pitch that Diana was 'the chosen one'.

Charles, meanwhile, continued his relationship with Camilla. Just days before leaving to spend Christmas at Sandringham, he drove down to Wiltshire to give Camilla her present, a gold necklace. Diana received a book and a jumper.

In the New Year, Charles went skiing in Klosters, Switzerland. Although he still had serious doubts that Diana would make a suitable wife, his mind was made up in a late-night phone call to Camilla. She told him that even if he married Diana, she would be there for him 'always'.

He took a deep breath and replied: 'In that case, I shall allow my head to rule my heart.'

Charles telephoned his future bride and informed her he would be returning on 3 February and would like to see her three days later.

The proposal took place on 6 February in the nursery at Windsor Castle. When Charles first asked her to marry him, Diana collapsed in a fit of giggles. When he explained the seriousness of his proposal, she went quiet – and said, 'Yes please.'

She had agreed to become the second woman in Prince Charles's life.

Two days later, Diana joined her mother on her last private holiday. Her mother, Frances Shand Kydd, was living with her then husband Peter on a sheep ranch outside Canberra in New South Wales, Australia.

Diana, blinded by love and thinking Charles was in love with her, became worried when she had not heard from her fiancé two days into her ten-day stay. She telephoned his private offices at Buckingham Palace only to be told the Prince was not there. Disappointed, she hung up. She tried again a dozen times in the next twenty-four hours. No reply.

What Diana did not realize was that Charles, on the eve of his engagement, was in the arms of the only woman he has ever truly loved: Camilla Parker Bowles.

Stephen Barry was amazed no-one close to the Prince was taking his growing reservations about his marriage seriously. Barry said: 'The Prince was becoming more agitated by the day. The engagement was imminent, but he knew then that he was being forced into a marriage he really didn't want with a woman he really didn't know or love.

'I remember one day, just before the engagement was announced, I found him in his study. He was clearly worried. He said: "I'm making an awful bloody mistake."

'It was a terrible thing to hear him say. The whole country was captivated by Diana, everyone loved her – except the man she was going to marry. But Sir's problem was always that he felt he had to put duty first. He was thirty-three years old; marriage was inevitable. And Diana was the girl who had been chosen for him. If he ducked out now, there would be an almighty row. And he couldn't face that. Perhaps in his heart, he thought he might grow to love Diana. But he already knew in his heart who he truly loved, and that was Camilla. I thought of it rather like a Greek tragedy. Here was the man who appeared to have everything, yet the one thing he truly wanted was the one thing he could not have. And that was Camilla Parker Bowles.'

During their first post-engagement interviews with Press Association reporter Crania Forbes, Charles made a telling comment in response to the question: 'Are you in love?'

He replied: 'Whatever that may mean.'

During the interview, the couple barely exchanged glances and sat at opposite ends of a sofa.

Prince Andrew was heard to say a few days later: 'He's not in love with her, you know. Let's keep our fingers crossed that he will learn to love her or at least learn to live with her in a civilized manner.'

On 26 February, Diana was examined by the Queen's loyal gynaecologist Dr George Pinker and was pronounced fully fit – and a virgin.

The engagement was announced to a jubilant country at eleven in the morning, 28 February 1981.

The previous evening, Di had packed her bags at Coleherne Court, the beloved flat she shared with old schoolpals Virginia Pitman, Carolyn Bartholomew and Anne Bolton. As she bade her loyal friends farewell, she begged them to stay in touch 'because I shall need you'.

Escorted away from the flat by her new Scotland Yard bodyguard Paul Officer, he quipped: 'This is the last night of freedom in your life, so make the most of it.'

She would later remark: 'Those words felt like a sword through my heart.'

Diana arrived at Clarence House, the Queen Mother's London home, later that evening. No sooner had the footman closed the door on her as she entered her new temporary home for the first time than Diana spotted a white envelope resting in the middle of the bed.

She later told a friend: 'I could not imagine what it could be. I naturally assumed it would be a welcoming note from Charles. I tore it open and then my heart sank. It was from Camilla. How the hell did she know where I was going to be unless Charles had told her in advance exactly what our plans were?

'For God's sake, I only knew the engagement was going to be announced on 28 February when the Palace called earlier that morning and told me I was moving to Clarence House that night in preparation for the announcement the following day.

'Camilla's note was dated three days earlier. That bloody woman knew before me.'

A friend of Camilla's says: 'Of course Camilla knew. The Prince tells her everything, always has. He keeps no secrets back from Camilla. She is his best friend so, of course, he rang her and told her that the engagement was imminent.'

In the note, Camilla invited Diana to join her for lunch. The pair met at Buckingham Palace three days later. It was a tense lunch. Camilla tried to talk to the nervous bride-to-be, but Diana clammed up.

According to a friend of Camilla's: 'It is unfair to see Camilla as the wicked witch in all of this. She truly wanted to help and guide Diana. But Diana was already being a stubborn little thing. Her back was up. She distrusted Camilla. Most importantly, she misjudged Camilla. What she failed to grasp was that Camilla's loyalty has always been to the Prince. Camilla hoped she would get along well with his new bride. If Diana was not exactly rude to Camilla, she certainly did not go out of her way to be friendly. Camilla left that lunch a little dejected. For the first time, she questioned herself about whether Diana was emotionally secure enough to cope with the mammoth task that lay ahead of her.'

Shortly afterwards, Charles left for a five-week visit to Australia. The world watched as Diana clutched at his arm at the airport and broke down sobbing.

What the world did not know was that Diana was heartbroken about an incident which had occurred just thirty minutes before they left for the airport. Diana was at his side in his private office in Buckingham Palace as he sorted out some last-minute paperwork.

The phone rang – and it was Camilla. Diana later claimed her fiancé asked her to leave the room so he could say goodbye to his mistress. She told friends her heart was 'broken into a hundred pieces' that morning.

But Charles's friends tell a very different story.

According to one: 'The phone went and it was Camilla calling to bid HRH farewell, as was quite within her rights as an old friend of twenty years to do.

'As soon as Charles picked up the phone, Diana flew into one of her tantrums. Charles didn't know how to handle her. She was like a petulant schoolgirl.

'He put his hand over the receiver and tried to talk to Diana. She was getting hysterical and saying something along the lines of "I suppose you want me to leave now?"

'He replied: "Of course not. You can stay here, I'll only be a minute." But he barely had time to get the words out of his mouth than Diana stormed out of the door, slamming it behind her.

'Charles was distressed by her behaviour. It was irrational and uncalled for. Camilla had simply called up to wish him well. Diana blew up the significance of the call out of all proportion. And it left Charles feeling perturbed. Even back then, he did not know what to do when Diana went into one of her rages. As their marriage progressed, she flew off the handle more and more.

'Of course, by this stage Diana was already suffering from bulimia, when she binged on food and then threw up. But Charles had no idea of her illness. He'd never encountered anything like that before. He knew the Spencer girls were volatile; he'd dated Diana's sister Sarah a couple of years before. But it worried him that the girl he had picked to be his future queen was acting in such a way.

'I remember him saying some time later: "I don't know what to do. Diana flies into a rage at the slightest thing. It worries me sometimes. Either I am so old and fuddy-duddy that I don't know what's going on – or she has some kind of psychological problem. I hope, for all our sakes, that the former is true. For if the latter is correct, I dread to think what might happen."'

Just five days before the wedding, Charles voiced his fears to John Barratt.

Barratt said: 'I knew Charles was still very much in love with Camilla and was having difficulties with Diana. Literally the week before the wedding he told myself and Lord Romsey that Camilla was the only woman he had ever loved. He told us: "I could never feel the same way about Diana as I do about Camilla."

'Lord Romsey simply assured him that his feelings would, most likely, change.

'The Prince was fascinated by the fact that Diana was still a virgin and he knew it was his duty to get married. But I knew that once his physical urges had been satisfied by getting Diana into bed, the marriage had no chance of lasting.

'Diana was very beautiful, but she lacked intelligence. Charles could talk to Camilla about anything, but that wasn't the case with Diana. She was young and had totally different interests. She hated hunting, shooting and fishing. She loathed his boring friends. She despised standing around for hours on freezing grouse moors. They had absolutely nothing whatsoever in common.

'It was only a matter of time before Charles gave up on her – and went back to Camilla. I knew Camilla well, and she clearly knew this too.'

In July, less than a week before the biggest day of her life, Diana entered the private offices at Buckingham Palace she shared with Michael Coleborne, the man in charge of the Prince's finances. She spotted a small package on his desk, beautifully wrapped up and tied with a small, pink bow. Unable to resist, she looked at the label. It was addressed to Camilla – from Charles. With trembling fingers, Diana opened the box. Inside, nestling on blue velvet, was a small gold bracelet with a blue enamel disc and the initials 'GF'. The initials stood for Gladys and Fred, Charles's and Camilla's nicknames for each other.

When a tearful Diana confronted Charles about the 'inappropriate gift' he replied: 'What's inappropriate about it? It's just a little thank-you to a dear friend.'

But Diana was not so sure. Just two days before she discovered the bracelet, she had overheard Charles ordering a bouquet of flowers to be delivered to Camilla – who was suffering a bad dose of the 'flu. She heard Charles instruct the florist to sign the accompanying card: 'To Gladys. Get well soon, old girl, love Fred.'

Diana was already harbouring grave suspicions that Camilla was more than just a friend.

Although she did not realize it at the time, her worst

nightmare was only just beginning. She voiced her fears to her closest friends and family, but they told her it was too late – the country was in the grip of royal wedding fever.

Diana's sister Sarah used Diana's childhood nickname when she told her: 'Bad luck, Duch. Your face is on the tea towels, so it's too late.'

Both Charles and Diana wanted to call the whole thing off. Just the week before the wedding, Charles told a friend: 'I feel like the whole thing is out of my control. I have not had time to even get to know this girl I am marrying. I will do my duty – and I pray for all of us that this thing works out.'

It was too late for both of them. The date had been set. St Paul's Cathedral was being prepared.

The Greatest Show of All was about to begin.

The Wrong Woman

'KISS HER! KISS HER! KISS HER!' The chant of half a million people packed into the Mall could be heard a mile away. It was the greatest day for decades in the history of the British monarchy

The Big Day, 29 July 1981, dawned fair and sunny. The hopes and expectations of the country rose to the occasion. Only two people were harbouring last-minute fears that this wedding might not be all it appeared. And they were the bride and groom.

As the crowd begged for the kiss to seal the perfect day, Prince Charles leaned back slightly and whispered to his mother, 'May I?' After a nod of approval from the Queen, Charles leaned forward and planted a kiss full on the lips of Diana, Princess of Wales. It was a picture beamed across the world as the final seal of 'love' on a perfect union. But what no-one knew as they watched the fairy-tale marriage unfold before their eyes that day was what had taken place just twenty-four hours before.

As he nervously awaited his fate, Charles stole his last moment of happiness – in the arms of Camilla. As the world thrilled to the impending wedding of Charles to Diana, he was in bed with his long-time mistress.

He had attended a dinner party hosted by the Queen in the Palace on the Monday night before the wedding. Earlier in the day he had arranged a secret rendezvous with Camilla in the London 'safe house' of a friend to present his mistress with the 'Fred and Gladys' bracelet – the same gift which had sent Diana into a blazing rage just a few days before.

After the small dinner party that night, the group moved on to a nearby ballroom for a bigger and more formal wedding dance. It was a memorable night, packed with eight hundred of Diana's and Charles's friends. The bar staff handed out a cocktail called 'A Long Slow Comfortable Screw Against the Throne'.

Charles danced twice with Camilla and then discreetly mingled with the other guests. Diana danced the night away too, before leaving shortly after one in the morning to spend the night at Clarence House. As she left the party, Charles's valet handed her a small package. Inside was a gold signet ring engraved with the Prince of Wales feathers and a card which read: 'I am so proud of you. When you come up, I'll be there at the altar for you tomorrow. Just look 'em in the eye and knock 'em dead.'

The note and the present made Diana feel more secure than she had in weeks. Before she fell asleep, she took a final look at her stunning £25,000 wedding gown, designed by Elizabeth and David Emmanuel, and smiled. Whatever fears she held were over-shadowed by her hopes and expectations for the greatest day of her young life.

Camilla's husband Andrew retired early. He was preparing for duty – riding alongside the royal carriage the following day on its way back from the wedding ceremony at St Paul's.

As the party reached its end, around half past two that Tuesday morning, the day before the wedding, Charles and Camilla slipped away.

As the Prince's valet Stephen Barry said: 'We all knew how he felt about Camilla. It was a very emotional last assignation for them both. But to do it on that night was truly incredible. Certainly incredibly daring, if not incredibly stupid.'

Another guest said: 'It was fairly obvious what was going on. Both Charles and Camilla had had a bit to drink, but neither was drunk. He left the room first and she seemed to be hanging on in a corner on her own. There was only a handful of people left in the room. Everyone was preparing to go home.

'Someone brought Camilla's coat in for her and she put it on. Then she said she had to nip to the loo. She left the room with her coat on. She never returned. Presumably, the idea was to give those of us who still remained there the impression that she had gone to the loo and then got into her car to go home.

'But no-one was that naïve. We waited for her by the main entrance for a while. But she had disappeared from sight. Everyone naturally assumed that she had been secretly escorted upstairs to the Prince's quarters.

'It seemed a rather foolhardy thing to do, but no-one really thought that much about it. I mean everyone needs to have a final fling.'

On the morning of the wedding, a select group of guests enjoyed a breakfast banquet at the Palace. Camilla had left by private car at around five o'clock.

It came as a surprise to most of the assembled guests that Camilla, the Prince's oldest and dearest friend, had not received an invitation. It was Diana's first act of defiance. According to one guest, Diana had absolutely refused to issue an invitation to Camilla on this, the biggest day of her life.

The guest says: 'Diana was adamant that Camilla should not be at the breakfast, When the list was being drawn up a month earlier, she simply put her foot down. She told Charles that "nothing and no-one" was going to spoil her wedding day. And she struck Camilla's name from the list. Charles was surprised, but he relented.'

The wedding was a glorious success.

Diana's brother Charles told author Andrew Morton: 'My sister was transformed that day. She was never one for make-up but she did look fantastic. It was the first time in my life I ever thought of Diana as beautiful. She really did look stunning that day and very composed, not showing any nerves, although she was slightly pale. She was happy and calm.'

As she walked down the aisle, her father leaning heavily on her arm, Diana had ample time to spot the assembled guests – including Camilla Parker Bowles. As she recited her wedding vows, 750 million people worldwide watched in awe.

Diana was later to say, with detached emotion: 'I had tremendous hope in my heart that day.'

As Charles and Diana rode back to the Palace for their reception, they were escorted by twenty-four horsemen of the Blues and Royals, dressed magnificently in their plumed hats and bright-blue jackets. Among them was Andrew Parker Bowles, the husband of the groom's mistress.

Camilla, who was among the guests at St Paul's, was again snubbed by not being invited to the reception. She celebrated with friends at a private dinner party.

Stephen Barry later recalled: 'The Prince told me he had stayed up the night before listening to the crowds singing "Rule Britannia" on the pavement beneath his window. He said he had found himself with tears pouring down his face. At the time, I thought they were tears of emotion at the tidal wave of patriotism that was sweeping everyone. Perhaps, though, those tears were tinged with sadness at the realization that he was marrying the wrong woman.

At Waterloo Station, as the day drew to a close, Diana and Charles boarded the royal train which was to take them down to Lord Romsey's Broadlands estate for the first three days of their honeymoon. The couple spent their first night in the Portico Room, the place where Charles had made love to Camilla for the first time, fifteen years earlier.

Charles, used to the mature affections of Camilla, was later to confide to a friend: 'That first night was nothing special. It was pleasant enough, of course. But she really was painfully naïve. It was clear she had absolutely no experience whatsoever in the bedroom.'

The friend commented that the words were spoken in a dull, emotionless voice.

He says: 'As for any man, Charles's big prize was Diana's virginity. But that was achieved without so much as a bang or a whimper. I was left with the impression that the whole accomplishment was rather an anti-climax for Charles. He was an experienced lover. He was used to sleeping with a woman who knew what to do. Diana hadn't a clue. In retrospect, it's jolly sad, but Charles would have preferred a night with Camilla any day of the week.'

Diana herself later complained of her husband's

'insatiable' sexual appetite. She said: 'He wants it all the time. I don't know what to do with him. I don't particularly care for it all that much.'

The newly-weds then flew to join the royal yacht *Britannia*, moored in Gibraltar, for a two-week cruise around the Mediterranean.

The honeymoon was a disaster from the start. Diana, already stricken by the bingeing and purging disorder bulimia, was already looking painfully thin. She gorged and vomited every day of what was supposed to be the most romantic time of her life.

One night she devoured an entire steak and kidney pie followed by a huge bowl of custard. While crew members marvelled at her ability to 'eat like a pig and stay skinny as a rake', as one put it, Diana rushed to the bathroom and made herself sick in secret.

Charles was later to tell Camilla: 'During the honeymoon, she smelled of sick the whole time. It turned my stomach. Of course I knew what she was doing. You only had to spend a few days with her to realize what was going on. She must be thick to think I don't know what she's doing.'

Diana, on an emotional rollercoaster after the wedding, made herself sick five or six times a day during her honeymoon. Her mental condition worsened when, alone in their stateroom during the first week of the cruise, Diana picked up Charles's official engagement book – the diary which listed all royal visits for the coming three months. As she moved the weighty book, two pieces of paper fluttered to the floor. Picking them up, Diana discovered to her horror that they were two private snapshots of Camilla. Diana stormed up to the main deck and confronted her husband of less than seven days.

Through her tears, she screamed: 'Why don't you just face up to the truth and tell me it's her you love and not me?'

Charles simply blushed and explained they were old pictures of a friend which he had forgotten to remove. Diana had thrown the photographs into a rubbish bin. Charles later sneaked downstairs and retrieved the crumpled snaps.

A few days later, during a state dinner aboard for Anwar Sadat, the Egyptian President, Diana noticed her husband was wearing a pair of gold cufflinks intertwined with two gold 'C's. Charles admitted they were a wedding gift from Camilla, but said rather hesitantly: 'Don't start getting ideas. Please, let's not start this marriage with any bother.'

But again his words did nothing to soothe Diana's troubled mind. She locked herself in their bathroom after the dinner and sobbed loudly. Emerging an hour later with red-rimmed eyes, she asked him: 'Why do you need these constant reminders of that woman? Why can you not forget her and concentrate on me? I am your wife now, she is nothing to do with us.'

Charles replied: 'But she is something to do with us. She is my oldest friend. If only you would realize that and try to become friends with her too. If you bothered to get to know her, you would get to like her.'

Diana simply shook her head and burst into tears.

By the time they returned to Balmoral, Charles was having his own doubts about the marriage.

He asked Stephen Barry: 'Is it normal for wives to be so obsessed by one's past?'

Barry was later to reflect: 'I told him it was quite normal. But I wanted to add that it was not normal for a man to make contact with his mistress so soon after marriage.'

For Charles had already decided not to give up Camilla's charms. He placed a ship-to-shore phone call to his mistress from *Britannia* on the fifth day of his honeymoon. He also secretly sent her a three-page letter describing his feelings.

Once back in Britain, their old routine of calling each other every day began again.

Barry said: 'Sir would be more discreet than he had to be in his bachelor days. He would make a point of calling Camilla direct from his office most days. If it was impossible to call, he would write a letter which would be smuggled out without the Princess's knowledge. It was extraordinary. The Prince simply had to be in constant contact with Camilla or he could not function properly. If he went without his daily phone call, he would become tetchy and ill- tempered. Camilla was a habit he could not break, an obsession he did not wish to conquer.'

Diana's fears and paranoia only worsened when, on the final leg of the honeymoon in Balmoral, she discovered two love letters from Camilla to Charles in his private quarters. According to a staff member, the letters 'were so intimate they revealed a long-term commitment between the two. Diana knew from the tone of the letters that Charles fully intended to continue his relationship with Camilla.

'She copied both letters. She had only been married a few weeks, but she was already thinking ahead. Diana still has those letters in her possession.

The Balmoral leg of the honeymoon left Diana depressed and miserable. Charles left her for hours on end to tramp the moors and spend endless days fishing. Diana became bored and fed up. He encouraged her to join him during his hunting trips. She refused. She begged Charles to cut short the trip and return to London with her, but he was in his element and refused point blank. He said: 'Who on earth ever heard of anyone cutting short their honeymoon?'

Diana plunged deeper and deeper into depression – and she began heaping the blame for her anger and unhappiness squarely on the shoulders of Camilla Parker Bowles.

Indeed, from the moment she discovered the secret love letters, Diana vowed never to use Camilla's name again. From that moment on, she always referred to Camilla in private as 'The Rottweiler'.

She would tell friends: 'The Rottweiler is the main reason I'm going through this hell. I honestly believe if she disappeared, I would at least have a chance to try and make Charles love me. But with that woman around, I have no chance. He's not even thinking about me; all he cares about is Camilla.'

But Camilla refused to turn her back on Charles – or allow his young wife's outbursts to affect their friendship.

A friend says: 'In the early days of the marriage, Camilla had no axe to grind against Diana. She truly hoped the marriage would work. But she could not give up on her friendship with the Prince. As the months went on, Camilla realized Diana was not making Charles happy. As he told her more and more about Diana's increasingly erratic behaviour, Camilla, in turn, came up with her own phrase for the Princess – she would refer to her as "that ridiculous creature".

'You have to realize, Camilla is not a malicious woman. But her loyalties lie firmly on the side of the Prince. Camilla has always been his most trusted friend. If it comes to taking sides, there is no doubt in Camilla's mind who she will side with. It is always Charles.

'At the very beginning, the two viewed each other with distrust. Within a very short period of time, that distrust degenerated into mutual loathing.'

Living a Lie

Diana was later to tell friends, when the fairy-tale marriage was finally exposed as the sham it had been from the beginning, that the 'spectre' of Camilla Parker Bowles had haunted her life from the start.

When she emerged from her honeymoon into the harsh glare of the public spotlight, everyone was shocked at how thin and frail the Princess had become.

By September 1981, Diana was convinced her husband was secretly telephoning Camilla behind her back. She was absolutely correct. What she did not know was that Camilla and her Prince had made a 'gentleman's agreement' between them – that, although there was no question of them giving up their friendship, that was all it would be after his marriage.

A friend of Camilla's says: 'After the wedding, Camilla was quite prepared to stand back and allow Charles and Diana to get on with their lives. She told the Prince that a continuing physical relationship was out of the question. He accepted that sex ban. He genuinely wanted to make the marriage work.

'But Charles quickly realized he had a major problem with his new wife. They simply had nothing in common, and he had no-one to voice his fears to. His family were still congratulating themselves on the morale-boosting wedding. He found it impossible to have rational conversations with Diana. There was only one person he could confide in and trust – and that was Camilla.

'He began telephoning her regularly. Camilla, being a devoted friend, willingly offered her advice.

'Diana would fly off the handle at the slightest thing. She was always provoking screaming rows with Charles about Camilla. She accused Charles of the most outrageous things. She was quite paranoid. She would scream at him that he was still "fucking Camilla". Diana looked like this sweet little girl – but she had a foul mouth on her.

'She put him through the third degree. Charles had hoped that after the excitement and chaos of the wedding, life would settle down into some kind of normality. But Diana was having none of it. She became paranoid and erratic. If he left the room to make a phone call, she would accuse him of ringing "that fucking woman".

'He was in a no-win situation. Of course he telephoned Camilla, she was his dearest friend. But they were not having any kind of a physical relationship at that stage. That was something Camilla was adamant about. Charles would probably have happily gone back to having a physical affair straight away. But Camilla wanted him to do everything he could to make the marriage work.

'Increasingly, even she became more and more dismayed by Diana's outbursts.'

At the beginning of October, Charles was convinced his new bride had deep-rooted psychological troubles. Just eighteen months earlier, she had been a fun-loving kindergarten teacher. Now, she was the most famous woman in the world. And the pressures of her new high-profile life were clearly getting to her.

He telephoned Camilla and she sensibly recommended he seek professional help for Diana. She told him: 'She needs proper help. This is something you cannot deal with alone.'

Throughout October 1981, Diana was visited dozens of times at the Palace by a succession of psychiatrists and therapists. Charles's own doctor, Michael Linnett, was called in to help the tormented Princess. He in turn called in top psychiatrist Dr Michael Pare, an expert in the field of depression.

Charles and his wife attended joint counselling sessions on at least three occasions. The Prince also met the experts separately in a bid to 'understand more' about Diana's torments.

But it was all to no avail.

Said a senior courtier: 'Charles did not fully understand his wife's problems. He believed it was something she would grow out of. Diana was getting more and more depressed. She even began making suicidal threats. But the psychiatrists assessed the possibility of her actually committing suicide as "low-risk". They explained her outbursts and threats were more because of her acute loneliness.'

Diana was also counselled by experts in the field of eating disorders. Mostly, they prescribed her tranquillizers, but Diana refused to take them. For, just fourteen weeks after the wedding, she learned she was pregnant.

The pregnancy served only to make Diana's behaviour more erratic.

Lady Colin Campbell, herself the author of two best-selling books about the royal family, says: 'Diana was and is the consummate performer. To the public, she was this wonderful, fairy-tale goddess when she first burst on to the scene. She smiled sweetly for the cameras and looked like a movie star. The cameras adored her and, of course, the public fell in love with her.

'But, in private, she put Charles through hell. Her mental problems were kept secret from all but those closest to the family. But I was hearing tales of her bizarre outbursts right from the start. Diana was an unpleasant shock to the whole family. The royals were not used to dealing with a young girl who was moody and quiet one moment and then a screaming banshee the next. They simply did not know what to do with her.

'Of course Charles sought advice from Camilla. Camilla has always been a port in a storm to him. When Diana started going mad, Charles sought the sanity of his friendship with Camilla.'

During her first Christmas at Sandringham, Diana suffered a minor nervous breakdown.

In Andrew Morton's best-selling book *Diana: Her True Story*, which was later revealed to be based on a series of taped interviews with Diana herself. The princess provided details of a string of suicide attempts. She portrayed herself as a girl suffering deep depression, who received no help or support from her husband or his family in her hour of need.

According to Morton's book, Diana – by now three months pregnant with Prince William – first tried to kill herself by hurling herself down a flight of stairs at Sandringham in January 1982. Diana said that Charles looked at her with disdain as she lay sprawled on the floor and then coolly turned on his heel and went off to saddle his horse for a day's riding around the estate.

On another occasion, Diana hurled herself against a glass display cabinet, and on another she tried to cut her wrists with a lemon slicer.

Lady Colin Campbell dismisses the suicide stories as 'absolute nonsense'.

She says: 'It's just Diana trying to go for the sympathy vote again. If the girl was serious about killing herself, she would not have tried to cut her wrists with a lemon slicer, of all things. What was she trying to do, peel herself to death? No, those suicide stories were something she made up to gain sympathy from the public. It was just another ploy to turn public opinion against Charles. On another occasion, Diana claims she took an overdose of paracetemol tablets. The Prince was at Highgrove and when he refused to drive back to London to see Diana, as she was insisting he do, she called him back an hour later and said she'd taken an overdose. In fact, the Prince had had a headache the evening before and had gone to the medicine cabinet in search of painkillers. There were four left. He took two and left two. He was disgusted that she'd tried to trick him like that. But he didn't want to take any chances. He got on to their doctor and had him go over to Kensington Palace to check up on Diana, Of course, she was perfectly OK and went out that same evening.'

Indeed, just two weeks after the alleged 'suicide attempt by stairs', Diana and Charles went on holiday to the Bahamas with Lord and Lady Romsey.

Royal watcher James Whitaker says: 'There were no signs that the couple were anything other than blissfully happy. In fact, Diana and Charles behaved like all newly-weds, standing in the water for ages with their arms around each other's necks, kissing constantly. All of which makes the suggestion that, only a couple of weeks earlier, Diana had thrown herself down the stairs at Sandringham completely laughable. I knew about the stairs incident at the time. I spoke to a contact who was on the scene almost immediately Diana had fallen and, far from Prince Charles walking away as she lay there, he was extremely concerned and called a doctor straight away. He waited with her while she was examined and the doctor announced that the foetus was unharmed. He acted with the utmost care and love.'

After the doctor gave Diana the all-clear, Charles took her for a picnic lunch on the Norfolk coast. Her mood instantly improved.

Charles would later say: 'It was amazing how violently her moods would swing. She could be sweet and nice one moment and then terrible the next. She could be dark and gloomy and then happy and smiling a few moments later. I have never, ever known someone who can change so suddenly not just day by day, but literally hour by hour.'

Lady Colin Campbell adds: 'Diana's whole life was a public-relations coup. She knew how to handle the media and she knew precisely what to do to appear to the public as some kind of saint.

'Charles's friends knew the truth. She was a scheming, manipulative little minx.

'She knew she wanted to marry Charles and she conned him right from the start. When he started courting her, she pretended she loved the outdoor country life. She said she "simply adored" hunting and fishing. In fact, she loathed everything about his lifestyle. But Diana wanted one thing more than anything, and that was to win his hand. From the moment she knew she was in with a chance, her mind was made up. She was totally and utterly determined to marry her prince. She successfully managed to con the Queen Mother and Camilla too. They both fell for her little "Shy Di" act.

'Once she had won the main prize, her whole attitude and behaviour towards her husband changed.

'From the start she would chide him for being old and fuddy-duddy. He is a deeply sensitive man who genuinely wanted his marriage to work. But Diana twisted everything. If she broke a fingernail, it was Charles's fault. She blamed her bulimia on Charles. As Charles started drawing away from her, recoiling in horror at this complete loony he had married, she started spreading the word that he was back bonking Camilla. At the time, nothing could have been further from the truth. But, in time, Charles did go back to Camilla.

'I will always believe, as will everyone who knows the Prince, that he desperately wanted the marriage to work. He has always put duty before anything else. He married out of duty but he also hoped to find a woman who he could walk through life with. Within a few months, Charles realized he had married a woman he wouldn't choose to walk to the corner of the street with. He felt conned.

'But Diana was nothing if not resourceful. Once she had determined in her own mind that Charles was closer to Camilla than he was to her, she was determined to knock Camilla off her perch. Camilla's position as a royal confidante carried an enormous amount of social kudos and clout. Her position was superior to most in the royal household and only marginally below that of Diana herself. Diana knew this and was determined to raise merry hell to get rid of Camilla,'

In fact it was Diana who encouraged the late Lady Dale 'Kanga' Tryon to renew her friendship with the Prince.

Diana invited Kanga – who had known the Prince well in his bachelor days but who had drifted apart from him during his marriage – to lunch at San Lorenzo restaurant.

Subsequent photographs of the two women lunching together gave Kanga's image as a royal confidante a boost. Diana later invited Kanga to join the royal family at Balmoral.

A royal aide says: 'It was Diana's way of trying to dilute Camilla's influence. She thought that by creating the image of Kanga as a confidante, Camilla would feel usurped. Of course, nothing of the sort happened. Camilla knew her position in Charles's life, she knew he considered her his main ally. And Diana's cosy plan backfired. Camilla and Kanga got along famously. Kanga quickly realized Diana was a flighty, mentally-confused young woman. She and Camilla would often discuss the Prince's problems together. They became close and dear friends and remained so up until Kanga's death.'

Prince William was born on 21 June 1982. As the country rejoiced at the birth of a son and heir, Diana's behaviour worsened.

A former member of staff recalls: 'She was throwing up ten or twelve times a day. She locked herself away. She was so convinced Charles was back with Camilla that she refused him his marital rights for weeks on end.

'Charles was devoted to William from the start. He adores children and he's quite wonderful with them. But Diana started using the young baby as a foil.

'If Charles wanted to spend time with his son, Diana would say William was sleeping. Diana even instructed William's nursemaid to telephone her every time Charles entered the nursery. Then, she would go upstairs and start a row.

'She was deeply troubled by this point. For example, after her shoes were cleaned she insisted on them being put back in her closet in precisely the straight lines they were in when they were taken away. She was obsessed that everything had to be perfect.

'What had to be perfect above everything else was herself. She started exercising to excess. She was doing 100 sit-ups in the morning and then another 100 at night. She was bingeing and purging all day long. She would go to official functions and pick at a lettuce leaf and then she would binge by eating a whole chocolate cake when she got back home and then throw it straight back up again.'

Charles simply could not cope. He turned more and more to Camilla for advice and comfort.

'I just can't ever have a reasonable conversation with Diana,' he would complain to Camilla.

Camilla, as always, would offer a sympathetic ear and wise advice. In the early years of his marriage, she would counsel Charles to be more understanding and try to explain to him that his new wife was under enormous pressures in her very public role.

'She is young and naïve,' Camilla would say. 'You must be patient with her and allow her to grow into the job. None of us can truly understand what she is going through. The girl's only problem is that she will not listen to anyone's advice.'

Camilla even encouraged Charles to spend more time with his new bride. In the early days of the marriage, he wrote a letter to his closest friends informing them that he intended to devote 'more time' to his family life. He gave up taking so many skiing trips. He stopped going to Iceland to fish every August.

A friend says: 'He was genuinely doing everything he could to make a go of it. He even cut back the amount of time he devoted to his friendship with Camilla. But he had to keep in contact with Camilla. He was living with a whirlwind, a flighty woman he simply did not understand. Camilla always understood. She was the only person he could confide in and know he was totally safe with. He would phone Camilla in tears sometimes, beside himself with anger and frustration. He knew the marriage was a disaster. The only friend he had in the world was Camilla.'

The situation came to a head when Diana overheard her husband making a phone call on a portable telephone from his bath. She heard her husband whisper: 'Whatever happens, I will always love you.' Enraged, Diana stormed into the bathroom and screamed hysterically at her husband for a full ten minutes as he lay in the bathwater.

A former royal aide says: 'The story of Charles's dressing down in the bath soon went around like wildfire. People thought the mental image of the future king sitting stark naked in the bath tub as he had a strip torn off him was rather amusing. In retrospect, it was rather sad. Most of us felt quite sorry for the Prince. He really had no idea how to handle the situation. He started spending more and more time alone. He simply retreated into his shell.'

In fact, Camilla too bore the brunt of Diana's growing obsession with the fact that she believed Charles was having a new affair with his old love.

A friend of Camilla's says: 'As Diana became more erratic, she would take to calling Camilla's house at all times of the day or night. If the Prince was out on official business and dared be even a few minutes late, Diana would call Camilla's home every half an hour, hanging up as soon as Camilla answered.

'Of course, Camilla knew who it was. But it was horrid for her. Most of the time, Prince Charles wasn't even there. But she'd have to put up with the nuisance calls constantly.'

Dame Barbara Cartland, Diana's step-grandmother, recalled her frequent tantrums.

She said: 'I always got along well with the Prince. One day as he told me, Diana asked him, or rather ordered him, to pour her a cup of tea,

'He has a dry sense of humour and he quipped back: "We have people to do that for you here, darling. Why don't you simply ring the bell and get one of the servants to oblige you?"

'She was so boiling mad at him, she picked up the entire teapot and hurled it across the room at him! Can you imagine!'

On another occasion at Sandringham, Charles drove off mid-row with Diana to have lunch with the Queen.

As he stepped into his car in the courtyard, Diana opened an upstairs window and screamed: 'That's right, go and have lunch with your mother and leave me here all alone! You're so bloody selfish.'

Then she ran downstairs and ran alongside him as he drove off in his Land Rover, yelling: 'Yes, dump me like garbage! Leave me on my own again – go on!'

Tales of their frequent rows soon became the talk of the household staff.

Late one evening, raised voices were heard coming from the couple's private quarters.

Diana's voice reached screaming pitch: 'What am I supposed to do all day while you're off enjoying yourself – die of boredom? Call yourself a husband? All you want is to be a husband in the bedroom when it suits you. You can go fuck Camilla if that's all you're interested in.'

One retired staff member says: 'Diana was always ranting and raving. She never cared who heard their rows.

She would be forever criticizing her husband to the staff, something we found slightly improper. I remember after one particularly nasty row, she asked me: "It's wrong what he's doing, isn't it?"

'I replied: "I simply could not say, Ma'am." It was embarrassing. Diana was breaking the golden rule of never discussing your personal problems with the staff. When Charles found out she was talking to everyone, he tried to gently explain to her that her behaviour was "inappropriate" for a woman in her position.

'She merely threw another fit and screamed: "Well, who the hell would you like me to talk to? You never talk to me any more!"'

In September 1982, Diana came face to face with her main rival when she and Charles attended a house-warming party at the Parker Bowleses' new residence. The couple had sold Bolehyde Manor and moved into Middlewick House near Corsham, Wilthire, just twelve miles from Highgrove.

Another guest says: 'Diana was quite rude and objectionable. She arrived, had a glass of water and then started moaning about how she didn't feel well and wanted to leave. Charles was publicly embarrassed. He apologized to Camilla and drove Diana back to Highgrove. He went to his study to work and Diana, who was supposed to be feeling sick, went into the kitchen and ate a huge tub of ice cream. Then she went upstairs and threw up. She refused to talk to Charles for twenty-four hours. She wanted to punish him for dragging her along to the party.'

Charles began seeing Camilla regularly again. They often met on the hunting field as they both rode out with the Beaufort Hunt or crossed paths when he spent the weekend at Highgrove.

Camilla's old friend Carolyn Benson remembers: 'After Charles married Diana and their marriage got into problems, Charles turned to Camilla for help. I think Camilla found herself in a position which got more and more involved without realizing what was happening. Wales was a naughty boy.'

Diana, by this stage, decided she was 'bored' with life in the country, and began spending many more of her weekends in London, meeting friends from her carefree bachelor-girl days at private dinner parties or going out with them to her favourite Knightsbridge restaurant San Lorenzo.

But despite the fact that Charles and Camilla were again growing close, friends insist there was no physical relationship between them.

Camilla told a friend: 'He just needed someone to talk to. By this stage, he could barely stand being alone with Diana. She made his life totally miserable with her antics.'

At the beginning of 1984, Diana became pregnant again – with Prince Harry. As her pregnancy continued, Prince Charles was growing ever closer to Camilla.

A friend says: 'The Prince could not stay away. When Diana was pregnant with Harry, he was on the phone to Camilla five or six times a day and seeing her at every opportunity. It was clear to everyone that the inevitable was going to happen.'

Harry was born on 15 September, 1984. Not long afterwards, Charles went to bed with Camilla again. Their 'gentleman's agreement' not to have a physical affair was over.

He knew Diana had used Harry's birth to score another 'publicity coup'. She had allowed friends to leak a story to the newspapers that Charles was so anxious for the baby to be a girl that when he saw the new baby boy he said: 'Oh, it's a boy – and it's got rusty hair' and then went off to play polo.

Diana was later to tell Andrew Morton: 'Something inside me died. I knew it was the beginning of the end.'

Charles, for his part, knew it was the end too. He angrily telephoned Camilla to tell her how yet another untrue story had somehow been 'leaked' to the press and arranged to see her late one night during that first week after Harry's birth.

After she had consoled him over Diana's publicity stunt, Charles leaned over and kissed Camilla for the first time since they had met up for that final night of passion on the eve of his wedding. Then he led her by the hand upstairs and into the marital bed he had shared with Diana.

Lady Colin Campbell says: 'It was inevitable that Charles would end up back in Camilla's arms and that she would end up in his bed. Charles was livid about the way Diana had used Harry's birth to score points. In fact, Charles was thrilled at Prince Harry. He stayed with Diana at the hospital for hours. He did play polo, but that was the following day. It was hardly as she portrayed it, with him running out of the hospital to go and play.'

The couple's sex life had become non-existent. Diana told one friend: 'He's seldom here to notice me.' And a friend of the Prince would later say: 'Diana may have had this image of a sex goddess, but she was as cold as a fish in the bedroom. The Prince once joked that his wife was so cold, he didn't close his eyes and think of England, he would close his eyes and think of Camilla.'

In fact, it was Diana who initiated the end of their sexual life together. As a bulimic, she was already dissatisfied with her body. A former maid once told how she walked into Diana's bedroom one day to find the Princess standing stark naked in front of a full-length mirror. She was pulling on her flat tummy, trying to pinch any fat that remained.

'It was quite strange,' the maid said. 'The poor girl had nothing there, but she was looking for any minor lump or bump. She always wanted reassurance that she looked lovely before she would leave the Palace. Everyone thought she was beautiful. But she always thought she was fat.'

Convinced that she was overweight, and suffering the headaches and sore throats which accompany violent bingeing and purging, Diana began to push Charles away. When he tried to make the first overtures of love to her at night, she would turn her back and pretend to fall asleep.

A friend of the Prince says: 'He tolerated it for a while, but he soon became peeved by her behaviour. He found it insulting, to say the least. He would often complain in private that his wife was "as cold as a fish". Diana did nothing to encourage him. In fact, her bulimia was a total turn-off for Charles. He would often hear her making herself sick behind the locked bathroom door. Then she would clean her teeth and crawl back into bed. He could smell the sickly combination of toothpaste and vomit on her breath. It was hardly a combination conducive to a night of passion.'

The couple began sleeping apart in their private rooms at Kensington Palace.

Shortly before he died, Diana's father Earl Spencer admitted: 'My daughter was pure when she married. To my knowledge, she has only ever slept with one man in her life – and that is her husband.

'In any case, the trouble with her is that she tells me she doesn't like sex.'

Her brother Charles confirmed: 'Hand on heart, the only man my sister has slept with is the Prince of Wales.'

Diana would often retire to bed at nine in the evening, a habit which irritated Charles.

One member of staff said: 'She'd go off and he'd retire to his study, staying up until all hours listening to opera at full blast. When he'd finished for the night, he'd slip upstairs and began sleeping in a single bed which was prepared for him in his dressing room, which adjoined the master bedroom.

'Diana didn't seem bothered by this arrangement. She knew the marriage was on the rocks.'

While Charles's friends knew he was again having a full-blown affair with Camilla, they maintained a discreet silence. The couple had several 'safe' houses in which they would meet.

One of their closest circle says: 'Once the affair was back on again, there was no problem in Charles and Camilla meeting. They knew lots of people who were more than willing to put themselves out to allow them to meet up in their homes. Everyone knew how Diana had behaved to the Prince and they felt sympathetic towards both him and Camilla.'

But Diana did have some sympathizers.

The unsettled Princess even began behaving erratically in public. At the 1984 State Opening of Parliament, she turned up late with a brand new hair-do which bared her neck for the first time. The Queen was reported to be 'furious' that her daughter-in-law had turned an important state occasion into a front-page fashion statement.

The royal family were, by now, fully aware they had a major problem on their hands. The future king and queen were barely speaking to each other. They were spending weekends apart and the only times their paths crossed were on official engagements planned several months before.

The press had leapt on the story of their bitter feuding and the ongoing 'War of the Windsors' was making almost daily headlines.

Prince Philip was angry at his son for placing the future of the monarchy in jeopardy by continuing his friendship with Camilla. He summoned Charles to a one-on-one meeting at the Palace. Tough-talking and blunt, Philip held nothing back. His face red with rage, he criticized Charles for acting selfishly and told him to 'get his bloody act together'.

Charles, who had never enjoyed a close bond with his father, was flabbergasted. He tried to explain that he was living with a woman who had irrational outbursts and who was suffering from a physical illness.

'Well, bloody well learn to deal with it,' was his father's curt reply. 'This situation cannot go on. It is up to you to put an end to all this nonsense.'

'It's not my fault,' responded Charles,

'I don't care whose bloody fault it is, just end this idiotic situation now!' replied his father.

The row did nothing to improve Charles's mood. He began to realize he had only one true friend who genuinely cared for him – and that was Camilla.

By the end of 1984, Diana began carrying out official engagements on her own. It gave her a chance to enjoy the mass adoration she thrived on, and Charles was not forced to take a back seat to his wife's latest fashion statements as he had done so many times in the past.

Charles continued to meet regularly with Camilla after she had moved to Middlewick House in Corsham,

Wiltshire, a magnificent manor house set in 500 acres and just a ten minute drive from the Prince's home at Highgrove

Diana's main comfort in 1985 was the arrival of Sarah Ferguson. The bubbly redhead was an old friend and when she appeared on the scene as Prince Andrew's girlfriend and then wife, Diana was initially pleased.

But having fun-loving Fergie around soon turned into a chore for the Princess. Charles would say to her: 'Why can't you be more like Sarah?'

The royal family instantly warmed to Fergie, who shared their love of outdoor pursuits and was relaxed and comfortable with the rest of the family. Diana soon began to resent Sarah, She tried to imitate Fergie's fun-loving personality by poking a friend's bottom with the end of an umbrella at the Ascot races and by giggling with her friend during serious state occasions, but her childish behaviour merely served to irritate her husband further.

'I wanted a wife, but I've married a bloody schoolgirl,' he would complain to friends.

After Fergie married Andrew that July in Westminster Abbey, Diana and Charles embarked on a bucket-and-spade holiday to Majorca as the guests of King Juan Carlos of Spain at his Marivent Palace. Rumours would later emerge that Diana and King Juan Carlos spent endless hours flirting with each other.

During this holiday, the rift between Charles and Di became public. They barely spoke to one another and seemed keen to put as much distance between them as possible.

As James Whitaker recalls: 'When Charles came up from his air-conditioned quarters to go windsurfing, she walked off in the opposite direction. When she went diving off the boat, he deliberately looked the other way.

They never once addressed a single word to each other. The five-year-old marriage was dead.'

The final death knell was sounded when Charles cut short his holiday by two days – and flew straight into Camilla's arms. He headed for Balmoral, where Camilla was a guest of the Queen.

By now, Diana was in no doubt that her husband was again sleeping with Camilla.

She said to a friend: 'What I simply cannot understand is what he sees in her. I mean, she's hardly an oil painting. And she is so blunt and rude. What the hell has she got that I haven't?'

What Camilla had was a deep understanding of Diana's husband, something Diana had never been able to attain.

By the beginning of 1986, the fairy-tale marriage was a sham. Diana moved her personal possessions out of Highgrove and into her own rooms at Kensington Palace.

Highgrove had a new mistress – Camilla.

Charles V. Diana

At the beginning of 1987, it was clear to the select few who were invited to spend weekends at Highgrove that Camilla was firmly ensconced as the mistress of the household.

It was Camilla, not Diana, who would greet weekend guests at the door. It was Camilla, not Diana, who would sit at the opposite end of the table from Charles at dinner. It was Camilla, not Diana, who would share his bed at the end of the night.

One member of Charles's inner circle says: 'If Diana's name ever came up during those weekends, which it rarely did, Charles would simply say she had chosen to spend the weekend in London.

'Quite frankly, it was clear by this stage that he'd all but given up on the marriage. Diana never fitted in at Highgrove the way Camilla did. She loathed the conversations at the dinner table, which were often

111

philosophical and highbrow. Camilla revelled in them. She is far more intelligent than Diana ever was; she and Charles are always finding obscure writers to read. They are both prolific bookworms. They never run out of things to say to each other.

'They are one of those couples who seem to know what the other is thinking before any words are spoken. They share private little jokes together. Camilla can say something and then give Charles a secret look and he'll smile back knowingly. They are in absolute unison.

'Camilla's body language gave it all away She was so relaxed at Highgrove. Had one not known that both she and Charles were married to other people, one would quite happily have concluded they were an old married couple.

'Camilla was always fussing over Charles. She isn't a wimp, don't get me wrong. It's just that she clearly has a deep affection for him. She would always be plumping up the cushions on the sofa, fixing a picture frame which was wonky on the wall. Just small things like that, things which the lady of the house would normally do.

'She would often talk with pride about the roses she was growing in the garden. Very often, she would sunbathe in the rose garden in her bikini. They were, to all intents and purposes, living as husband and wife.

'Camilla, unlike Diana, was quite prepared to change her diary to fit in with the Prince's plans. On the weekends he was at Highgrove, she was there all the time for him. To be frank, the food was not always the best but the conversation was always sparkling and the company very exclusive. The conversations about history were always first-class.'

People invited to Highgrove included dozens of Camilla's and Charles's oldest friends.

One visitor was Lady Sarah Keswick, wife of a banker

and daughter of the Earl of Dalhousie. She too shared the Prince's love of music and laughter. Like Camilla, Sarah became a target of Diana's wrath.

One night, Charles invited Sarah to a night at the opera in the royal box at Covent Garden. Diana walked in late and began screaming at them both.

A person sitting in a nearby box said: 'It was quite something. She didn't give a damn who heard her. She behaved more like a fishwife from Billingsgate than a royal princess. I'll never forget it. I had no idea she had such a foul mouth on her.'

Diana contemptuously described her husband's friends as 'that fuddy Highgrove Set' or 'the wrinklies'. But their company suited Charles. They shared his interests: country pursuits, painting, environmental issues, architecture, politics, literature, classical music. Diana, by contrast, liked loud pop music, dancing and the noisy London life – something Charles longed to escape.

His Georgian manor house became his refuge during those darkest days of his marriage – when he knew it was on the rocks, but when he was desperately trying to keep up the pretence of the fairy-tale for the world – and the monarchy. He was never happier than when he was working in his garden at Highgrove or walking around the estate with his gamekeeper – or with Camilla.

He and Camilla even hired portrait painter Neil Forster, who lived a few miles away in Sherston, Wiltshire, to give them painting lessons. They would spend hours in the garden at Highgrove, sketching and painting and talking.

And it was at Highgrove that he was able to enjoy his children. The *Sun*'s royal photo-grapher Arthur Edwards disputes claims put out by Diana's friends that Charles is a cold and distant father.

Arthur says: 'Nothing could be further from the truth.

The thing is, he doesn't push himself forward as a loving parent the way Diana does. I've seen him many, many times with the boys and they both adore him. I've seen both William and Harry spontaneously fling their arms around their dad and tell him how much they love him.

'He's a wonderful father. At Highgrove, he could relax with his sons away from public scrutiny. He spends hours with them, talking to them about their lives and what lies ahead. He has a great rapport with both boys. He is forever taking them out cycling, fishing or even hunting. They both admire their father enormously. But, most importantly, they love him very much too. Any talk of Charles being a cold dad is nonsense. He is a fine father. Considering the cold upbringing he himself endured, it is remarkable that he is so relaxed and open with his own children. Perhaps that is why he is such a good father. He knows what it felt like to have a cold, tough father and a mother who was rarely there. He is determined to have a much closer friendship with his own children. And he has succeeded.'

Arthur told how, in November 1991, he watched Charles say goodbye to his sons, who were flying home after joining him and Diana aboard the royal yacht *Britannia* on an official visit to Canada.

He said: 'The little Princes were clearly upset to be leaving to go home to England without their parents. Charles took it the worst. As Prince Charles watched his two boys walk away, there were tears rolling down his cheeks. It was obvious how he felt.'

Diana would still pay the occasional visit to Highgrove during early 1987. She would tell her friends: 'I have to go down to the prison this weekend – unfortunately.'

In one of her rare visits to the estate, on a weekend during which Charles spent most of his time fishing in a bid to avoid any more fighting, Diana pushed the last-number-recall button on his mobile phone. Her call went straight through to Middlewick House, Camilla's Wiltshire home. She flung the phone to the floor in anger.

She also discovered a secret stash of letters from Camilla in the drawer of the Prince's dressing table in his bedroom.

Camilla and Charles have exchanged hundreds of letters through the years. It is a habit they continued until only recently. Some of the letters are loving and intimate. Others are friendly and chatty. They are a relaxed form of correspondence both enjoy.

The discovery of the letters infuriated Diana. She already had in her possession the 'love notes' she had discovered on honeymoon, but a former staff member says she pocketed another letter. Later, she would tell friends, 'I plan to use them in my divorce action.'

She dined alone that night in her private study and left early the next morning to drive back to London.

Her worst fears were realized when she turned up at Highgrove again three weeks later. Arriving early in the morning, around eight o'clock, with just her detective accompanying her, Diana saw a car driving out of the front gates in the opposite direction. Inside, the Princess saw the familiar blonde head of Camilla.

Storming into the downstairs family room, she discovered her husband having breakfast. 'What was Camilla doing leaving here this early?' she demanded.

Charles simply ignored her and carried on reading his newspaper.

Diana went upstairs to the main bedroom. The four-poster bed she and Charles had shared was unmade, the sheets crumpled and slept in. The Princess then ran into the spare bedrooms; none was disturbed.

She later said to a friend: 'I was hysterical. It was clear the main bed, our bed, my marital bed, had been slept in by two people. I went downstairs and screamed at him for sleeping with that woman in my bed. He wouldn't answer. I was shouting at him and crying but he wouldn't say anything. I kept asking him why he was bonking her. It was the worst moment ever. I felt like it was all over. I knew for sure he was sleeping with that bitch. I seriously thought about topping myself there and then. I knew there was no chance. I knew he loved her and not me – and always had done.'

A friend said: 'Right the way through the difficult time, when the marriage was deep in the mire, Diana always secretly nursed the hope that Charles would realize the error of his ways and run back to her. When it was confirmed to her that day that Charles was sleeping with Camilla, she knew it was over.

'Charles had had enough. He was sick and tired of her antics. He became stubborn. Don't forget, this is a man who has grown up being told everything he does is wonderful. His surroundings have always been controlled. Diana was like a mad bull in a china shop.

'At first he couldn't cope or understand. Eventually he gave up even wanting to understand what was wrong with her or their marriage.

'The fundamental problem has always been that Charles wanted to be loved. Camilla always loved him. Diana was happy to be loved and worshipped by the masses. She never understood Charles.'

In *Diana: Her True Story*, Andrew Morton spoke extensively to used-car salesman James Gilbey – a man whose name was linked with Diana's in the infamous 'Squidgey' tapes.

Gilbey told Morton: 'Diana was never able to get Camilla out of her mind. As a result, their marriage was a charade. The whole prospect of Camilla drove her spare. I can understand it. I mean what the hell was that woman doing in her house? Diana saw the whole thing as a gross injustice.'

In April 1987, Charles went on a solo painting holiday to Italy. Camilla stayed in a neighbouring villa. They used the holiday to continue their secret affair. When word leaked to the press that Camilla had been staying less than ten minutes away from the Prince, her family rushed to her defence.

Andrew's brother Simon said: 'It's nonsense to even suggest any impropriety. Camilla was there with her husband.'

Former Highgrove police officer Andrew Jacques revealed the extent of Camilla's relationship with the Prince in a devastating story in the *Sun*.

Under the headline SEPARATE HOMES, Jacques told how he had once sneaked a peep through the living-room window of Highgrove when Charles was home alone with Camilla.

He said: 'I was patrolling outside the house when I noticed a light on in Princess Diana's private sitting room. The curtains were closed, but through a chink between the drapes, I spied Camilla and Charles dancing cheek to cheek. They were smooching to very romantic music. Then I saw them sitting side by side on the sofa. Then they embraced. They disappeared behind the sofa for a few moments. I could see the Prince's face, but Camilla ducked out of my sight. It was as if she was on her hands and knees. A few minutes later, they re-emerged from behind the sofa and the Prince appeared to be doing up his trousers. Camilla was adjusting her dress. They had obviously been engaged in an intimate sexual act.'

Jacques added: 'The fights and rows erupted frequently between Diana and Charles. Their marriage grew more distant by the day. At the start of their marriage, they were like an ordinary couple. But within a couple of years, they seemed to want as little contact with each other as possible. They never laughed or did anything together.

'The only time they would meet up was if Diana brought the boys down for the weekend. They would meet at mealtimes and very often those meals ended with a blazing row for all to hear.

'They stopped sleeping together. Charles moved his favourite brass bed from Kensington and had it installed in his private dressing room. It was a very masculine room, with no feminine touches.

'The main bedroom with the four-poster was Diana's when she was there. It had her mark all over it. There was a row of forty or fifty cuddly toys like My Pet Monster propped up on a settee. She would bring books with her like the *Relate Guide to Marital Problems*.

'They barely spoke to each other. They were living a lie and it was clear to see. Sir was besotted by Mrs Parker Bowles and the Princess knew it.'

The 1987 marriage of the Marquess of Worcester to actress Tracy Ward showed the depths to which the Waleses' marriage had floundered.

Charles spent the night locked in conversation with Camilla, leaving early. Diana stayed up all night furiously dancing with a succession of men. One of the men she lavished attention on that night was Philip Dunne, a handsome Old Etonian. In full view of the assembled crowd, Diana ran her fingers through Philip's hair and pecked him on the cheek.

Dunne was twenty-eight years old and, according to a friend of the Princess, 'exactly her type'. His father was the Lord Lieutenant of Hereford and Worcester. His long-time girlfriend was the Honourable Katya Grenfell.

Dunne and Diana were soon spotted enjoying dinner at London's exclusive Ménage à Trois restaurant together. Rumours quickly circulated that Diana was enjoying her own fling with Dunne. The rumour reached epic proportions when Dunne was photographed sitting by Di's side at a David Bowie concert that summer.

A couple of weeks later, it was revealed that Diana had spent the night at Dunne's family home in Herefordshire, Gatley Park. His parents were away for the weekend. Charles was alone at Highgrove. Days later, Philip was invited to be a member of the royal party – at Diana's specific request – at the Ascot races. He was photographed sharing a joke with Di in the winners' enclosure.

When news of the non-existent 'affair' hit the newspapers, Dunne received a telephone call from Prince Charles's private secretary He was told, in no uncertain terms, to stop seeing Diana.

To this day, Diana's friends deny any affair. 'She was simply using Dunne to get back at Charles,' says one. 'He was never a serious contender. But he was fun, and he amused her greatly. She never did anything more than flirt with him.'

During an official trip to Madrid in April 1987, Diana made light of rumours of her alleged affairs. She quipped: 'When we first got married, we were everybody's idea of the world's most perfect couple. Now they say we are leading separate lives. The next thing is I'll start reading that I've got a black Catholic lover.'

It was a joke that fell flat, for, by this stage, dozens of rumours were circulating that the Princess did indeed have a few male friends of whom her husband did not approve.

Lady Colin Campbell says: 'Diana embarked on a string of flirtations with chaps from the right background. If, as she claims, she was not sleeping with them, she certainly gave all the right signals. She was trying to rattle her husband's chains. Unfortunately for her, he was beyond caring.'

In 1988, Diana met the Life Guards officer Major James Hewitt. He began giving the Princess and her sons riding lessons at Conermere Barraks near Windsor. Hewitt was young, sexy and fun, and again, 'exactly her type', according to friends.

Within a short space of time, William and Harry began treating Hewitt as an 'uncle' figure. Diana regularly took her sons to spend weekends at Hewitt's parents' home in Devon – something the Prince voiced his 'strongest objections' to.

In his book *Diana v Charles*, royal expert James Whitaker interviewed Hewitt's former personal valet Lance-Corporal Malcolm Leete at length.

Leete told him: 'One particular morning I got a call at 3.30am to say that Diana was coming to ride at seven. The usual happened, she arrived, gave Hewitt a peck on the cheek and said hello. But I remember from that day they became much more friendly towards each other. Princess Diana's visits changed from once a week to three days a week, regularly – Mondays, Wednesdays and Fridays.

'They always went into the Park, but this particular morning there was no lady-in-waiting. They went out by themselves. I thought it was quite peculiar. She would have had someone with her like a detective. They became closer and closer to each other.

'She started sending him presents, buying him things, always in a flash carrier bag – Harrods or other big stores. I never paid much attention to it all, but I always had to press the clothes before he wore them and that made me think that whenever he wore them, he was always going to see her.'

Leete told how one morning, the couple disappeared

inside the indoor riding arena. Overcome by curiosity, he stood on a mounting block and looked through a window.

He said: 'The pair of them were in the corner. I wasn't quite sure what I saw, but they were certainly cuddling.'

Lady Colin Campbell says: 'It was far more than that. Leete said he saw Hewitt put his hand up the Princess's blouse. Her blouse was outside her jodhpurs and his hand was clearly up inside it. There was nothing innocent about that encounter at all.'

When Hewitt was sent to serve in the Gulf, Diana wrote him long, intimate letters and watched TV newscasts of the unfolding war for hours on end. She would sign all her letters 'Dibbs', Hewitt's affectionate pet name for her. She also kept a photograph of him in her bedside locker drawer. She told a friend she was 'frantic about James' when he failed to telephone her one night as planned.

Hewitt's girlfriend, Emma Stewardson, also received letters. She later told the story of how he had spurned her affections in favour of the Princess to a Sunday newspaper. She told how Hewitt became 'infatuated' by the Princess and regularly arranged to meet her at weekends.

Pictures of the Princess with Hewitt soon appeared. In one, she throws her head back in laughter and thrusts her hips forward as she presents him with a polo trophy. In another, she leans provocatively back against a Land Rover while she talks to him.

Lady Colin says: 'The body language is there for all to see. This was a woman sending out all the signals.

When Hewitt's girlfriend spilled the beans about the relationship, Diana was furious. She called a friend, saying: 'Why the hell can't I have my own life when no-one seems to care that my husband is having his way with the Rottweiler?'

In fact, Diana had not chosen her friend wisely. In

March 1994, Hewitt was to betray her by selling his story of their 'intimate' friendship to the *Daily Express*. Just a few months earlier, the dashing Major caused further embarrassment to the Princess when he was cited in the divorce papers of TV weathergirl Sally Faber and her husband, the Conservative MP David Faber.

In the words of one former friend of Hewitt's: 'He always did have a problem keeping his flies done up in the company of pretty girls. He was a flash so-and-so, he loved the chase, if not the kill. God gave him a pretty smile, lovely eyes and a big dick, but not much up top in the old brains department.'

In fact, Hewitt's revelations about Diana were a big disappointment. Despite receiving a reported six-figure sum from the newspaper, Hewitt shied away from the facts, hinting at an affair with the Princess, but giving no details.

He said: 'When we first met, we started talking about riding and she told me how she had lost her nerve a long time ago and had always thought about trying to regain it. I said that I thought I could help and I started giving her lessons.

'Naturally, I had to clear our meetings through the army and we began riding together. It was all very surreptitious. Yes, we built up a rapport easily. I think she is great fun, with a good sense of humour. I found her interesting and intriguing. She is terribly loyal, affectionate and caring.

'Obviously when I first met her I was as unaware as anyone who wasn't a close friend how unhappy she was with her marriage. But as you become friendly with people, you get a feeling as to what upsets them and what makes them happy. Occasionally she was upset, and occasionally she was happy. She wanted friendship.

'She was in a situation where it is very difficult to make friends. Remember, she was still developing and was interested in meeting a variety of people. She is the sort of person that, once she feels she has your trust, she opens up very quickly because she is a very giving person.

'I'd defy any man not to find her attractive.'

Talking about how the friendship developed to 'another level', he added: 'All the time, in my gut was the warning bell of the fear of getting too close.'

Hewitt was forced to lie low in Switzerland when his 'kiss and tell' appeared.

As one royal observer says: 'It was so, well, *tacky*. Honestly, one would have thought the Princess of Wales could have chosen a man with a little more class. One wonders how she felt when this chap she invested so much faith and hope in turns up the next minute plastered all over some downmarket newspaper selling his rather boring little stories about her. To be frank, it just confirmed what everyone thought – that the Princess had her head turned by a small amount of flattery from a chap who is clearly on the same intellectual level as her. It was a rather mucky affair. He just came out of it rather like a bimbo prepared to tell all for a nice fat cheque. Everyone refers to him as a *him*-bo now.'

At the same time as Hewitt's kiss-and-yawn was appearing, the *Sun* carried a far racier interview with Paula Campbell, a busty blonde telephone operator who readily admitted enjoying Hewitt's 'notable assets' while he was stationed in Germany.

She said: 'He used to call up and tell me he wanted to lick my body all over from the toes upwards and then he'd ask me to talk the same way to him.

'He arrived at the telephone exchange and there was just me on night duty. The switchboard office had a small room off it. It was about eight foot square. There was room in there to lie down. He just put into practice all we'd been talking about on the telephone.

'It was all rather disappointing. His talk was better than his performance. But he is big where it matters.'

In 1988, when the Princess's friendship with Hewitt first became public, it was the breaking point for Prince Charles.

On 22 September 1988 the Prince flew to Balmoral.

For thirty-seven days, he did not see his wife. He spent his time painting, fishing and hunting. His only company were his old friends Lord and Lady Tryon – and Camilla. He and Camilla happily spent days alone, away from the prying public gaze, walking through the heather and sharing their love of painting,

A friend of Camilla's says: 'Camilla spent a couple of weeks up there, then she returned home for a few days and then she flew back up to Scotland. The Prince was very depressed at the start of the trip. He told Camilla he was at "breaking point". He would only refer to Diana by this stage as "the mad woman".

'The Prince was fed up with everything. But mostly he was fed up at his silly airhead wife and his miserable marriage. Camilla was seriously concerned by his unhappy mental state. She spent hours and hours talking to him. She consoled him and comforted him. Camilla felt an enormous amount of guilt at this time, because she had been the one who had been so forthright about Diana being the right girl for Charles. But it wasn't Camilla's fault. At first glance, Diana did appear to be the best on offer at the time Charles was looking for a bride. Charles felt he had done everything he could. But his pride made him feel there was always more he could do. He'd never failed in his life before, but slowly it was dawning on him that he was failing in the most important things of all: his marriage and his family.

'Camilla never passed judgement. She was never particularly nasty about Diana. She was just a great, great friend, someone who would listen for hours and never get bored.'

Her greatest test came in June 1990, when the Prince broke his right arm badly in two places when he crashed from his pony during a polo match at Cirencester Park, Gloucestershire. The fall was so bad that spectators who were standing more than fifty yards away heard the bone snap.

An initial operation was unsuccessful. The Prince was moved to Nottingham General Hospital, where he spent three long weeks in his own room.

The recuperation was long and painful. He spent months recovering at Balmoral or Highgrove. His normally full diary of public engagements was empty, cancelled on the advice of his doctors.

Loyal Camilla hardly left his side. As the break took more time than expected to heal, Camilla buoyed his spirits. Camilla was given her own suite of rooms at Balmoral, adjoining the Prince's. She developed a close friendship with Sarah Key, the pretty Australian physiotherapist hired to help the Prince rebuild the strength in his arm.

According to one visitor who went to Balmoral during that time: 'Camilla did everything for the Prince. She would sit there for hours reading to him, she helped him with the exercises he was given to do, she would cut up his food and help him eat it. She comforted him when the pain was bad. She was devoted to him. She was always fussing around him. In the evening, they would sit in his private drawing room together for hours. Sometimes they would talk, other times they would listen to classical music. On other occasions, they would sit there in silence for ages. But it was never a painful silence. It was the silence of a couple so secure in the love they share that they do not need words to fill the gaps.'

Diana was furious that Charles did not wish to see her – preferring to be nursed by Camilla. Diana remained at Kensington Palace.

But seeing Diana was the last thing the Prince wanted. The accident gave him ample time to consider the state of his marriage. And he decided he could not stand it.

As he later told a friend: 'That time was bad for me. The fracture left me in permanent pain and I felt useless and helpless. There was nothing I could do to speed up the healing process. I wanted to get back to work. Camilla was an absolute rock.

'But what the accident did give me was more time to reflect on my life. And I decided it wasn't going the way I wanted it to.'

Charles was deeply troubled. For the first time, he told his mother he feared he 'could not stick out' the marriage.

Their most poignant meeting came over lunch at Balmoral one day. The Queen tried to offer some wise advice. Her own marriage to Prince Philip had not been without difficulties.

She knew Philip had enjoyed his own 'discreet liaisons' through the years.

She told her son: 'Divorce is out of the question. We must come to some arrangement with Diana. I am not asking you to give up Mrs Parker Bowles. As you know, I am extremely fond of her myself. But Diana must be kept in check. She is a flighty girl; who knows what she might do?'

The Queen wrote Diana a long letter. She invited the Princess to dine with her privately on her return to Buckingham Palace.

Recalling that dinner, Diana told a friend: 'The Queen

stressed the importance of making the marriage work. She told me Charles was willing to give it another go. I promised I would do my best. But I insisted he end his friendship with Camilla. I remember the Queen looking at me over her glasses and saying: "Why are you so concerned about Camilla? All men have certain urges. Camilla is married, she is no threat to you. Try to put her out of your head. You have nothing to concern yourself with there, my dear."'

Diana realized at that moment that Camilla had more than one powerful ally inside the royal family.

Privately, the Queen confided to her aides that she feared Diana was 'a bolter' – someone who would bolt from the family, leaving them in turmoil if she could not get her own way.

Diana's chop-and-change past did nothing to allay those fears. Even as a teenager, Diana had had difficulty committing herself to anything.

After leaving her Swiss finishing school, she enrolled on a cordon bleu cookery course under teacher Elizabeth Russell, but lasted only ten weeks. Then she decided she fancied training as a dance teacher, so she signed up on a three-year teaching course with Madame Betty Vacani, who had taught the Queen and Princess Margaret to dance. A month later, Diana went on a skiing holiday – and never returned to the dancing school.

Madame Vacani says: 'She never gave a reason or an explanation, but I think she felt the course was too all-embracing. I imagine she thought teaching at a kindergarten would be less demanding.'

Diana began teaching at the Young England kindergarten, but only part-time. She said: 'I prefer only being a part-time worker. It leaves me free to do my own thing. I loathe being tied down by restrictions.'

But in 1988, Diana felt suffocated by restrictions.

Another death knell was sounded in the marriage during the terrible Klosters skiing tragedy on 10 March 1988. Diana, Charles, Fergie and Charles's friends Major Hugh Lindsay and Charles and Patti Palmer-Tomkinson were sharing a small, secluded chalet at Wolfgang, near Charles favourite Swiss resort of Klosters,

One day, after a morning on the slopes, Di and Fergie returned to the chalet while the Prince and his party ventured further up the mountain to pursue their favourite off-piste skiing.

An hour later, the two women heard a helicopter fly overhead. Shortly afterwards, Charles's press secretary Philip Mackie entered the chalet stony-faced. He told them there had been a terrible accident. The Prince's party had been engulfed in an avalanche. He said no further details were known except that a male member of the party was dead.

A few minutes later, a clearly shaken and upset Prince Charles telephoned. Major Hugh Lindsay, a former equerry to the Queen, had been killed outright. Patti Palmer-Tomkinson had been revived by mouth-to-mouth resuscitation. She had suffered severe injuries and was, at that moment, undergoing a seven-hour operation at a local hospital to save her shattered legs.

Diana and Fergie packed Hugh's belongings into a suitcase. Prince Charles accompanied Patti to a nearby hospital. He stayed at the hospital late into the night until Patti left the operating theatre. He was by her side as she came around. He then paid a sombre last visit to see Hugh's body in the hospital morgue, where he spent more than twenty minutes alone in the room with his old friend, saying his final farewells, The following day, the tearful royal party flew back to RAF Northolt. Diana comforted

Hugh Lindsay's wife Sarah, a member of the Palace press office, who was six months pregnant.

Those close to Diana circulated the story that 'cold-hearted' Charles did not even want to return to England with his friend's body; that he suggested they were all over-reacting and should continue their skiing holiday.

In fact, nothing could be further from the truth. Charles was heartbroken by the tragedy. For the first month after the accident, he would called Sarah Lindsay on a daily basis. He still contacts her regularly to make sure she is doing well. A friend says: 'It was Charles, not Diana, who offered Sarah her greatest strength in her hour of need. He was a rock. He telephoned her constantly, he sorted out all the financial arrangements for the funeral. He did absolutely everything he could, and more, to help her. She will be forever grateful to the Prince for what he did for her in those dark days after Hugh's death.

'The Princess was there the day of the accident. She looked suitably miserable for the cameras at the airport. But she hardly went out of her way in the months to come. She probably telephoned Sarah once or twice. Charles was on the phone constantly.'

The accident also brought the Prince and the Palmer-Tomkinsons even closer together. Today, they are still among his closest circle of friends.

Lady Colin Campbell says: 'The Prince's circle of friends is small, elite and utterly devoted to him.

'They know the true character of the man and they all stick together through thick and thin. Charles was deeply affected by the loss of Hugh. He was totally supportive of Patti Palmer-Tomkinson as she recuperated. He visited her many times in hospital and again at home as she recovered. Far from wanting to stay on in the resort skiing, it was Charles who stayed up throughout the night making arrangements to fly the body and the rest of the party home. For Diana to try and cash in on that incident was shameful. Charles's friends never forgave her.'

At this time Diana was receiving treatment for her bulimia, now at a critical stage, from Dr Maurice Lipsedge, a world-renowned expert on eating disorders, at Guy's Hospital in London. The Princess would pay three one-hour visits to Dr Lipsedge's office each week. She was asked to fill out a special eating-diary, logging the high points and low points of each day and monitoring each morsel of food which passed her lips.

It was during this time that Diana is said to have confronted Camilla during the fortieth birthday party of Camilla's sister Annabel Elliot. According to one witness, Diana stormed up to Camilla and said: 'Why don't you just leave my husband alone?' Camilla turned on her heel and left the room. Charles followed closely behind.

A friend of Camilla's says: 'The incident only served to make Camilla even more contemptuous of Diana. Camilla never spoke to the Princess from that day on. Any pity or sympathy she may have had at the back of her mind for her had died. From that moment on, it was all-out war over the affections of the Prince. And it was pretty clear who was going to win.'

Diana's Revenge

Andrew Parker Bowles was admiring the fillies being paraded before him at Ascot. It was June 1992, and Andrew was now a brigadier with the illustrious title of Silver Stick in Waiting to the Queen. He was also in charge of the Army Veterinary Corps.

He and Camilla had been invited to Ascot as the personal guests of the Queen that year. His wife's affair with Charles was now so commonly known among their own circle that people rarely commented on it any more.

The Duke of Marlborough's younger brother, Lord Charles Spencer-Churchill, having enjoyed several glasses of champagne, caught sight of Andrew as he walked across the Royal Enclosure.

Churchill called over to his friend: 'Ernest Simpson! Hey, Ernest Simpson! Why don't you come over here?'

Andrew's back stiffened. He, of course, fully condoned his wife's extra-marital affair, but to be mocked publicly and referred to in the same breath as the cuckolded husband Wallis Simpson had ditched half a century earlier to marry the Duke of Windsor, was something he would not tolerate.

In front of dozens of witnesses, he calmly turned around to face Churchill. 'Come over here,' he commanded. A rather shaky Churchill lurched across the paddock.

Andrew grasped him by the arm and thrust his face towards him. 'I don't ever want to hear you talk to me again like that, do you hear? NEVER!'

Spencer-Churchill himself told best-selling royal author Nigel Dempster in his book *Behind Palace Doors*: 'He was very, very angry indeed. He pummelled my right arm and shoulder extremely hard. The next day I was black and blue with bruises. I thought it was just a tease, a bit of a giggle. But Andrew didn't find it amusing at all.'

Spencer-Churchill added ominously: 'I told him, "Mark my words, it will end in tears. When you play around with the monarchy, you play around with fire."'

A few months later, Parker Bowles was sitting in his favourite chair at his gentleman's club, Whites in St James. Lord Soames, one of Andrew's oldest friends and the father of Andrew's former 'flame' Charlotte Hambro, sat down beside him and proceeded loudly to chastise him for his 'ungentlemanly' behaviour.

Parker Bowles was so upset by the old man's criticism that he immediately stood up and left the club. As he walked towards the exit, he overheard a fellow club member whisper: 'There goes the finest man in Britain. He is so loyal to the Crown that he is prepared to lay down his wife for the sake of his country.'

Although he was happy with his unconventional marriage at that time, these snide jibes wounded him deeply.

At home, the Parker Bowles marriage was much as it had been for years. Camilla was still deeply devoted to both the Prince and her husband. She loyally ran her own household and the Prince's household at Highgrove. She and her husband enjoyed a passionate, if volatile, relationship.

A family member says: 'Camilla and Andrew always loved each other very deeply. They had an enormously strong marriage, despite the opinion of others. The marriage was an open one; they both had other partners, but when they were together they were very happy with each other's company. But the constant jibes were beginning to gnaw away inside Andrew. He was still enjoying his own discreet friendships outside the marriage, but the constant criticism he was facing over Camilla's ongoing affair with the Prince was becoming unbearable.'

A friend says: 'The facts of the matter were that Camilla and Andrew's marriage was slowly falling apart They remained good friends, but sexually, the relationship was in deep trouble They were spending increasing time apart and often, when Andrew was at home, he would choose to sleep in a separate bedroom. The holes in the marriage were getting bigger.

'Privately, both Andrew and Camilla would insist they wanted to remain married for the sake of their two children. They said divorce was out of the question until their daughter Laura was grown up. But the writing was already on the wall – they would remain married, for the time being.'

Within the royal family itself, the ranks were divided. Princess Anne, who never liked Diana, sided with her brother. She steadfastly refused even to talk to the

Princess. She believed some of the negative stories about Charles which were appearing in the newspapers had been planted by Diana's allies.

Diana had built up her own circle of trusted friends who would call sympathetic reporters almost daily with new tales of the Princess's anguish – and fresh sordid stories about Charles's heartlessness.

One prominent Fleet Street royal watcher says: 'When the Princess came on the scene it was the first time any of us began getting inside scoops from a source within the royal family itself. Of course, none of the boys in the pack were complaining. We were all sympathetic to Diana. Her side did all the talking. You never got a peep out of Charles's cronies. They still simply couldn't bring themselves to break their vow of silence. But Diana's lot were far more open. Diana had wooed the press. She knew the full value of the tabloids in getting her story across to the people. And she milked the tabloids for everything they had.

'If there was even the slightest chance of getting on to the front pages, Diana could turn a routine visit to a children's hospital into a front-page story simply by giving a great quote. She learned that early on. As the marriage started crumbling, she started consolidating her public position through the newspaper columns. She wanted to make sure that if, and when, the walls came tumbling down, she would emerge as the victim in the whole sorry saga.

'The phone would go at all times of the day and night. The tipsters were all Diana's friends and their information would be spot on.'

On one memorable occasion, one of Diana's tipsters told photographers the Prince was enjoying a 'romantic boat trip with a mystery blonde'. It was enough to send

Fleet Street's photographers into a feeding frenzy. When the pack arrived at the location, they managed to get several good pictures of a relaxed and unsuspecting Charles, aboard a small dinghy with his 'mystery blonde': Camilla Parker Bowles.

On another occasion, Diana's friends tipped off the press that Camilla was spending the weekend at the Queen Mother's Deeside Lodge with the Prince, After a three-day stake-out, the photographers got their picture of Charles leaving the house with Camilla a few steps behind. What no-one mentioned was that a few paces behind Camilla was her husband.

In May 1988, when Charles was on another painting holiday in Italy, he was informed on the flight out that Prince Harry had been taken to hospital for an emergency hernia operation. He immediately wanted to fly to his son's side, but Diana said no.

She told him it 'was only a little op' and that there was 'absolutely no need' for him to return. Charles checked in with the hospital every hour from then on, so great was his concern for his son.

The next day's headlines said it all. Diana's informants painted the Prince as a cold-hearted father who ignored his son's illness while 'saint' Diana had spent the night sitting on a hard chair at the end of Harry's hospital bed at Great Ormond Street Children's Hospital in London.

Later, in June 1991, when Prince William was accidentally hit by a fellow pupil swinging a golf club at Ludgrove School, it was again Diana who scored the 'good parenting' points. When the accident occurred, Diana was having lunch at San Lorenzo and Charles was at home at Highgrove.

The pair both raced to the Royal Berkshire Hospital in Reading where William was undergoing X-rays. When a compressed fracture of the skull was discovered, the child was rushed to Great Ormond Street Hospital.

Later that day, the Prince was due to attend a charity gala performance of the opera *Tosca* at Covent Garden. It was an important meeting of European and British ministers. The event had already been postponed once because of the Prince's broken arm.

William's surgeons told Charles it would be 'fine' for him to go. But Prince Charles insisted on carrying a pager so he could be alerted immediately if there was any worsening of his son's condition.

Diana, meanwhile, talked to her 'friendly' journalists. She told them that while she had slept in a small chair at the end of William's bed all night, hard-hearted Charles had gallivanted around town.

The following morning's headlines said it all. WHAT SORT OF DAD ARE YOU? asked the *Sun*.

A former staff member at Great Ormond Street says: 'The Princess asked for all that morning's newspapers to be delivered to William's room. She spent ages reading through them. She seemed quite pleased at the favourable press coverage she had received.'

Charles – and the rest of his family – were becoming increasingly angry at the continuous smear campaign against him. First, it was unfair. Second, it was untrue.

As one former royal aide says: 'The constant diet of negative stories about the Prince which appeared in the press greatly wounded him. He is someone who takes his position in life and his family very seriously. But Diana was much cleverer than him at media manipulation. It took the Prince years before he could catch up. His problem was that he'd been brought up to believe that *anything* was better than airing one's dirty laundry in public. Now he had this wife who was washing her smalls in public on a daily basis. It infuriated and maddened him.'

Another woman close to the Prince says: 'Diana proved herself to be extraordinarily difficult. Many people who got to know her during her marriage to HRH came to the conclusion she was very unpleasant. It is not in the Prince's nature to answer back. He has not been brought up like that. There was always an intellectual gap between them, but Diana was the one who went running to the press.

'Right from the start, it was the Prince who worked hard to try and make that marriage work. He hired all manner of psychiatrists and eating-disorder doctors to try and help his wife. But she always wanted more. What she really wanted was to take over. She loved being the Princess of Wales, she loved all the attention and the glory. But she wanted to be the Princess of Wales without the Prince of Wales. And that is an utterly ridiculous notion. But Diana believed her own press. She thought she was above and beyond anyone else in the family. Newspaper polls were constantly deeming her the most popular royal. She thought she could get away with anything.'

Princess Anne once confronted Diana about the daily diet of royal tittle-tattle which was appearing. 'It is astonishing,' she told Diana during one of Anne's rare visits to Kensington Palace. 'Before you joined, there were hardly any leaks. Now the ship is so full of holes, it's no wonder that it's sinking.'

Diana looked back at her, dumbstruck. 'I wouldn't go telling too many tall tales if I were you,' Anne added, 'They might just come back to haunt you one day.'

Princess Anne had never had anything in common with Diana. She despised Diana's constant dieting and her cover-girl image. Anne, who had spent years rebuilding her reputation into a woman now considered Britain's most hard-working royal, felt put out of place when Diana came along and stole her thunder simply by wearing a new outfit or flaunting her trim body in a bikini at the beach.

Anne was overhead saying: 'She's nothing more than a horse, a clothes horse. If she were a real horse, I might like her more. At least horses have a brain.'

One another occasion, Anne observed that Diana's dresser in the early days of her marriage, Evelyn Dagley, had eight O level passes. Diana had none. It was a passing comment made flippantly at dinner, in full earshot of the Princess of Wales. The jibe did not go unnoticed.

Diana was later to say: 'She never liked me. She was jealous.'

Anne purposely did all she could to avoid meeting Diana. On state occasions, she would stand as far away from the Princess as she could, literally putting distance between herself and Diana.

In private, Princess Anne spent most of her time at Gatcombe Park, her estate in Gloucestershire. Once, when Diana was due to arrive to pick up Prince William who had spent the day at a birthday party at Gatcombe for Anne's daughter Zara – Anne saddled up her horse and rode off, returning only later that night when the Princess had come and gone.

A handful of Charles's friends decided, unilaterally, to fight back on his behalf.

One says: 'Diana's manipulation of the media was so unfair and so unbalanced it was getting ridiculous. The Prince is not as photogenic as she is, but he is the future king and he still has a massive groundswell of support in the country.

'It is no coincidence that we saw pictures of Princess Diana and the boys at Alton Towers and Thorpe Park. *She* was the one who made sure the photographers knew where she would be. She was the one with the eye for the main photo opportunity. Prince Charles has always taken the boys to school, and he is constantly taking them on outings. He spends hours fishing, cycling and walking with them. But you hardly ever see a picture of it because it is not his style to cash in on his children to boost his public image. In fact, not only is it not in his nature to push the boys forward, the exact opposite is true. The Prince wants to shield the children. He doesn't want them to constantly be in the public eye. The constant stream of pictures of them being squired around by their mother upsets him.

'Several of us made the decision that, whether he liked it or not, we simply had to counter the relentless onslaught in the media that he was being subjected to on an almost daily basis by Diana.'

The Princess's thirtieth birthday party provided Charles's friends with their first chance to strike back publicly.

Diana had 'let it be known' to her circle of press informants that Charles was so aloof and uncaring that he could not be bothered to attend her birthday celebrations. In fact, for several months, the Prince had been begging Diana to allow him to throw a lavish party in her honour at Highgrove.

'I don't want to go to any party you might organize for me,' she had said. 'I'd rather be on my own.'

Charles had insisted he would foot the bill and invite only her friends, not his, but 'she rejected him out of hand', according to a close friend of the Prince.

This story was leaked to the press by someone very

close to the Prince. The subsequent story, splashed all over the front page of the *Sun* under the headline: DI DON'T WANT TO DANCE, enraged the Princess.

Like a petulant child who had failed to get her own way, she stamped her foot and shouted: 'He can't do this! He can't do this to *me*!"

In the end, Diana spent the day alone with Prince Harry, joining her sister Jane in the evening for a quiet dinner. Diana 'leaked' her own quote-of-the-day to the press, telling a friend to instruct Fleet Street's finest that she 'had spent the evening quietly at home, with the only man in my life – Prince Harry'.

The Prince's friend said: 'She preferred to sit around being bored and miserable than to give her husband even the slightest joy at organizing a party for her. It was small-minded and petty. Charles was upset, but it said more about Diana than anything else. She was prepared to bite off her nose to spite her face.'

While Charles's friends fought back, he found an enemy within his own camp, in the shape of his father. Prince Philip was at war with everyone. He viewed Diana as a 'silly little girl' but he was furious at Charles for not taking a firmer stand against her.

Philip and Charles had never enjoyed a close relationship. From childhood, Philip had been determined that his eldest son should be 'a man's man'. It was Philip who insisted Charles went to his old school, Gordonstoun, a rigidly tough boarding school in Scotland. Charles loathed the cold-shower mentality of the place and still refers to it as 'an institution rather than a school'.

It was Philip who decided, when Charles was barely a teenager, that his son should follow his footsteps into the Royal Navy. It has always been Philip who has drummed into Charles the importance of his future position in life, as head of the British monarchy and of the Church of England.

A former equerry says: 'Philip was the one who was forcing Charles to get married Charles would happily have stayed a bachelor all his life. But Philip kept insisting he should get married and would goad Charles that people would begin to think he was a queer if he didn't hurry up and walk down the aisle. Philip has always ruled his son with a rod of iron. Privately, Charles is still frightened of his father. When Philip added his voice to the growing call for Charles to marry Di, the Prince felt he had no doors left open to run through.

'The whole philosophy that Philip drummed into Charles's head was to put duty and the Crown before everything else. Philip has spent *his* life putting duty and the Crown before everything else. He found it very difficult, in the early days of his marriage to the Queen, to take a back seat and allow her to be centre stage. But he always remembered his sense of duty. Philip's deep-rooted loyalty has never wavered.

'Philip was always shockingly blunt to Charles, who was always too sensitive for the old man's liking.

'Prince Philip knew what it was like to put up and shut up. He'd done it all his life. And he understood Charles's need to take a mistress. But he was enraged that Charles and Camilla were being openly discussed in the newspapers.'

For several months, Philip tried to broach the subject of his son's affair with Camilla. He even wrote Charles several letters, expressing his 'fears' that his personal life was becoming 'increasingly complicated'. But each time Philip tried to talk to his son, Charles would change the subject or avoid it altogether

Finally, Philip cornered Charles on a shooting field at

Sandringham. According to witnesses the conversation went along the following lines: 'What the hell is going on?' the older man enquired. 'The whole bloody court is talking about you and Camilla. You're playing with fire. I don't care if you want to have a shag on the side, but for God's sake, deal with Diana. That's your problem. You always avoid problems until they become so enormous they overwhelm you. You have got to stand up and be a man.'

Charles, red-faced with annoyance, tried to turn away.

Philip physically grabbed him by the arm. 'You are *not* going to walk away this time,' he shouted.

Charles began to try and explain his predicament: 'Diana is impossible. We have absolutely nothing in common. I would dearly love to get out. Why the hell did no-one do anything to stop me getting into this situation in the first place?' he exploded.

Philip was furious. To him, it was just his weak son trying to make yet more excuses. He shook Charles by the arm: 'For God's sake, grow up,' he yelled.

Then Philip jumped into his Land Rover and drove off.

It was the last conversation between the two for more than four months.

A former equerry says: 'From that moment on, every time Charles walked into a room, Philip would walk out.'

Charles's only ally was the Queen Mother. He began spending a considerable amount of time with her, both at her London home, Clarence House, and at her Scottish estate, Birkinhall.

An insider says: 'Charles has always been closer to his grandmother than he has to his parents. When Camilla was not around, he would talk to the Queen Mother. She tried to intercede in the growing feud between Charles and Diana. She even tried to play matchmaker by inviting them both to Clarence House one Friday evening. But Diana could not face the old lady. She always felt terribly uncomfortable around the Queen Mum. She cried off at the last minute, claiming she had a migraine.'

Nothing, it appeared, was going to happen to prevent the inevitable. The fairy-tale marriage was so badly damaged that no-one and nothing could save it.

Prince Charles himself sought help and guidance from a professional. He began visiting the offices of one of Britain's top psychotherapists, Dr Allan McGlashan. The Prince would arrive at the doctor's Sloane Street offices at 6.30pm at least once a week during this difficult time. Dr McGlashan proved 'enormously helpful' to the Prince, according to a friend.

She says: 'They would discuss Diana's eating disorders and the best ways for the Prince to react to and deal with those. The Prince fundamentally blames all the problems in his marriage on the bulimia and on deep-rooted, long-term psychological problems he believes Diana suffered since childhood.'

The Queen herself tried to smooth the waters. She would often personally call Diana to try and resolve problems. One such problem occurred when Diana's beloved father Johnnie Spencer died on 29 March 1992.

The couple were in Lech, Austria, on a skiing holiday. The year before, Charles had taken a solo skiing trip and had been widely criticized for not taking Diana and the boys. Buckingham Palace had decreed that this year they should, for all intents and purposes, put up the pretence of playing Happy Families.

Both Charles and Diana had agreed to go on the holiday for the sake of their sons. The announcement that Charles was to accompany his family on their skiing trip was made at the last minute. He had planned to spend the week at Balmoral with Camilla. But two days before Diana and the Princes flew to stay at the Arlberg Hotel in Lech, Charles bowed to the wishes of the Palace and announced he would go too.

But the couple barely spoke to each other in private. Charles flew into Lech separately and very publicly greeted his two sons outside the hotel. It was later revealed that Diana had been banned from the photocall for the world's media,

A Palace insider said: 'The Prince wasn't wild about having his picture taken with the boys, but he agreed to do it on the advice of his staff. They told him he simply had to start redressing the balance. He had to start projecting himself in a positive light. Reluctantly, he agreed.'

The following day, Charles had an impromptu snowball fight with his sons in full view of the Schneiderhof Hotel, where most of the photographers and reporters were staying. The candid and happy snaps were published all over the papers the next day Charles, who had for so long allowed Diana to manipulate the media, was fighting back. And Diana was livid.

When the news came that Spencer had died, Diana instantly packed her bags. She intended to fly home, leaving her husband and sons behind. A specially-ordered Queen's Flight was despatched to bring her home.

But the Palace was adamant it would look terrible if Charles was seen to be ignoring his wife in her hour of need.

'Why are they bothering about him ignoring me now?' said a grim Diana 'He's been ignoring me for years already'

Finally a call was put in to the Queen, who was at Windsor Castle. She telephoned Diana directly, and spoke to the upset Princess for more than twenty minutes. When the call ended, Diana agreed, reluctantly, to bow to her

he spotlight once more, Prince Charles and Camilla pose for the cameras at the cial announcement of their intention to marry.

Kiss me quick! The first public kiss between Charles and Camilla at the 15th Anniversary reception for the National Osteoporosis Society attracted much media attention.

rles and Camilla make their first
lic appearance at the 50th birthday
y of Camilla's sister, Annabel Elliott.
y are greeted by a barrage of press
tographers (*inset*).

Above: A young Camilla and her sister as bridesmaids in 1952.

Below: Camilla on her own wedding day – marrying Andrew in 1973.

…milla's coming out party in 1965. She is pictured here with her mother,
honourable Rosalind Shand.

A glamorous Camilla at another coming out party.

ove: An early encounter between the young sweethearts – Camilla and Charles chat at
olo match.

low: A night out in the West End, 1975.

An untroubled, happy Camilla in the early years of her marriage to Andrew.

equally relaxed Charles, in later years, before the Camillagate story broke.

A family portrait that could not have foretold the drama of divorce and drug allegations that would unfold.

two women in Charles' life. Camilla approved of Diana as a choice of wife for
rles, but Diana would later say that there were three people in her marriage...

Above: Andrew Parker Bowles escorts the royal carriage during Charles and Diana's wedding.

Below: Andrew and Camilla during happier years of their marriage.

rles and Diana put on a brave face as their marriage falls apart.

Diana's boys brought great happiness to her life.

mother-in-law's wishes and allow Charles to travel back with her.

The couple did not exchange a single word on the plane. A witness said: 'Charles, at one stage, tried to put his hand on her arm, but she brushed it away.'

When the plane touched down, Diana scored her own publicity coup. Despite professing to be devastated by her father's death. she refused her husband's offer to carry her suitcases off the plane at RAF Northolt The subsequent photographs and stories condemned the Prince for allowing Diana to struggle with her own bags in her darkest hour of grief.

But one of Charles's aides says: 'It simply wasn't like that at all. It was so unfair what she did that day. The Prince offered to carry her bags, but she had insisted on carrying them herself. It seemed astonishing to all of us that day that Diana was still out to score brownie points.'

The pair travelled to Kensington Palace together. Later that night, Charles drove down to Highgrove to see Camilla. They remained together throughout the next forty-eight hours.

A former staff member at Highgrove says: 'They barely emerged. The Prince and Camilla locked themselves away for hours. There was clearly something serious going on. When anyone entered his private living room to bring in food or drink, they would be talking about Diana and the problem she had become. But they would become quiet when the servants entered. Both of them have too much style to wash their dirty linen in public.'

The Prince did fly to Northamptonshire for the funeral on 1 April aboard a red Wessex helicopter of the Queen's Flight. But he left before the cremation service. His aides said he had 'prior, important business' to attend to. He actually went to meet Camilla.

By this stage, Charles was taking the most extraordinary risks to be with the woman he loved. Most Friday afternoons, he would drive down from London in his gleaming Aston Martin and leave the M4 motorway by Exit 17. On the drive down, he would be followed by a police back-up car containing two sergeants from the royal protection squad. His own personal protection officer would follow on behind.

The Prince believed his security detail thought he was leaving the motorway to take a back-road route to Highgrove; he would instruct the protection officers to leave him at the motorway exit and allow him to continue alone.

But his affair with Camilla was known to all of those close to the royal circle.

One former aide says: 'The Prince, of course, never knew we'd twigged what was going on. He would tell us he wished to make the final short drive home alone and would only allow his personal protection officer to follow him from Exit 17 onwards. That officer would then follow him to the gates of Camilla's home and would wait there. Sometimes he would wait for an hour, sometimes two – sometimes he would sit in his car at the gates throughout the night.

'Of course we all knew what was going on. As the Prince would drive off, we'd all sing in unison, "We know where you're going!"'

On other occasions, when Charles was staying at Highgrove, he would drive an unmarked Ford estate car the twelve miles between his estate and Camilla's home, Middlewick House.

An estate worker says: 'It was a fairly scruffy car, dirty on the inside from carrying machinery and dogs, and it smelled to high heaven. But Charles used it because it offered him anonymity.

'I remember talking to a friend over at Middlewick and they told me the first time the car appeared in the driveway, they were contemplating towing it away because it was so filthy. Then they were told it was the Prince's vehicle, which surprised everyone, since they were all used to seeing his Aston Martin parked outside Mrs Parker Bowles's house. But the Ford was what he preferred to use. There were often reporters hanging around outside both places. I guess the Prince believed they would never think to keep an eye out for him in a scruffy old car.

'The car was so filthy that we cleaned it up one day before the Prince arrived that Friday night. When he saw it had been washed, he wasn't too happy. He left instructions that it was to remain dirty. He preferred it that way because it didn't draw attention to itself or him. But everyone knew what was going on.

'It was common knowledge to everyone even remotely attached to the royal family that the marriage of Charles and Diana was over.

'And it was common knowledge that Charles was very much in love with Camilla. You only had to look at his eyes when they were together to tell he was besotted with her.

'The only people who didn't know were the British public. And it was only a matter of time before they found out.

History Repeats Itself

Princess Diana first demanded a separation from her husband as early as November 1989. Fed up with 'living a lie', as she would later tell friends, she confronted Charles in his study at Kensington Palace and told him she wanted out of the marriage.

He dismissed her demands as 'ridiculous'.

He told her: 'There is absolutely no way a separation would be acceptable either to me, my family or the palace. If you find me intolerable, you do not have to see me. But the marriage remains. I shall never, ever allow a separation to occur.'

For Charles knew that no matter how bad the marriage was, any separation would spark a constitutional crisis on a level with the devastating drama which had rocked the monarchy some fifty years earlier when his great uncle Edward VIII had abdicated the Crown for the love of American divorcee Wallis Simpson.

To those inside the royal household, history could not be allowed to repeat itself in such a damning way. The House of Windsor had survived one crisis – it could not survive another.

Edward VIII became king on the death of his father George V in January 1936. Within twelve months, he had created the biggest scandal in British history and was banished to live out the rest of his days in exile all for the love of a woman.

The comparisons between Edward and Mrs Simpson and Charles and Camilla are almost eerie. Both were long-time love affairs. Both involved strong women who captivated the heir to the throne. Both were affairs which remained secret from the British public for years while they were openly gossiped about and discussed in aristocratic circles. Both caused a scandal which rocked the monarchy to its foundations when they first burst into the public arena.

One ended with the then monarch renouncing the throne and living out his days in a lonely, self-imposed exile with the woman he loved, but who was never accepted or embraced by the royal family. The other involved a woman who *had* been embraced by the royal family – but who could never be allowed to marry the man she loved.

History could not be allowed to repeat itself.

The affair of Edward and Wallis Simpson began in 1931 when both were invited to a house party hosted by the society 'grande dame' Thelma, Viscountess Furness. According to one royal biographer, 'Wallis set her sights on Edward immediately. She knew what she wanted, and that was the ultimate prize. Nothing was going to stop her.'

She was totally unsuitable as a partner for the future king. Divorced from her first husband, a US naval officer Earl Winfield Spencer, she was separated from her second husband Ernest Simpson when she met Edward.

From their very first meeting, she captivated Edward. In his personal ledger, Edward was to write shortly after their affair began in June 1931: 'She is the most intriguing, fascinating, unpredictable creature I have ever met. I fear I am falling . . .'

The similarities between Wallis and Camilla are uncanny.

Neither was a raving beauty in the conventional sense, but both had an earthy quality which captured the heart of the heir to the throne. Wallis was strong, confident and self-assured, just like Camilla. According to friends, Wallis 'could always muster a turn of phrase to banish Edward's dark clouds of depression and make him feel loved, wanted and needed' – the same qualities which attracted Charles to Camilla. Both have been described with words like 'rock-solid, trustworthy, loyal'.

Between Charles and his great-uncle too, there were similarities. Both were sensitive men, craving affection after a childhood of loneliness.

Edward told a previous mistress, Freda Dudley Ward, 'In my childhood I never ever knew love. There were servants who seemed to love me but I could never forget it might be because I was heir to the throne. I never knew real affection from my own parents.'

Charles too would say: 'Growing up, I never knew the comforts of a loving family environment. My nannies seemed to love me, but I did not know if it was because of who I was or who I would become.'

Like Camilla, Wallis soon became the 'accepted' mistress. She played hostess at Edward's private home, Fort

Belvedere, near Ascot. She would sit at the head of his table and would refer to Edward quite openly as 'my boy'.

In his book *Fall of the House of Windsor*, author Nigel Blundell gave the account of a guest who attended a dinner party at Belvedere: 'It was a very lively evening with a great deal of conversation and jollity. The party went on until around 2am. As a house guest, I retired to my bedroom. I do know that night Edward went to Wallis's room. Those of us who knew him well enough could see that he, and all of us, were heading for trouble. The man whom I admired so much was going to destroy his great heritage. He was blinded and astounded by Wallis and nothing could move him from the path he was taking. He believed, in his distorted thought, that he could make everything work out in a way that would suit everyone, that he could take Mrs Simpson as his wife and she would sit beside him when he became king. That was how the infatuation with her had taken over his thoughts. I think sometimes he did allow himself to consider the worst, that he would be prevented from marrying her. And I think in those moments, he had decided long before the abdication that he would quit his royal life for her. Sad, but true.'

Yet while London society was abuzz with talk of Edward's 'inappropriate' affair, the British public knew nothing of the growing scandal. The British papers studiously avoided any mention of the affair – only announcing it like a bombshell just days before the abdication.

The British public felt cheated and conned when they learned the devastating truth. As one newspaper editor of the time said: 'They had the wool pulled over their eyes. The American press and the European press had been writing about the affair between Edward and Mrs

Simpson for years. But the British public knew nothing of it. When they found out they had been deceived, the public outcry was enormous. Edward was personally hugely popular. The public outcry on his abdication was unprecedented.'

Edward and Wallis would openly attend parties around London, she lavishly dressed in the latest fashions, dripping with jewels. Like Camilla and Charles half a century later, they seemed oblivious to the constant criticism of their relationship from within their own circle.

Edward's mother, Queen Mary begged her son to 'rid yourself of that woman for the sake of the country – and the Crown'.

Like Charles all those years later, Edward replied: 'I cannot do so, Mama. She is the woman I love.'

In September 1935, Edward and Wallis holidayed in Europe. It was then that Edward made the decision to renounce the throne. He was implored to change his mind by the Prime Minister of the day, Stanley Baldwin, and by his own family – but his mind was made up.

'I cannot live without the woman I love,' he would say, over and over again.

But in the 1930s, the idea of a twice-divorced American on the throne of England as the country faced up to war was unthinkable. The crisis built up over a period of months. Finally, the decision was taken. On 10 December 1936, Edward signed the abdication papers and George VI, the present Queen's father, was announced as the next king.

In an emotion-packed radio broadcast the next day, the nation listened in stunned silence as Edward revealed the true reason he had placed the Crown and the country in crisis, He said: 'It is impossible to carry the heavy burden of responsibility and discharge my duties as king as I would wish to do without the help and support of the woman I love.'

Two days later, Edward went into exile in France. On 3 June 1937, he married Wallis at their new home, the Château Le Cande outside Paris. The royal family allowed them to use the courtesy title of the Duke and Duchess of Windsor, but always denied Wallis her greatest dream – to have the honour of being addressed as Your Royal Highness.

Only on his death on 28 May 1972 was the Duke of Windsor accepted back by his family. The Queen arranged for his body to be flown back to London and then on to the royal graveyard at Frogmore in Windsor Great Park for burial.

For the remainder of her days, Wallis remained in France. When she died on 2 April 1986, her body was flown back to Frogmore, to rest beside the man who had paid the ultimate price for loving her. Her simple headstone reads: 'Wallis: Duchess of Windsor 1896-1986'. Even in death, the royal family denied her that which she most craved: the letters HRH.

To the present royal family, the abdication crisis has always been regarded as a story of how one man's selfishness and weakness almost destroyed the House of Windsor. The present Queen Mother loathed Wallis for causing a situation which meant her 'beloved Bertie' was forced to take the Crown, a position she believed his poor health and nervous disposition made him unsuitable for. When he died early, aged just fifty-four, she blamed 'that terrible woman' for placing him under a burden which wrecked his health. Even today, the Queen Mother never refers to Wallis by name. On the rare occasions the abdication crisis is referred to in the royal household, Mrs Simpson is simply 'that dreadful woman'.

When the crisis between Camilla, Charles and Diana became evident, Elizabeth, the Queen Mother said curtly: 'History will not be allowed to repeat itself. Absolutely not. Never, *never*, NEVER!'

But, by 1989, history *was* repeating itself.

Charles was to tell friends he was haunted by one particular statement which reverberated down through the years.

Sir Alan Lascalles, an adviser to Edward VIII, told the King at the height of the abdication crisis: 'Sir, you can have the throne, or you can have the woman. You cannot have both.'

Prince Charles was to confide to his closest circle of friends: 'That statement went round and round my head. I was in the same damnable situation. And I did not know what to do.

'I was trapped between the devil and the deep blue sea.'

After Diana had made her first demand for a separation, Charles informed his mother. The Queen summoned Diana and the Prince to a private lunch at Buckingham Palace. She implored them to try and make their marriage work, at least in the eyes of the public.

According to Palace insiders, Diana listened as the Queen stressed the importance of maintaining 'an outward sense of propriety' for the sake of the Crown. At the end of the meeting, Diana said calmly: 'I know where my duty lies.' But while Diana outwardly agreed to the Queen's demands, inwardly she was already plotting her escape.

Diana was further outraged when, in June 1992, at the height of speculation about the state of her marriage, Camilla was invited to the Queen's Cup polo match at Smith's Lawn in Windsor Great Park. She was a personal guest of the Queen and was warmly welcomed by Her Majesty in the royal box.

With typical humour, Camilla loyally wore a two-piece Prince of Wales check suit.

A fellow guest says: 'Camilla made a joke that it was the only suit she had clean that day, but the irony wasn't lost on anyone. Camilla's always had a very dry wit. That suit was her way of making a silent statement. The Princess of Wales was furious.'

It was a public declaration of the Queen's continuing support for Camilla – and a public rebuke for Diana. The wind of change was blowing against the Princess.

Lady Colin Campbell says: 'Diana knew she needed something so devastating that it would give her the clout and power to demand anything of the family. She was firmly ostracized by this stage and she knew she needed a powerful weapon on her side.

'She knew that no-one inside the royal inner circle would knowingly do anything to harm the Crown.

'So she conned a top security adviser. She told the man she wanted to *save* her marriage to the Prince, but that she needed some proof of his affair with Camilla in order to do so. Diana played her finest little-girl act. The whole idea, she said, was to trap Charles on the phone to Camilla and then use that to force him into giving Camilla up.

'Of course, the master plan was to entrap Charles and use any taped evidence to blackmail him into meeting her every demand.

'The security adviser used a call-tracking device which was locked on to Charles's mobile phone.'

The notorious Camillagate conversation was recorded on 17 December 1989. The conversation, which is examined in detail later in this book, was the bombshell Diana needed.

She arranged to have the conversation broadcast repeatedly over a mobile phone line. It was a blatant act of 'treason' by Diana which was later to backfire horribly. The conversation *was* picked up and recorded by a member of the public. But it was to remain private and unpublished for another two years.

Diana reneged on her promise to use the tape to save her marriage – in fact, she wanted to use it to sabotage what was left of the marriage.

Days later, Diana went to see her husband again.

A source close to the Prince says: 'She walked into his office cool as anything and said: "I have been sent this tape. It proves you and Camilla are having an affair. I want a separation – *now!*"

'Charles told her what he had told her a few weeks earlier, that a separation between a Prince and Princess of Wales was "unthinkable". He refused to give in to her demands. He ridiculed her threats as "the rantings of a deranged mind".'

But although the Prince believed his wife was calling his bluff, he informed his private secretary and his other closest advisers. They took the news of the secret tape far more seriously. For they knew Diana, unstable and angry, would stop at nothing to win what was now viewed as her full-scale war, not only against her husband but against the entire royal family.

They decided to fight fire with fire.

They knew all about Diana's own 'liaisons' outside the marriage. By this stage, it was common knowledge at the Palace that she was enjoying an intimate friendship with the used-car salesman James Gilbey.

When Diana arrived to spend Christmas at Sandringham just two days before Christmas Day, she had no idea that *her* private phone inside her bedroom was being tapped.

The Palace did not have to wait long to get exactly what they wanted. On New Year's Eve, Diana and Gilbey duly provided Charles's side with the infamous 'Squidgey' tape.

Revelations

It was the bombshell which exploded the myth of 'the perfect Princess'.

'And so, darling, what other lows today?' asks James Gilbey.

The unmistakable voice of the Princess of Wales replies: 'I was very bad at lunch. And I nearly started blubbing. I just felt really sad and empty and I thought: "Bloody hell, after all I've done for that fucking family."'

The infamous 'Squidgey' tapes had been sitting in the safe at the *Sun*'s offices in Wapping for more than two years. The sensational recording had been made by amateur radio buff Cyril Reenan at his home in Abingdon, Oxfordshire, during the New Year of 1990. A £900 scanner on the roof of his house had picked up the conversation which had been secretly recorded and broadcast by Prince Charles's aides.

Reenan, a highly respectable retired bank manager,

159

instantly recognizing the value and importance of what he had overheard, turned the tapes over to the *Sun*. The paper knew it had a ticking timebomb which would explode the fairy-tale image of the woman regularly voted the most popular royal by its readers.

During the rambling, rather cringe-making twenty-three-minute conversation, Gilbey calls Diana 'darling' fifty-three times. He calls her 'Squidgey' fourteen times. She gushes and blows kisses down the phone to him. They talk about masturbation and her fears of getting pregnant.

In one memorable exchange, Gilbey says: 'Oh Squidgey, I love you, love you, love you, love you,' to which she replies: 'You are the nicest person in the whole wide world.'

In fact, within ten days of receiving the tapes in 1990, the *Sun* sent a reporter to Gilbey's London flat in Lennox Gardens, near Kensington Palace. When the reporter asked him directly about the 'Squidgey' tape and repeated a few of the choice phrases from the tape, his mouth fell open and he turned white.

'He just stood there looking stunned,' says a witness. 'He knew the game was up. He didn't say a word. Once he'd got his act together he just ran into his car and drove off at high speed. It was pretty obvious he knew we had him bang to rights. To this day Gilbey has steadfastly refused to comment on the tape.

The decision was taken that the tapes could not be published at the time, because, according to one top executive at the paper: 'We knew the tapes could cause enormous damage to the Princess of Wales and the entire royal family and we were not prepared to do that. We had the tapes checked out and authenticated, but we did not publish them. To be frank, we wondered whether they would ever be made public. They were simply devastating. The idea that the Princess of Wales would be talking so intimately to a man other than her husband, a man who repeatedly whispered that he loved her and was so relaxed with her that he was calling her "Squidgey" was a bombshell which could possibly have destroyed Diana's image for ever.'

But, by the summer of 1992, the royal family seemed intent on destroying itself. Princess Anne was divorced and embroiled in a new love affair with Commander Timothy Laurence. Fergie was estranged from Prince Andrew and the infamous 'toe-sucking' pictures of her in the south of France with her 'financial adviser' Johnny Bryan had just been splashed all over the newspapers. Prince Edward, for his part, was making headline news by declaring: 'I'm not gay!' in response to a question which was not even asked. The marriage of Charles and Diana was clearly a sham – and both sides had been regularly 'informing' on each other to their favourite Fleet Street contacts for years. Diana had openly co-operated with author Andrew Morton on his devastating exposé of her unhappy marriage, *Diana: Her True Story*.

The 'Squidgeygate' tape, which just two years earlier had been deemed too racy for publication, was now justifiably newsworthy for it showed the full extent of the depths to which the marriage of the Prince and Princess of Wales, future king and queen, had sunk. It also showed the hypocrisy of the advisers at the Palace. For years, Fleet Street had known the marriage was over. For years, the Palace had consistently denied there was even a hint of discord. It was almost laughable.

Those within the royal circle knew Diana and Charles were leading separate lives. Everyone in Fleet Street knew the marriage was over. Diana's friends were calling up on an almost weekly basis to throw some more 'dirt' at the Prince. And yet the Palace doggedly released hollow press statements to try and perpetuate the myth that the Waleses were a couple.

In reality, the pair had not slept together for more than five years. They never spoke to each other unless they were arguing. It was a sham marriage – and the public had a right to know.

On 24 August 1992, the *Sun* decided to run the 'Squidgey' tapes. An American newspaper, the *National Enquirer*, was planning to publish the full transcript.

Unlike fifty years earlier, when the British public were the last to know about the affair between Edward and Mrs Simpson because of a blanket ban on coverage in the British press, the public would not be duped again.

Four million readers woke up the next day to the headline: MY LIFE IS TORTURE, DIANAGATE TAPE OF LOVE CALL REVEALS MARRIAGE MISERY. The tape had been made while Diana was alone in her bedroom at Sandringham shortly after Christmas 1989, lonely and bored during one of what she described as the 'interminably boring' Christmases with the royal family. Gilbey was stationary in his car in an Oxfordshire lay-by – talking on his mobile phone, number 0860 354661.

In fact, Diana was later to say the publication of the taped conversation was 'a great relief' to her, because, for the first time, the full extent of Diana's loathing for her husband and the break-up of the marriage was out in the open.

She later told a friend: 'It was a huge weight off my shoulders. For the first time, everyone knew the hell I was going through. I'd known about the existence of the tapes for two years. I felt like the Sword of Damocles was hanging over my head. Once they came out, it was a nightmare, but it was also a big relief.'

Prince Charles was furious. He felt that publication of the Princess's rather painfully naïve conversation with her admirer, packed with innuendo and crude sexual references, had embarrassed the royal family immeasurably. He was seen as the cuckolded husband and he believed it showed his wife 'as a total airhead'.

The question of whether Diana ever slept with Gilbey is one still hotly debated among their friends. Most tend to concur with the view that the relationship never went beyond the heavy petting stage. Yet certain extracts of the tape suggest the relationship was more intimate. On the tape, Diana is heard saying: 'I don't want to get pregnant.'

Gilbey replies: 'Darling, it's not going to happen. You won't get pregnant.'

Diana: 'Yeah.'

Gilbey: 'Don't get like that. It's not going to happen, darling. You won't get pregnant.'

Diana: 'I watched *EastEnders* today. One of the main characters had a baby. They thought it was by her husband. It was by another man.'

Gilbey: 'Squidgey, kiss me. Oh God, it's so wonderful, isn't it, this sort of feeling. Don't you just love it?'

Diana: 'I love it. I love it. Never had it before. I've never had it before.'

Gilbey: 'Darling, it's so nice being able to help you.'

Diana: 'You do. You'll never know how much. You'll never know how much.'

Gilbey: 'Oh, I will, darling. I just feel so close to you, so wrapped up in you. I'm wrapping you up, protecting.'

Diana: 'Yes please ... yes please ...'

One part of the conversation was omitted from the original *Sun* story as being too personal and intimate for a family newspaper.

Gilbey says: 'Darling, umm, it's just like, umm, sort of . . .'

'Playing with yourself?' replies Diana.

'What? No I'm not, actually,' says Gilbey.

'I said it's just like . . . just like,' she says.

'Playing with yourself,' he says.

'Yes,' says Diana.

Gilbey responds: 'Not quite as nice. No, I haven't played with myself actually. Not for a full forty-eight hours. Not for a full forty-eight hours. Ummm, tell me some more . . .'

Diana: 'I haven't for a day.'

Gilbey: 'You haven't?'

Diana: 'Not for a day.'

Some royal watchers believe Diana *did* engage in a full-blown affair. Lady Colin Campbell says: 'Diana keeps putting out these stories that her relationship with Gilbey was nothing more than an innocent flirtation. It sounds rather more than that when you listen to the tapes. If Diana is talking about getting pregnant, it pretty much leaves it clear that they were sleeping together.'

Gilbey, at first sight, seemed an unlikely suitor. He ran the Holbein Motor Company, an upmarket used-car dealership in Battersea. That company finally ended up in liquidation, crashing with heavy losses.

Gilbey had, in fact, known Diana from her carefree bachelor-girl days at Coleherne Court.

A friend of Gilbey's says: 'James has always had an eye for a pretty girl and another eye on the main chance. When he was reintroduced at a party to Diana in the late eighties, he was straight in there, like a rat up a drainpipe, so to speak.'

Their friendship first hit the headlines in October 1989

when the Princess was photographed coming out of Gilbey's rented one-bedroomed apartment in Lennox Gardens, Knightsbridge. It was later revealed she had dismissed her private detective, Sergeant David Sharp, some two hours earlier. Gilbey later said: 'We were simply playing bridge. It's hard for the Princess to keep up old friendships.' He said the Princess made up a foursome at bridge that night. But that was impossible: she was the only visitor to his apartment the whole evening.

In fact, according to aides close to Prince Charles, Diana's friendship with the rather unsuitable car dealer was common knowledge at the Palace.

One says: 'Everyone thought it rather amusing that Diana had finally found someone of her own class. Of course, everyone knew she was having this thing with him. They met up all the time, and she couldn't dismiss her royal protection officer without us knowing. The first thing he did was radio back to the Palace to alert us that Diana was in this man's rather modest flat, unguarded. A second car was sent out there without her knowledge. There was no way we were going to leave her unguarded. Don't be ridiculous.'

Perhaps the most worrying thing for the Palace was Gilbey's co-operation with Andrew Morton on *Diana: Her True Story*. Gilbey was quoted extensively in the book and was the person responsible for telling Morton some of the juicier stories about Diana.

A Palace aide says: 'What was of great concern was that Gilbey was considered an unsuitable confidant for the future queen. He'd already proved that by co-operating with Andrew Morton. Even the Princess was privately concerned that he'd gone "over the top" in some of the stories he gave Morton. Claiming the Sandringham stairs incident was a serious suicide attempt when, in fact,

Diana had simply taken an accidental slip was over the top, to say the least.'

But Diana was determined to pursue her friendship to spite those at the Palace who warned her of Gilbey's unsuitability.

Diana's main ally in her growing 'friendship' with Gilbey was Mara Berni, the owner of the fashionable Knightsbridge restaurant San Lorenzo. Mara would allow Gilbey to drop off letters for Diana at the restaurant, which she would pass on to the Princess discreetly at a later date. She also allowed Diana and Gilbey to dine alone in a private room in the restaurant.

A former waitress says: 'They would go in there, the order would be taken and delivered and then no-one was allowed to go into the room apart from Mara. It was quite strange. They often stayed in there alone for hours. You'd never hear a peep out of them apart from the occasional high-pitched giggle from the Princess.'

On the 'Squidgey' tapes, Gilbey says: 'Darling, forgetting that for a moment, how is Mara?'

Diana replies: 'She's all right. No she's fine. Can't wait to get back [from holiday].'

Gilbey: 'Can't she? When's she coming back?'

Diana: 'Saturday.'

Later on, the conversation returns to Mara and a planned meeting at her restaurant.

Gilbey: '. . . I love it when I hear you laughing. It makes me really happy when you laugh. Do you know I am happy when you are happy?'

Diana: 'I know you are.'

Gilbey: 'And I cry when you cry.'

Diana: 'I know. So sweet. The rate we are going, we won't need any dinner on Tuesday.'

Gilbey: 'No, I won't need any dinner, actually. Just seeing you will be all I need.'

In fact, Charles's friends knew all about the Mara Berni connection.

One says: 'Of course he knew. Diana would go over to San Lorenzo all the time to meet Gilbey. The Prince was hardly going to complain. The more time Diana spent away, the more freedom it gave him. He didn't want her anywhere near. His only objection was that she chose someone so clearly not of her class. He thought it shameful that she should have a fling with Gilbey, a used-car salesman, of all people. It just confirmed to the Prince that Diana's head was turned by anyone with a good line in chat and a sympathetic ear to listen to her whingeing.'

Those who believe Diana's explanation that Gilbey was simply infatuated by her point to the fact that, throughout the entire conversation, it is he who continually professes love for her – while she remains quietly detached and aloof.

A friend of Gilbey's says: 'James put Diana up on a pedestal. It's rather like listening to one of those pathetic sex phone-in lines. Diana's never been much interested in the down-and-dirty of real sex. To her, the idea of some chap sitting in a lay-by getting all steamed up about her was about as close as she gets to a sexual thrill. She just loved leading him on and flirting.'

In another portion of the tape, Diana talks about another of her former admirers, James Hewitt. She talks about how she 'spent a fortune' kitting the guardsman out with a new wardrobe.

Gilbey: 'I like those ordinary Italian things that last a couple of years and then I chuck them out. It was a sort of devotion to duty. I was seeking an identity when I bought my first pair of Guccis twelve years ago.

Diana: 'Golly!'

Gilbey: 'And I've still got them. Still doing me proud like.'

Diana: 'Good.'

Gilbey: 'I'm going to take you up on that, darling. I will give you some money. You can go off and spend it for me.'

Diana: 'I will. Yah.'

Gilbey: 'Will you?'

Diana: 'I'm a connoisseur in that department.'

Gilbey: 'Are you?'

Diana: 'Yes.'

Gilbey: 'Well, you think you are.'

Diana: 'Well, I've decked people out in my time.'

Gilbey:'Who did you deck out? Not many, I hope.'

Diana: 'James Hewitt . . . entirely dressed him from head to foot, that man. Cost me a lot, that man. Cost me quite a bit.'

Gilbey: 'I bet it did. At your expense?'

Diana: 'Yah.'

Gilbey: 'He didn't even pay you to do it?'

Diana: 'No!'

Gilbey: 'What an ext ... very extravagant, darling.'

Diana: 'Well, I am, aren't I? Anything that will make people happy.'

Gilbey: 'You mustn't do it for that, darling, because you make people happy. It's what you give them ...'

Publication of the tapes came as a complete shock to one woman: Gilbey's long-time girlfriend Lady Alethea Savile. The daughter of the Earl of Mexborough was totally unaware of the relationship between her boyfriend of two years and the Princess. In fact, up until the day the tapes were published, Lady Alethea was planning to marry Gilbey.

After the publication of Andrew Morton's book a few weeks earlier, Alethea had accompanied Gilbey on holiday to Italy – with Diana's brother Earl Spencer and his then wife Victoria Lockwood. But the romantic holiday could not save the relationship.

Lady Alethea refused to comment on her boyfriend's 'betrayal', saying only: 'The whole thing is mind-blowing.'

One of her friends says: 'She went crazy. She felt completely betrayed. Whether James was or was not sleeping with the Princess, the fact was he bloody well wanted to. And that was appalling to Alethea. Just a couple of days before the tapes appeared in the *Sun*, he'd been in her bed, making love to her. The next thing she knows, he's all over the newspapers making verbal love to another woman – and the Princess of Wales to boot. Alethea was appalled. She is a lovely woman from a good family. Her family had been dismayed when she'd taken up with Gilbey in the first place. Once those tapes appeared, it was curtains for him as far as the Savile family went.

'James tried calling Alethea, but she simply refused to even talk to him. She was distraught over the whole affair. She went to pieces.'

In fact, a year later, Alethea wrote a piece for the *Daily Mail* which talked about how she was admitted to the Sierra Tuscon rehabilitation clinic in Arizona suffering from severe depression. Alethea admitted being 'in floods of tears' after the publication of the tapes and she underwent therapy at the clinic to ease her heartache and 'enormous depression'.

A close friend of Alethea's says: 'She could not cope with the publicity. All the press attention and the endless speculation sent her crazy. It was Alethea who dumped James.'

Tragically on 17 September 1994, Alethea was found dead at her London flat after taking a massive drugs overdose. Friends said that, despite the treatment for her addiction, she had lapsed back into a spiral of depression.

One said: 'Poor Alethea never really recovered from the tapes scandal. She always suffered from severe depression and all the attention and publicity became too much to bear. She was a tragic figure who was always threatening to end it all. Sadly in the end, she succeeded.'

Gilbey refused to talk about the tapes at the time or since. He was reported to be 'devastated' after Alethea's suicide. Shortly after the tapes were first published, he went to work in the promotions department of the Lotus Formula One team based in Norfolk. According to someone who knew him well: 'James arrived at Lotus rather shell-shocked by the whole experience. For a few weeks, he would stiffen and leave the room if the Princess's name came up. But after a while he became more relaxed. He actually seemed rather proud of his royal connections. He's not the most attractive of men, rather slight of form and balding, To him, it was a massive ego boost that the most gorgeous girl in the world spoke so intimately to him.'

In fact, Diana had not spoken to Gilbey since the end of 1993.

Dianagate, as the affair was dubbed, left Diana even more anxious to break away from the royal family.

She was also devastated to learn of the existence of a second tape – one which recorded her speaking from her bedroom at Kensington Palace to one of her 'friendly' journalists. The tape, which still remains in the hands of Prince Charles's advisers, is damning proof that not only did Diana co-operate directly with Andrew Morton on his book – but that she was continuing to 'feed' unflattering stories to the newspapers about her husband.

On this second tape, Diana and Gilbey discuss the Morton book. Diana instructs Gilbey to continue to 'keep up the good work' – supplying pro-Diana stories to the papers.

A Palace insider says: 'Diana was actually made aware of this tape at the time. It proved, conclusively, that she co-operated with the Morton book. No one knows for certain where that tape is, but you can rest assured it is somewhere safe in the Palace.'

The situation reached crisis point three days after the 'Squidgey' tapes were published.

Diana, in Balmoral with the rest of the royal family, again demanded a separation. She wanted out of the marriage.

An emergency closed-door meeting was held at Balmoral between Diana, Charles, the Queen and Prince Philip. The Queen, sympathetic to Diana's cause, advised her that it would be wise for her to accompany Prince Charles on a planned visit to Korea in November 1992. She said that if Diana did not go on the trip, it would only lead to a greater press feeding frenzy about the state of the marriage. Diana agreed. The Queen suggested a three-month 'cooling off' period for both Charles and Diana to 'give serious consideration' to their future plans.

The possibility of an informal separation was also discussed. Prince Philip explained a full-blown divorce was out of the question. He explained to her, in no uncertain terms, that if she were to go for a divorce, she would lose custody of the two young Princes. Since they were second and third in line to the throne, custody would remain with the royal family. It was unthinkable for it to be otherwise. Diana realized the family meant it.

Despite all that had happened, Diana now saw her only

trump card was the role she played as mother to the future king and to the second in line to the throne: Wills and Harry.

She told a friend: 'It'll be over my dead body that they try to take the boys away.'

She therefore made an agreement. She would stick with the marriage until the end of the year. She would accompany the Prince and her sons on a summer cruise to the Mediterranean. She would go on the tour of Korea. But if, when she came back, she still felt the same way, a separation would be announced. It was agreed that Diana would be allowed to remain in her own private quarters at Kensington Palace while the Prince would be set up in a new London home at St James's Palace. He would also retain his main home at Highgrove, a place the Princess 'loathed' anyway.

In fact, Charles met with Camilla shortly afterwards to seek her advice about a major refurbishment of Highgrove. Camilla oversaw the whole redecoration process as the pretty pastels and flowery prints of the Diana-era were removed and a more 'manly' style was introduced to the house.

An estate worker says: 'It was as if the Prince wanted to erase any memory of Diana from the house. Camilla oversaw all the renovations and redecorations. She was at the house the whole time, even when the Prince was away. She masterminded the whole thing. And he was thrilled with the result. Camilla's taste in decor and furnishings is completely in line with his. As a result, the house is a lot more comfortable than it was in Diana's day when it was full of chintz and flowery things.'

The Queen, meanwhile, still lived in hope that Diana would not 'bolt' from the family.

A royal aide says: 'Even at that stage, after the

publication of the "Squidgey" tapes, the Queen was doing all she could to preserve the marriage and the dignity of the monarchy. She was always sympathetic to Diana and she hoped against hope that Diana would stick it out. I think in her heart, though, she knew all was lost. It was something she could not even bring herself to think about.

'But the Queen was always more than fair to Diana. She was always sympathetic and she personally intervened when the marriage broke down. She still talks to Diana to this day. They are in contact far more regularly than people would imagine. Of the whole family, the Queen is the one who has bent over backwards to be fair and supportive to the Princess.'

A few days later, a clothes rack was unceremoniously placed in the office of the Prince of Wales at St James's Palace. The metal rack on wheels contained grey and black clothes bags crammed from end to end. Inside, the Prince of Wales's uniforms were stacked up high. A small box also appeared. It was crammed with personal papers and small items of jewellery, including the Prince's modest collection of cufflinks – among them the pair with the intertwining 'C's which Camilla had given him as a wedding gift.

A Palace aide says: 'It was a clear signal that the Prince of Wales was moving all his stuff out of Kensington Palace. The uniforms and cases of his other personal possessions were later taken by car down to Highgrove. Some were taken to his new quarters at St James's Palace.

'It was very sad. It was like seeing the Prince of Wales thrown out on the street. Very sad indeed.

'He refused to even go back into the Kensington Palace rooms while Diana was there. He waited until she'd gone out for the day and then went back and packed a few more personal possessions. He took all his letters, all his personal journals. He didn't want to leave anything behind which Diana might find and use against him in the future.'

In the summer of 1992, Diana went on a cruise of the Mediterranean with Prince Charles on a luxury yacht owned by Greek shipping tycoon John Latsis. The media hyped the holiday as 'a second honeymoon'. It was wishful thinking.

The couple were accompanied by Princess Alexandra and her husband Sir Angus Ogilvy, Lord and Lady Romsey and their children and Princes William and Harry.

Sadly, the Prince and Princess hardly exchanged a single word. Diana preferred to eat separately from the main party, she spent mealtimes with the children, and slept in a small cabin at the other end of the yacht from her husband.

One day, they passed each other in the ship's galley. He simply ignored her. He fetched a glass of milk and then left.

In an updated chapter in his book *Diana: Her True Story*, author Andrew Morton later revealed that Diana went into the state-room to make a phone call back to England to check on the condition of her AIDS-stricken friend Adrian Ward-Jackson. She picked up an extension and heard her husband in the middle of a long ship-to-shore call to Camilla from the main ship's satellite phone.

Morton says: 'It merely provided further fuel for Diana's suspicions regarding her husband's relationship with Camilla, if any were needed.'

In October 1992, Diana was to come face to face with Camilla once more. The setting was Westminster Abbey; the occasion, a service to mark the fiftieth anniversary of the Battle of El Alamein.

Camilla, dressed in black, went to the service with her father Major Bruce Shand, a Military Cross winner. She had considered backing out at the last minute, knowing Diana would be there and the press interest would thus be 'overpowering', but out of love and devotion to her father, she went.

An audible buzz went through the Abbey as Camilla entered, her head held high, and walked slowly with her father to their allocated seats. A few moments later, Diana walked in with Prince Charles. As she walked down the centre of the Abbey to the front pew, Diana turned and gave Camilla a frosty stare.

Said one witness: 'It was enough to chill you out. Camilla, being Camilla, did what she always does when Diana is being a petulant child: she just ignored her.'

Afterwards, Camilla was rushed by a crowd of photographers outside the church. She later quipped: 'It was like going into the lion's den. But I guess all they're going to care about was the fact that my hair was in a mess.'

Sure enough, the headlines branded Camilla a 'frump' and repeated the question: how could Charles possibly dump the most beautiful woman in the world for a woman so remarkably *plain*?

Later that evening, the Prince phoned Camilla to apologize for his wife's 'childish' behaviour and for the 'barrage of abuse' she had been subjected to.

According to a family friend, Camilla replied: 'There is no use in apologizing, darling, it's not your fault. I'm afraid Diana is not in the best of health these days. I know people want to see me as the wicked woman in all of this, but you know the truth – and that is all I care about. If I have your support, I can endure anything.'

The publication of Andrew Morton's book that

175

summer and its subsequent serialization in the *Sunday Times* had caused Camilla enormous pain, and incredibly, Diana was still 'cashing in' on the book even after the furore blew up.

Just a few days after the first extract of the book was serialized in the *Sunday Times*, a well-spoken woman telephoned a top executive at the *Sun*. The executive was advised to 'get' a photographer around to the house of Carolyn Bartholomew, one of Diana's friends who had fully co-operated with the Morton book. Bartholomew's obscure address in Fulham was given.

When the photographers arrived, they were greeted by the sight of the Princess of Wales leaving Carolyn's house. The two women hugged and embraced for a full five minutes. It was Diana's way of showing that she stood by what was in the book.

The Princess steadfastly refused to sign a statement confirming she had not co-operated with the book. She refused to disown either the contents or her friends who had co-operated with the publication.

Prince Charles was devastated by this blatant act of betrayal.

He later told Camilla: 'From this moment on, I shall never forgive her – and I shall never forgive or forget what she has done.'

He immediately launched a 'counter-attack'.

Several 'positive' articles about the Prince appeared. The author Penny Junor, who had become close to the Prince and his circle of friends when she produced a biography of him, wrote a piece for the now defunct *Today* newspaper under the headline: CHARLES: HIS TRUE STORY.

The article told of the Prince's 'extreme dis-appointment' with his marriage and of his 'sense of betrayal' by his wife's behaviour. Junor was quoted as saying: 'It is time to put the record straight once and for all. The Prince has suffered in silence long enough.'

She added: 'It would take a miracle for the marriage to survive. I fear too much damage has been done. As heir to the throne, Charles will one day be Defender of the Faith. One of the cornerstones of the Anglican faith is the sanctity of marriage. Charles acknowledges that to live a publicly dishonest marriage is incompatible with his faith and position.

'On the other hand, this marriage has come to this state because of Diana's illness and for no other reason. If she could be treated and cured, I am sure that Charles would be willing to work to repair the damage.

'The trouble is, Diana is a very sick woman. In public, she is a wonderful princess, charming and beautiful.

'But Charles has lived with a very different woman. She screams, shouts, is vitriolic and unreasonable with him.'

While Charles's aides attempted damage control, Camilla's life was made 'a living hell' by the mounting crisis. Reporters were camped out at the door of Middlewick House. Camilla lost more than a stone in weight through the upset. She also began chain-smoking.

A close confidante says: 'Camilla went through hell. But she would never even think to go public with her side of things. As ever, she remained steadfastly loyal and quiet. She was being subjected to the most awful abuse. She was branded a scarlet woman and every other name under the sun. In the end, she left and went to stay at a friend's house for a few weeks. She simply could not cope with all the fuss. I am sure Camilla would love to have set the record straight. But she maintained her dignity and silence.

'But she never stopped speaking to the Prince.

Throughout the whole scandal of the Morton book, when Diana's so-called friends put the blame for the Prince's marriage failure firmly on her doorstep, Camilla remained firm friends with the Prince.

'Throughout it all, Camilla showed she had one thing in which the Princess of Wales was sadly lacking: class.'

One member of Camilla's immediate family says: 'She believes the old adage that silence is golden. If you look at what Diana's side have said and done, you would think Camilla is the Wicked Witch of the West, the woman who "stole" the Prince from the fairy-tale Princess.

'It wasn't like that at all. The Prince was the one who refused to give Camilla up. Truth is, she's the only woman he's ever loved, always will be. You cannot blame Camilla for everything. The marriage was a disaster from the start. The only person who has helped the Prince survive over the past few years has been Camilla. After the Morton book, even after the 'Squidgey' tapes, Camilla was always there for him. He knew he had a true friend in Camilla.

The four-day trip to South Korea undertaken by the Prince and Princess of Wales that November was an unmitigated disaster from start to finish. The trip had been planned by the Prince's deputy private secretary Peter Westmacott two months earlier – but even he did not know that Diana intended to accompany Charles on the trip until seventy-two hours before they were due to leave.

Another Palace insider said: 'It was chaos. Everything was up in the air. No-one really knew what was going to happen. Diana was still threatening to duck out three days before they were due to set off.'

The pair had a blazing row on the Queen's Flight on the way over to Seoul and were clearly not speaking to each other from the moment their VC-10 plane touched down on the runway after the fourteen-hour flight.

On the eve of the trip, Diana put out a press release denying that there was any truth in reports that a rift had developed between her and the Queen, but adding the tell-tale line that there were 'difficulties' in her marriage.

Hopes by the Palace for a 'love tour' bit the dust. The Prince and Princess could barely stand to look at each other. At joint functions, their body language made it clear for the world to see that theirs was a mutual hatred and loathing. They would purposely stand as far away from each other as possible. Diana frequently rolled her eyes skyward when her husband spoke in public. She physically turned her shoulders away from him when they were forced to sit or stand side by side.

A friend of Diana's says: 'She was clearly unhappy to be there. She felt she had been pressurized into going to fulfil her part of the deal she'd made with the Queen. But she knew from the start it was a big mistake. Just seeing Charles there made her mad. And knowing he was going back and telephoning Camilla made her even madder.'

At a cocktail party at the British Embassy, the pair walked to opposite sides of the room and refused to say a word to each other.

One observer says: 'They kept as far apart from each other as they could. They didn't even exchange glances across the room.'

When they were apart on that trip, both relaxed and smiled for the cameras. Diana returned to her 'normal' cheerful self and the Prince visibly cheered up. But when they were together, the stony silence and long faces returned.

The headline writers back home summed them up as THE GLUMS.

In a car taking them to a state dinner, both looked solemn and grim. They purposely fixed their eyes firmly in opposite directions and turned their bodies away from one another. The Prince then spoke the only words to his wife anyone was to hear during the next four days:
'You get out of that side,' he said as the car arrived at its destination.

The diplomatic mission of Britain's royal ambassadors had turned into a cruel, crude farce. Said one witness: 'It was like the War of the Roses. They both had their own camps of people and their own agendas. When they were together, you could have cut the tension with a knife. It was appalling. Their Korean hosts simply could not work it out. They had expected this wonderful fairy-tale couple, and they got the *Nightmare on Elm Street*.'

In a desperate attempt to salvage something from the trip, Westmacott called James Whitaker to one side. He explained to the royal correspondent that the Prince and Princess were 'distressed' by what they considered 'gross' intrusions into their private life through the constant reports about the unhappy state of their marriage.

Whitaker replied: 'Peter, are you trying to tell me this is a happy marriage?'

Westmacott replied: 'No, I am not trying to say that. But I am saying it has been unfair and exaggerated.'

The story made the headlines on that night's television news back in Britain – it was the first time a Buckingham Palace official had recognized, on the record, that the marriage was in trouble.

The couple did not even travel home together. Diana returned to London alone, while Charles continued on for a private trip to Hong Kong.

An aide says: 'The Prince knew the Korean trip had been a disaster. He said one day: "She is impossible. She won't even make the effort any more. And, to be frank, I don't think I can be bothered any more. It's time for things to take their natural course. I'll be damned if I have to put up with that woman any more."'

Shortly after she returned home, Diana told a friend that she had inadvertently picked up the telephone at a hotel in Korea – to find her husband in the middle of an affectionate late-night call to Camilla.

She said: 'It's all over. I want out of that bloody family and I don't care what the repercussions are.'

Prince Charles celebrated his forty-fourth birthday on 15 November 1992. His wife ignored the event, choosing not even to buy him a card or a present.

Camilla telephoned him to wish him many happy returns. She and Charles spent more than an hour on the phone together.

Twenty-four days later, on 9 December, the Palace issued a terse statement: the Prince and Princess of Wales were announcing their official separation.

Winning the Battle,
Losing the War

It was Prime Minister John Major who finally made the announcement the world had been waiting for:

Standing on the floor of the House of Commons on 9 December 1992, he said:

> 'It is announced from Buckingham Palace that, with regret, the Prince and Princess of Wales have decided to separate. Their Royal Highnesses have no plans to divorce and their constitutional positions are unaffected. This decision has been reached amicably, and they will both continue to participate fully in the upbringing of their children.
>
> 'Their Royal Highnesses will continue to carry out full and separate programmes of public engagements and will, from time to time, attend family occasions and national events together.

'The Queen and the Duke of Edinburgh, though saddened, understand and sympathize with the difficulties that have led to this decision. Her Majesty and His Royal Highness particularly hope that the intrusions into the privacy of the Prince and Princess may now cease.

'They believe that a degree of privacy and understanding is essential if Their Royal Highnesses are to provide a happy and secure upbringing for their children, while continuing to give a wholehearted commitment to their public duties.'

In fact, Diana had again 'forced' the royal family into making the announcement.

A few days after she returned from the disastrous South Korean trip the previous month, she went to see solicitor Paul Butner of Wright, Son and Pepper in London. Mr Butner has never spoken of the meeting but it is known Diana asked him to hammer out a separation agreement with the Queen's solicitor Sir Matthew Farrer.

Then she instructed her solicitor to insist the separation announcement be made by the Prime Minister. A royal aide says: 'By this point, everyone knew any attempt to paper over the cracks in the marriage would be worthless. So the Palace allowed Diana to start making the first moves for a separation. But they were aghast when she demanded the Prime Minister make the announcement. It was just Diana attempting to show, once again, how much clout she had. She was being a prima donna right to the end.'

When the Palace initially turned down the Princess's demands, she produced the ace up her sleeve. Princess

Anne was to marry Commander Timothy Laurence on 12 December 1992. A petulant Diana threatened to make her *own* announcement of the separation on that day, stealing what little positive publicity the Palace was hoping for from Princess Anne's happy wedding. The Queen was furious – but she backed down. She was determined that no-one, and certainly not the Princess of Wales, would be allowed to ruin Anne's big day.

She told a close aide: 'I suppose we shall have to give that tiresome girl what she wants again. I shall not have anyone ruining Anne's day. Instruct the Prime Minister accordingly.'

Prime Minister Major was due to meet European Union heads of government in Scotland on the day of the announcement. But, in response to a private telephone conversation with the Queen, he abandoned his plans the previous evening and flew back to London.

Diana thus had her separation announced in the House of Commons, just as she had requested.

Lady Colin Campbell says: 'The Palace was livid that they had had to give into the whims of this headstrong young woman yet again. It left a very nasty taste in people's mouths.

'Diana was now openly considered an outsider within the royal circle. What she had done, in those last months of 1992, had provoked the crisis at the heart of the monarchy which everyone had tried to avoid. Her actions were considered shameful and appalling.

'She was effectively frozen out of the royal circle from that day forth. Of course, in public, as the mother of the future king, she was accorded a certain amount of civility by the other members of the royal household. But in private, she was a social outcast. She had let the side down, and the Queen was not amused.'

For her part, Camilla refused to comment on the separation, saying loyally: 'I will not be making any statement. Obviously, if something has gone wrong I feel very sorry for them.'

Her husband said: 'Like everyone else, one feels sad about what has happened.'

A short time after the official announcement, the Palace instructed Diana that William and Harry would be spending Christmas at Sandringham with their father and the rest of the royal family. Diana tried objecting, but her objections fell on deaf ears. She spent what she later described as 'a lonely and tearful' Christmas with her brother Earl Spencer on the Althorp estate.

Bitterly she told her friends: 'They took the boys off me for Christmas. I try fighting them, but I am weary of the fight. There seems nothing I can do any more. If I complain too much, they take the boys away. And the boys are all I have left now.'

Slowly, Diana was beginning to realize she had won the battle to destroy her marriage and destroy the reputation of the future king but that she was losing the war.

Thirty-six days later, the 'Camillagate' scandal erupted with the force of a tornado.

Damage Limitation

'Your great achievement is to love me,' he says.

'Oh darling, easier than falling off a chair,' she replies.

'You suffer all these indignities and tortures and calumnies.'

'Oh darling, don't be so silly. I'd suffer anything for you. That's love. It's the strength of love. Night, night.'

The 'Camillagate' tape, published on 13 January 1993, revealed, for the first time, the full extent of the depth of feeling between Prince Charles and the woman who had been his mistress for nearly a quarter of a century. It was devastating. For the first time, the world heard the most intimate conversation of two people desperately in love – two people each married to someone else.

The bedtime call took place at around one in the morning, on 18 December 1989, when Charles was staying at the home of an old friend, Anne, Duchess of Westminster. He made the call from his personal mobile phone. Camilla was alone in bed at her home in Wiltshire. Her husband was in London.

She and Charles spoke with the frank openness of lovers secure in the knowledge that the intimate details of their conversation would go no further. Neither could have had any idea that their six-minute, 1,574-word conversation was being secretly bugged and that it would come back to haunt them more than three years later, causing a scandal unparalleled in modern times.

The affair which Prince Charles had denied and tried to hide for more than two decades was about to become known around the globe.

In fact, transcripts of the tapes had been at the offices of both the *Sun* and the *Daily Mirror* for months; in November 1992, both newspapers had written articles which mentioned the existence of the tapes. Andrew Knight, the former chief executive of News International, which owns the *Sun*, had written an article in the *Spectator* magazine as early as July 1992, claiming the newspaper had 'highly damaging material' about the royal family locked in the safe in his offices at Wapping. One element of the 'damaging material' was the 'Squidgey' tape of Diana – the other was the 'Camillagate' tape.

Again, the British press chose not to be the first to publish; the 'Camillagate' scandal was put into motion on the other side of the world when the mass-circulation Australian magazine *New Idea* revealed it had obtained a copy of the tape and that it was going to publish and be damned.

Prince Charles had actually considered seeking an injunction, banning publication of the tapes. He was fully aware that they were in the possession of British newspapers. But after long discussions with his advisers, he had vetoed any legal action because of the added pressure it would put on the one person he cared about most – Camilla.

A friend says: 'By the time the tapes appeared, the Prince had known about them for at least six months. He knew their content and he knew they would surface eventually. He had discussed the repercussions of them several times with Camilla. She knew the score, too.

'Charles decided he was prepared to stand up and face the public fall-out. If he had attempted to ban publication of the tapes, it would have led to an even greater scandal. People would have wondered what he was trying to hide and he would have been found guilty by default anyway. And he knew if he tried any kind of legal action, Camilla would again be brought into the fray. He wanted to do every-thing he could to prevent the woman he loved from being subjected to such a nightmare ordeal.

'He knew once the papers had the tape, he was standing on the end of a very short plank. The only question remaining was how long would he have to stand there before he was forced to jump?

'But I don't think even he realized quite how enormous the reaction would be. I think secretly he believed that after the Diana and James Gilbey "Squidgey" tapes, the public might not be so shocked by the conversation between him and Camilla. But, of course, they were.'

The news agencies Reuters and Associated Press had already put out extracts from the tape on the foreign wires. The British papers had no alternative but to run them.

Wednesday, 13 January 1993 was to be forever known within royal circles as 'Black Wednesday'.

Prince Charles was awoken at half past six that morning by the Queen's private secretary Sir Robert Fellowes. It was the start of what he would later describe as 'what felt like the longest bloody day of my life'.

Fellowes, the husband of Diana's sister Lady Jane Spencer, has always been one of the Prince's closest friends. After the scandal of 'Squidgeygate' and the Andrew Morton book, he had effectively cut all links with his sister-in-law. As one of the most 'true blue' royalists, he considered Diana a 'traitor to the cause'.

Charles was in Scotland, visiting the Shetland Islands to help islanders who had suffered horrendously after the *Braer* oil tanker had disgorged 80,000 tons of crude oil on to their shores. Fellowes telephoned the Prince and told him the 'Camillagate' tapes had been made public. The Prince's reaction was a simple and forlorn: 'Oh God.'

The Prince's private secretary Commander Richard Aylard was the next to call. He arranged to meet the Prince later that day 'to discuss damage control'. Damage control was perhaps an understatement of what the Prince would need. The tapes were so intimate, so personal and so embarrassing that, he later told a royal aide, 'It took all the strength I could muster to go downstairs for breakfast that day – I couldn't even face the servants. The thought of facing my own family filled me with dread.'

In fact, his first reaction was to telephone Camilla to forewarn her. She already knew. Her home had been besieged by reporters and photographers since the crack of dawn. She was told the news about the tapes by a reporter from the *Sun* as she emerged from her house in the small hours. Her first reaction was to say: 'Oh my God, I can't believe it. I must speak to my husband.' She then disappeared inside Middlewick House and took the phone off the hook. Ironically, therefore, when the Prince tried repeatedly to call Camilla to warn her of the impending scandal at seven that morning he could not get through.

The blatant passion of the conversation between the Prince and his mistress stunned everyone. According to one aide: 'It was staggering to hear the depths of passion that still existed in their conversation. Everyone close to the Prince knew that he and Camilla had renewed their romantic liaison several years before. But this is a couple who had known each other for nigh on twenty years, and they were talking with the excited passion of newly-weds. It took us all by surprise. It proved they were even more in love and more deeply involved than anyone could have guessed.

'You'd be hard pressed to find a married couple who'd known each other that long and who still had that burning passion between them.

'They speak without any hang-ups or embarrassment. They have no qualms about talking to each other in the most intimate way. They come across as a couple who want and desire each other equally.'

Throughout the conversation, the language is colourful, intimate and raunchy.

Camilla: 'Mmmm, you're awfully good at feeling your way along.'

Charles: 'Oh stop! I want to feel my way along you, all over you and up and down you and in and out.'

Camilla: 'Oh!'

Charles: 'Particularly in and out . . .'

Camilla: 'Oh, that's just what I need at the moment.'

Charles: 'Is it?'

Camilla: 'I know it would revive me. I can't bear a Sunday night without you.'

Charles: 'Oh God.'

Camilla: 'It's like that programme *Start the Week*. I can't start the week without you.'

Charles: 'I fill your tank!'

Camilla: 'Yes you do.'

Charles: 'Then you can cope.'

Camilla: 'Then I'm all right.'

Charles: 'What about me? The trouble is I need you several times a week.'

Camilla: 'Mmmm. So do I. I need you all the week, all the time.'

Charles: 'Oh God, I'd just live inside your trousers or something. It would be much easier!'

Camilla: (*laughing*) 'What are you going to turn into? A pair of knickers? Oh, you're going to come back as a pair of knickers?'

Charles: 'Or God forbid, a Tampax. Just my luck!'

Camilla: 'You are a complete idiot! Oh, what a wonderful idea.'

Charles: 'My luck to be chucked down the lavatory and go on and on for ever, swirling round at the top, never going down!'

Camilla: 'Oh darling!'

Charles: ' . . . until the next one comes through.'

Camilla: 'Or perhaps you could come back as a box.

Charles: 'What sort of box?'

Camilla: 'A box of Tampax, so you could just keep going. Oh darling, I just want you now.'

Charles: 'Do you?'

Camilla: 'Mmmm.'

Charles: 'So do I.

Camilla: 'Desperately, desperately, desperately!'

The couple talk about meeting up at a safe friend's house. Camilla refers to her husband as 'it'.

Part of the conversation revolves around the couple's attempts to link up. They discuss the 'ambulance strike', a bitter dispute which had been going on for six months. Camilla's husband Andrew Parker Bowles played a key role in providing army ambulance services as back-up. Charles and Camilla talk about how they both wish the dispute would continue – to allow them to meet. Furtively.

Charles says: 'Oh God, when am I going to speak to you?'

Camilla: 'I can't bear it. Um . . . '

Charles: 'Wednesday night?'

Camilla: 'Oh, certainly Wednesday night. I'll be alone, um, Wednesday, you know, the evening. Or Tuesday. While you're rushing around doing things I'll be, you know, alone until *it* reappears. And early Wednesday morning. I mean, he'll be leaving at half past eight, quarter past eight. He won't be here Thursday, pray God. Um, that ambulance strike, it's a terrible thing to say this, I suppose it won't have come to an end by Thursday?'

Charles: 'It will have done.'

Camilla: 'Well, I mean, I hope for everybody's sakes it will have done, but I hope for our sakes it's still going on.'

Charles: 'Why?'

Camilla: 'Well, because if it stops, he'll come down here on Thursday night.'

Charles: (*groaning*) 'Oh no.'

Camilla, as well as offering him a passionate physical relationship, also offers him a motherly ear. She asks him for a copy of a speech he has just written which she longs to read.

Charles says: 'I'll be working on the next speech.'

Camilla: 'Oh no, what's the next one?'

Charles: 'A rather important one for Wednesday.'

Camilla: 'Well, at least I'll be behind you.'

Charles: 'I know.'

Camilla: 'Can I have a copy of the one you've just done?'

Charles: 'Yes.'

The couple talk anxiously of 'how wonderful' it would be 'to have just one night together'.

Camilla suggests a number of 'safe houses' where they could rendezvous. It was an anguished conversation for them both – after so many years of intimacy, they are still not free to meet and love each other in the open. They both know they will never be together permanently. But they both agree they cannot face life without meeting regularly.

When they finally hang up on each other, Charles says he will ring off by 'pressing the tit', the button on his mobile phone. Camilla replies: 'I wish you were pressing mine.'

A close friend of Camilla's says: 'Despite the shocking frankness of the conversation, what cannot be denied is the closeness between the two.

'She reassures him throughout, she tells him how much she loves him. She tells him she will always be there for him, She reassures him of how much he is loved and she tells him how clever he is.

'They tell each other they love each other because they truly do, not because they just want to hear the words spoken.

'When the Prince tells Camilla her greatest achievement is to love him, one gets the impression not of arrogance, but that he is enormously grateful that he is deserving of her love.

'The fact that Camilla was anxious to read his speech, shows she genuinely cares about his work and is interested in every aspect of his day. She is constantly bolstering him up, giving him support in all areas of his life.

' 'A lot of people poured scorn on Camilla, but everyone close to her and the Prince knows what a valuable source of strength she has been to him. He has no-one else to talk to except Camilla. And of course he adores her.

'Everyone who knows Camilla adores her. She's smart, she's very funny and what you see is what you get. She is loyal to a fault and if she is your friend, you know you have a friend for life. Camilla is the one person all of us know we can call for some solid advice. But she is someone who never particularly unburdens herself on others; that is not her style. She is very strong and confident in herself as a woman. Her attitude towards the whole scandal was that, deep in her heart, she knew the truth and those she loved knew the truth. That was all that truly mattered to her.'

Within twenty-four hours of 'Camillagate' first breaking it had appeared on the front pages of fifty-three newspapers around the world – and was being broadcast on television news stations in countries from Japan to South Africa, America to Australia.

The mockery that followed the publication of the 'Camillagate' tapes was almost unbearable for the Prince. He returned to the Queen's estate at Sandringham in shame.

'How can it have all gone wrong so quickly?' he would ask his loyal private secretary Richard Aylard, over and over again.

According to those close to him, he seriously considered leaving Britain, renouncing the throne and 'running away' to his beloved Italy. A friend says: 'It completely knocked him for six. The ridicule was staggering. In Italy, they were referring to Charles as the Prince Tampacchino, the "little Tampax Prince". In stores across Britain and America, girls were asking for "Charlies" instead of tampons.

'The Prince heard all these stories, of course. And he was heartbroken. He felt like he had let down himself, let down the Queen, and more importantly, let down his country.

'He seriously talked about going to Florence. He was at the point of just clearing off. He is someone who has always believed totally in his destiny. But, for once, and for the briefest time, he questioned whether his future was going to be as it had always been mapped out. He was totally disillusioned and fed up. He was as depressed as anyone had ever seen him.'

The Prince even ordered his rooms at St James's Palace and the every single room at Highgrove to be swept for telephone bugs. None was found – but it was too late anyway: the irreparable damage to his reputation had been done.

The Prince started to take sleeping pills to help him rest at night. A friend says: 'He was surviving on one or two hours' sleep a night. He was shattered. In the end, his doctor gave him some mild sleeping pills just to help him get some rest.

'He hardly smiled for months, he went around with this dark gloomy storm cloud above him. He was truly a very sad and pitiful sight. He would lock himself away for hours. He was often red-eyed. It was clear he'd done a lot of crying.'

Another close friend who saw him at a dinner party more than a month after the tapes were published said: 'He was almost on the verge of tears all evening. He tried talking about what he was going through, but it was clear he was deeply distressed. Only when he talked about Diana did he get angry. He felt, indeed he still feels to this day, that he tried to make the marriage work in the early days. He would have stuck in the marriage even when it was clear it wasn't working. It was Diana and her problems which caused the rift. She was the one who forced the separation. She was the one who was determined to get out.

'He kept saying how he never meant any of this to happen, how he couldn't understand "the whole bloody mess".

'He was genuinely confused and miserable. There were a few of us that were seriously concerned about his depression. He was so vulnerable, he felt so alone, anything was possible at that stage.

'He even made a passing joke about suicide. He said: "Perhaps they'd all prefer it if I was six foot under. Then what would they do?"

'He forced himself to laugh when he'd said it. He was making a big joke. But privately, a lot of us were worried. He was about as depressed as anyone had ever seen him. All his life, he had wanted to be taken seriously. Now, in a six-minute phone conversation, he had blown years of hard work. He was being laughed at by everyone – everyone except Camilla. In his darkest hours, it was Camilla he turned to once again. She comforted him and offered him a strong shoulder to lean on. She was constantly giving him advice. She encouraged him to face the battle head on.'

The pair would talk on the phone at least once every day. According to friends, these conversations would sometimes be two or three hours in length.

The Queen Mother, anxious about the welfare of her favourite grandson, invited him to lunch. According to one royal aide: 'The Queen Mother knows the depths to which the Windsor men can sink in despair. After all, it was she who watched as Edward VIII, the former Prince of Wales, sank deeper and deeper into the mire over Wallis Simpson. She knew Charles had always suffered from attacks of deep melancholia. She feared history might be repeating itself.'

The Queen Mother telephoned her grandson almost

every day in the weeks following 'Camillagate', and she invited him to lunch at Clarence House at the beginning of April. She asked Charles to tell her all about his visit to see the ageing Duke of Windsor when he was living in exile in France shortly before the Duke's sad and lonely death.

She ended by telling him: 'You have a duty, Charles. You have a duty to your country. Remember what happened before.'

Charles was later to say: 'It was a very clever move. She knew how deeply affected I had been by meeting my great-uncle. Talking about his circumstances helped put mine into perspective. I knew that, no matter what happened, I had to pick myself up by my shoestrings and carry on. History could not repeat itself.'

'She is a wonderful restorer of backbones,' one of the Queen Mother's ladies-in-waiting would later add with a smile. 'She made it clear to Charles, although it took some time for him to fully accept it, that no matter how grim and bleak things appeared, his duty was to the Crown. She told him that no matter how bad he was feeling, he could turn his time of crisis into a strength. He could use the lessons he had learned to rebuild – and look forward.'

Prince Philip was less understanding. He exploded in rage when he first read the 'Camillagate' extracts running in the newspapers.

'Now the whole bloody country knows who you're bonking!' he screamed at his son. 'It's not that you have been bonking the woman for years that bothers me – it's the fact you were so bloody idiotic, you got found out. What the bloody hell are you going to do next?'

Charles sat stony-faced and silent as his father berated him. Without saying a word, Charles left the room and went upstairs.

A courtier says: 'He felt abandoned by his father in his hour of need. On the one occasion when Charles truly needed fatherly advice, Prince Philip just screamed and ranted at him. Their relationship plunged further downward from that day on.'

After the 'Camillagate' tapes were published, Camilla's world was turned upside down. She was under siege at Middlewick while Andrew was in London. But, according to a close friend, publication of the tapes never seriously threatened their marriage at that time.

The friend said: 'Camilla and Andrew always knew where they stood with each other. The publication of the tapes didn't mean anything to that marriage. Camilla had known the tapes were in the public domain for months. Not only had she braced herself for their eventual publication, but she had also warned her husband.

'People who weren't in the know started speculating about whether Andrew would go for a divorce.

'But when the tapes became public, Andrew's first response was to race down to Wiltshire to be by his wife's side. He even spoke to the Prince on at least two occasions in the weeks following the scandal breaking.

'Camilla stayed strong throughout. Her nerves were on edge, but she's not the type to crack under pressure, unlike the Princess of Wales. Camilla hated all the attention, but she bore the pressure as well as anyone could. She is a very tough character; you should never underestimate Camilla.

'She maintained a resolute silence throughout. She allowed her name to be blackened without speaking out, because she knew if she spoke out, it would only fan the flames of scandal. She surrounded herself by family and friends and just kept her head down.

'Apart from the Prince of Wales, there are a few friends she trusts implicitly. Her sister Annabel was a rock to her and Annabel's husband Simon was terribly supportive. They rallied round. Camilla even tried to joke about the press pack outside her gate. She loathed all the attention, but, as always, her best defence mechanism was to laugh. She showed incredible strength of character throughout that whole ordeal.'

Carolyn Benson, who was a house guest at Middlewick that first weekend, said sadly: 'Whatever happened, they knew their lives would never be the same again. Andrew and Camilla were trapped.'

Another friend said: 'Andrew and Camilla had reached an impasse in their marriage. But they were still devoted to each other on a level no-one can truly understand. When "Camillagate" broke, Andrew stuck by his wife. It would not be his style to abandon her at a time of crisis. He, like she, knows where his duty lies.'

Camilla showed even more strength of character shortly afterwards when Andrew Parker Bowles was photographed leaving the same Carolyn Benson's London home at quarter to seven in the morning.

Andrew denied any impropriety and simply said: 'Of course I have stayed with Carolyn. I have stayed with a lot of people in a lot of premises and spent the night there as well.'

He told a friend: 'It makes me absolutely bloody mad what they're saying. I'm not standing for any of this much longer.'

Carolyn, who is godmother to Camilla's son Tom, said: 'I am a good friend of both Andrew and Camilla. I am not going to justify any malicious rumours by commenting further on the incident.'

One friend said: 'The whole idea was ridiculous.

Camilla told me she spoke to Carolyn later that same day. The two have remained firm friends ever since.'

And Carolyn's father Colonel Gerard Leigh told one writer: 'Carolyn has been friends with Camilla since they were children. Any suggested link between Carolyn and Andrew is ridiculous. If anything, Carolyn is better friends with Camilla than she is with the Brigadier.'

But another friend of the Parker Bowleses says: 'Andrew may or may not have been having an affair with Carolyn. It really doesn't matter. Camilla and Andrew had a rock-solid partnership. Dynamite couldn't blow them apart. They were firm friends with each other and they shared the same sense of humour. When you've been through what they've been through, you have to learn to laugh together.

'And when the chips are down, as they were when the tapes broke, they stuck together. There was no way either one of them was going to bolt from that marriage – not at that stage, anyway.'

A couple of days after the photographs of Andrew leaving Carolyn's house appeared, he and Camilla put on a show of force by holding a picnic lunch in the grounds of Eton school, where their son Tom was in his final year. Camilla's father Major Bruce Shand and her sister Annabel Elliot joined the family outing.

A friend says: 'They could not say anything about all the scandal, but they put on a dignified show of strength. That was typical of Andrew and Camilla. When things were as bad as they could be, and then got worse, they stuck together. They understood each other totally.'

At the picnic on the green playing fields of Eton, the couple laughed and joked and behaved just like any other proud parents. Their son Tom looked a little less jolly. For weeks, he had been subjected to the cruel taunts of some of his schoolmates calling his mother 'a tart'.

On one occasion, according to a former schoolfriend, Tom became embroiled in a fist-fight in defence of his mother. The friend says: 'The jibes had been going on behind Tom's back for years. It was to his credit that he was popular at Eton, He was a fine sportsman and an immensely likeable chap. He knew about the snide comments which were being made, but he chose to ignore them.

'One day, however, he walked into the changing rooms after rugby practice and one fellow challenged him directly to his face. He pretty much said Tom's mother was a tart who had brought shame on the royal family. Tom snapped: "Shut up. You don't know what you're talking about." But the other chap repeated the accusation. Tom leapt on him and gave him a pretty good working over. After that, the name-calling stopped.'

Incredibly, despite the heartache the 'Camillagate' tapes had caused, the two main players continued to talk regularly.

A former equerry says: 'I walked into the Prince's private study about a week after the tapes had been splashed all over the papers and he was deep in conversation with Camilla. He had his back turned to me and I heard him talking to Camilla in hushed tones. I quietly turned around and went out again. But I was shocked . . . I was truly shocked.'

Reshaping the Monarchy

'Just when I thought it couldn't get any worse, it has.'

Prince Charles was speaking to his grandmother shortly after the most difficult meeting of his life. It took place in his private rooms at Buckingham Palace nine days after 'Camillagate' broke.

Major Bruce Shand, Camilla's elderly father, had written to the Prince demanding a meeting. Shortly after four in the afternoon, the decorated war hero arrived and was ushered into the Prince's study where Charles sat working at his table.

Major Shand first refused to shake the hand of the man who had been his daughter's secret and now very public lover for years, then, despite the fact that he was near eighty years old, he refused the Prince's offer of a chair.

Instead, for ninety minutes, the old man became increasingly angry. He started speaking to the Prince in a bewildered and sad voice, but within minutes, he became red-faced with rage.

'My daughter's life has been ruined, her children are the subject of ridicule and contempt. You have brought disgrace on my whole family,' ranted the Major.

The Prince bowed his head in shame. Shand continued in the same vein. He told Charles that his wife was an invalid who had been 'deeply and profoundly upset' by the scandal. He said the Prince had 'made a mockery' of his entire family and their good name.

According to one source close to the Shand family: 'The Prince said nothing. He stood there like a young boy being torn off a strip by his father. He kept trying to murmur a few words under his breath, but the Major was irate. He was beside himself with rage. The Prince had known Major Shand for years, he had stayed at the family home many times in the early days when he had first got to know Camilla in the mid-seventies.

'The Major was like a second father to him. In fact, Charles got on better with Bruce Shand than he did with his own father.

'For him to be so upset by what had happened affected Charles deeply. Bruce demanded Charles sever all links with Camilla. He told Charles to "get out" of her life in no uncertain terms.

'He criticized his abilities as a father and as a husband. He said Charles, in his position and with his background, should have "known better" than to continue the affair with his daughter so publicly.'

'It was,' the Prince said later, 'the worst moment of my life.'

A friend said: 'It was a moment of total humiliation for Charles. The Major was someone who knew the royal family extremely well. He had known Charles for twenty years. He felt perfectly at liberty to tell him exactly what he thought. No-one had ever spoken to Charles in that manner before. He was genuinely shocked at the old man's anger.'

As the Major prepared to leave, his anger abated for a moment. Looking Charles straight in the eye, he said: 'For the sake of my family, for the sake of your family, for the sake of the country – you must stop seeing my daughter. I implore you, please, please put an end to this nonsense for ever.'

Charles nodded his head in silence. Then he promised the Major he would 'think about it'.

The words made Shand erupt in a final outburst: 'I don't want you to *think* about it, I want you to do what you know is the only course of action left open to you. You must sever all links with Camilla and you must do it now!'

The Prince responded to the old man's plea by bursting into tears.

On his first official visit to the City of London after the scandal broke, a man shouted from the crowd: 'You should be ashamed of yourself!'

The Prince's face reddened and he turned away.

His private offices at St James's Palace began receiving hate mail from members of the public – the same public he was set to rule over – condemning him for cheating on his beautiful wife. A daily diet of anti-Charles stories appeared in every national newspaper.

It was clear, above all else, that drastic action was needed to counter the anti-Charles sentiment sweeping the nation.

A former courtier says: 'The Prince had wrongly assumed that "Camillagate" would merely cause a small blip in the works. In fact, it soon became apparent to everyone at the Palace that they had a full-blown crisis on their hands. The future of Prince Charles was seriously in jeopardy. Newspaper polls were coming out on a daily basis proving his popularity was at an all time low.

'Even more serious was the fact that the royal family were embroiled in a scandal just as serious as the abdication crisis more than half a century earlier.'

Shortly after his harrowing meeting with Major Shand, Charles was summoned to a meeting with the Queen, Prince Philip, the Queen's private secretary Sir Richard Fellowes and the Prince's private secretary Commander Richard Aylard, an unstuffy former naval officer who was to become the kingpin in the almost military-style campaign to revamp Charles's image.

In a meeting which lasted more than an hour, the two private secretaries underlined the seriousness of the situation and the fact that the future king's reputation and image had sunk to an all-time low. Drastic measures were needed, and they were needed fast. The Queen agreed to a proposal from Commander Aylard that the Prince needed to embark on a 'positive public-relations' campaign.

The following Sunday, for the first time in living memory, photographers waiting outside the church at Sandringham after the royal family's traditional Sunday-morning service were staggered to find Prince Charles walking over to them with his two sons.

One photographer recalls: 'It was the first time anyone could remember that the Prince willingly put himself out and stood and posed for pictures outside the church with the two boys. It was clear a wind of change was sweeping the Palace.'

Charles knew he had important decisions to make to secure his future. There was no question in his mind that his duty lay where it always had done: in succeeding to the throne as King Charles III.

But he fully understood the growing crisis. During the darkest days after 'Camillagate', he was to recount one of his favourite historical quotes to friends, a quote made by the former German Kaiser Wilhelm: 'The monarchy is like virginity, once you have lost it, you can never, ever get it back.'

A close member of the royal circle said: 'He was facing up to the stark reality that his very future, the future of the institution he had been born into and which he had spent forty years in, was in jeopardy. Charles knew the situation was very grave indeed.

'His sense of duty and destiny made him determined to fight back.'

The trouble was that there was more and more very public dissent. A poll in the *Sun* newspaper shortly after 'Camillagate' revealed that, out of a staggering 20,000 readers who responded, the vast majority believed that the Prince's reputation was so tarnished that he would never be king. Seventy per cent of readers said they thought less of him after 'Camillagate'. More than sixty per cent believed he had to end the affair with Camilla.

Even Charles himself said: 'It's a bloody awful time. It's utterly bloody awful.'

The most damaging criticism came from within the ranks of the Church of England. Since Charles was the future Head of the Church, this criticism from churchmen was of great significance to the future of the monarchy.

The Venerable George Austin, Archdeacon of York and a tireless supporter of family values, went on the BBC Radio Four programme *Today* and made a comment which was to grab the headlines. 'My view,' he said, 'would be that Charles made solemn vows before God in church about his marriage, and it seems, if it is true about Camilla Parker Bowles, that he began to break them almost immediately. He has broken his trust and vows to God on one thing. How can he then go into Westminster Abbey and take his Coronation vows?'

It was a shattering blow. Austin, though not a bishop, was one of the most respected churchmen in the land.

The Archbishop of York, Dr John Habgood, fired a warning shot at the Prince. He said: 'He must resolve his personal problems before becoming king.'

The Bishop of Oxford, the Right Reverend Richard Harris, was a little more understanding. He joined the growing discussion: 'While one of the Queen's titles is Defender of the Faith, I don't think people take that literally now. It's been very good when monarchs have presented themselves as ideal role models, but it is not expected of them these days.'

So great was the growing criticism from the Church that the Queen summoned senior Church leaders to a meeting at Lambeth Palace, the Church of England's headquarters.

She told them: 'Although the misfortunes of the Prince of Wales's private life are a regrettable chapter in the monarchy's history, he will be king. No question about it.'

Although the Archbishop of Canterbury announced publicly that he was 'in full support' of Charles becoming king, the damage was done,

CHARLES NOT FIT TO RULE screamed the headlines.

It was then that Charles, and his advisers, realized their never-before-questioned belief that Charles would one day be king was in serious jeopardy.

The war was on.

But Charles's advisers were new at the game of positive public relations, and at the end of April 1993, the Prince made a massive PR mistake. He decided to fly to the funeral service of King Juan Carlos of Spain's father, Don Juan de Bourbon y Battenberg, in Madrid. At the same time, the British public's attention was firmly focused on the horrendous IRA bombing of a shopping centre in the northern town of Warrington. Two young boys, Jonathan Ball and Tim Parry, had been killed in the bloodbath. The whole of Britain was outraged by the callous slaughter.

Diana had asked permission to go to a memorial service in Warrington for the two young boys. The Palace refused her permission. Diana retaliated by telephoning the mother of twelve-year-old Tim Parry twenty-four hours before the memorial service. She had a long chat with the grieving woman and offered her 'warm words of comfort and condolence'.

Mrs Wendy Parry was later to say she was 'deeply touched' by the Princess's caring and compassionate nature.

Her husband Colin said: 'Wendy answered the phone and I noticed her face go slightly red.

'Then a smile as wide as the Mersey tunnel spread across her face as she said, handing me the phone, "It's the Princess of Wales."

'You could tell by her voice it was her. The Princess said she was terribly sorry about what had happened. She said she just wished she could give Wendy a big hug. They obviously spoke as mother to mother.

'She was just very, very kind and sympathetic with the things she said. She's great and it has meant such a lot to us. I think she feels deeply how much we have lost and she said exactly the same things you would expect any other mother to say.'

Mrs Parry also revealed that Diana had told her she had wanted to be at the memorial service, but that she had been refused permission from the Palace. It was Diana at her 'magnificent finest', according to the Prince's friends.

The subsequent angry reaction appeared on the front pages of newspapers across Britain the next morning.

SNUBBED DI RINGS BOMB FAMILY ran the front-page headline in the *Sun* . It was another publicity coup for 'Saint' Diana.

In fact, the Prince had visited Warrington a couple of days after the bomb had gone off. He and Commander Aylard studied the television tapes of the visit later. It was a disastrous trip.

Charles was seen on the BBC news saying to a woman who had lost her leg in the blast: 'Your courage has made my day.' He came across as being uncomfortable, unsympathetic – and wildly out of touch. He was bitterly disappointed by his performance.

Diana was still a bigger crowd-puller than Charles. Over a month-long period, in April 1993, Diana drew crowds of more than 10,000 on sixteen public engagements, while Charles's score was an average of just 132 spectators on twenty-five royal engagements. He was working harder, but he was not being *seen* to work harder.

The Palace swung into action. One of the biggest repackaging jobs of all time was about to begin; the Palace realized it had to get its public-relations machine in order.

Even the Queen responded to the call to 'bring the monarchy into shape for the twenty-first century'. First, she announced that she would start paying taxes for the first time ever. It was an announcement hailed as 'long overdue' but 'admirable' by both royalists and critics alike.

Then it was announced that Buckingham Palace would be opened to the public for two months each summer – August and September – for the next five years, beginning in 1993.

It was a tremendous success. Queues stretched for blocks, the Palace gift shop did a roaring trade – and the positive publicity around the world was fantastic. During that first summer a total of 377,000 visitors paid £12 a head to tour the Palace. Two million pounds profit was made from attendance fees and a further £1.2 million was raked in from the sale of souvenirs.

The Queen also agreed to contribute a major part of the rebuilding costs of Windsor Castle, devastated by fire in December 1992.

In June 1993, another meeting was called at St James's Palace. Sir Richard Aylard called on 'professional' help in rebuilding Charles's image after 'Camillagate'.

Among those chosen to revamp his fortunes were pop promoter Harvey Goldsmith, the TV arts presenter Melvyn Bragg and the editor of the *Times* Peter Stothard. While the Prince's image was discussed for more than an hour, Charles himself inexplicably failed to turn up.

Commander Aylard sent a handwritten memo to his boss, stressing the importance of him co-operating 'in the work we have before us'. On the bottom on the memo was the underlined word *please*.

A royal aide says: 'The Prince has not missed a meeting since.'

The marital battles of the eighties had now become a full-scale war for the hearts and minds of the British public and for the future of the monarchy.

Charles knew he needed to make still more changes if he was seriously to hang on to his chances of becoming king.

Throughout 1993, he continued to talk regularly to

Camilla on the phone. A source close to Camilla says: 'Despite all that had happened, the Prince still needed Camilla. There was never a thought in his head that he might have to give her up. They continue to enjoy long conversations, but always on a safe landline. They had learned their lesson the painful way from using mobile phones.

'The relationship was even more secret than ever. Only a handful of people were aware it was still going on. The Prince kept it secret from everyone, including his own father. He knew the process of rebuilding his image would be long and drawn out. He could not afford any negative publicity, and certainly no negative publicity about him and Camilla.

'They met only once or twice, both times at the safe houses of friends. They were meetings shrouded in secrecy. But they were meetings Charles needed. He simply could not live without Camilla. Even when things were at their lowest ebb, it was Camilla he turned to to get him through.

'He needed her emotionally and sexually. He needed to know she still loved him as much as he still loved her. They would arrive at the safe houses separately, they would leave under cover of darkness. No-one knew of these meetings, but they were going on.

'If anything, the crisis brought them closer together. They helped each other to stay strong during those dark days after "Camillagate" broke. Charles was still reluctant to trust anyone but Camilla. He valued her advice. And it was she who made it very clear to him that enough was enough; he had to start fighting back.'

By December 1993, Commander Aylard realized he still had one major problem with the Prince's image. The long affair with Camilla was out in the open, but the spectre of scandal still remained. Newspaper stories were once again surfacing, saying that the Prince and Camilla were continuing to enjoy a 'discreet' relationship.

One of Diana's friends was quoted as saying: 'After all that has happened, the Prince is continuing to call Mrs Parker Bowles on a weekly, if not daily basis. The Princess does not care any more. She simply wants to get on with her life.'

If the stories were allowed to continue, it was only a matter of time before the whole Camilla scandal would blow up again. While the shadow of Camilla lurked in the Prince's background, he would never be fully forgiven by the British public for allowing his affair to destroy the fairy-tale marriage.

A major solo tour of Australia by the Prince was being planned for January 1994. It was a make-or-break trip for Charles. Those close to him hoped the tour would show him at his best enjoying mass acclaim *without* Princess Diana.

In mid-December, Commander Aylard called a strategy meeting in the Prince's private offices at St James's Palace. Sitting around the polished mahogany table were Commander Aylard, the Queen's private secretary, Sir Robert Fellowes – and, of course, Prince Charles himself.

The meeting was to have devastating personal repercussions on the entire future of the man who had been groomed since birth to be king.

The three men began discussing the Australia trip. Their conversation dealt with mundane issues: at first where the Prince would visit, arrival and exit times and flight plans for the trip.

As in a military operation, the three even discussed minute details like which cufflinks would be packed for the Prince and how many bottles of his favourite Scottish mineral water would be aboard the Queen's Flight.

It was a normal strategy meeting to ensure the tour would be faultless, seamless and smooth, but, when the business of the day was complete, Aylard – a man who by now enjoyed a closer relationship with the Prince than anyone else at the Palace – cleared his throat. 'Sir, there is one final issue we must discuss.'

Then, the two loyal aides talked directly to the Prince about what had been referred to in royal circles for years only as 'that matter': Charles's twenty-four-year-long affair with Camilla Parker Bowles.

Over the next sixty minutes they held nothing back. They were brutal and to the point.

'Do you want to be king?' they asked.

Without hesitation, Charles's reply shot back: 'Of course.'

Their response was equally succinct. 'Well then, Sir, about Camilla . . .'

In straight language, man to man, they explained to him that the Australian trip would be the first, vital battle to rehabilitate his image. In simple terms he was told he would need to 'Tipp-Ex the Tampax', a crude reference to Charles's admission on the notorious tape that he wanted to come back as Camilla's tampons.

By the end of that meeting, Charles's mind was made up. He would say sadly: 'It's awfully difficult to see yourself as others see you. But I now know what I must do.'

He had been told by those closest to him that he had but one choice to make: it was the Crown or Camilla.

A royal insider says: 'It was D-Day, decision day for Charles. For the first time, the $64 million question had been put to him. It was explained, in no uncertain terms, that if he truly genuinely and absolutely wanted to be king, something would have to go. And that was Camilla.'

After twenty-four long years, the Prince was being asked to make the most difficult and heart-rending decision of his life. Like his great-uncle, Edward VIII, he was being asked to choose between the Crown . . . and the woman he loved.

Charles's Duty

When the end came, it was quick, deadly and decisive.

It was the week before Christmas 1993. Camilla Parker Bowles picked up the telephone and dialled the number which had become as familiar to her as her own. She heard the telephone ringing at the other end. Normally, it would ring a maximum of three times before he picked it up.

Today, it rang and rang and rang. Perturbed, she hung up.

She redialled the number. This time, the receiver was picked up at the other end. But far from hearing the calming tones of a friendly voice, a stranger answered.

Confused, but always impeccably true to form, Camilla gave a slight cough and said: 'Good evening, may I speak to His Royal Highness, the Prince of Wales, please?'

'Sorry, madam,' the curt stranger replied, 'His Royal Highness is unavailable.'

Hearing those few short words, Camilla knew it was

over. The greatest, and ultimately most tragic, love story of modern times was at an end.

For twenty-four long years, Camilla Parker Bowles and Prince Charles had enjoyed a relationship more binding, passionate and enduring than most marriages. But the Prince had made his mind up. He was faced with a choice between fulfilling his life's work and the love of his life.

As he was later to tell a friend: 'If being king is my duty, Camilla was my fate. But duty always comes before fate.'

Camilla knew it was over.

The number she had dialled was a private 'hotline' set up in Charles's private study at his Highgrove estate in Gloucestershire. It was 'Camilla's number'.

The special phone had been installed shortly after the devastating 'Camillagate' tape became public. No-one else, not even Diana, had the number. It was a special 'safe' landline, checked at random at least once a month by the Prince's security staff to ensure no-one would ever again be able to 'tap in' to his most intimate conversations. Camilla knew the stranger could have picked it up only on the specific instructions of one man: Prince Charles. And she knew Charles had finally sacrificed her love for the love of something greater and even closer to his heart: the Crown.

Fifty-four years earlier, Edward VIII had given up the throne for love. But history was not going to repeat itself.

A close member of Prince Charles's inner circle says: 'It was the toughest decision of his life. He spent days mulling it over in his mind. Of course, giving up Camilla is something he had been asked to think about many times before. But each time in the past, he refused.

'Camilla was like a drug to him, an addiction he could not give up. He always needed to have his "fix".

'Now, on the eve of the Australian visit, he knew he

had to end it. He knew that, above all else, he had to fulfil his destiny.

'The irony is that Camilla knew what he was thinking. They had been speaking on an almost daily basis. She was fully supportive, as ever. She told him she loved him; that she would always love him and be there for him – but that she would sacrifice her own happiness for his sense of duty. She actually told him: "You may be happy with me, but one thing is for certain, you will never be happy unless you fulfil your destiny."

'Even though Camilla knew she would suffer, she was prepared to make the ultimate sacrifice, She was prepared to pay the ultimate price of losing the love of her Prince so that he would never have to suffer the same indignities as his great-uncle.'

In the tragic and complex web of human emotions which had been his life for so long, Charles had reached an unwavering decision: his relationship with Camilla was the price he would have to pay for his future. But even after he had refused to take Carnilla's call that day he could not get her out of his mind. His business was unfinished. He called her from Sandringham on Christmas Day. The conversation lasted less than two minutes. He told her he loved her, but that his decision was 'irrevocable'.

Camilla, as ever, understood 'totally'.

The Prince's tour of Australia in January 1994 was a glorious success. For the first time in more than a decade, he was on a solo tour – and making headlines back home.

He delighted the crowds by popping into a pub for a pint, clowning about with a golf club and even giving an energetic demonstration of mouth-to-mouth resuscitation on a topless blonde plastic dummy.

Then, student David Kang fired a starter's pistol at the Prince during an event in Sydney. The cool calm and collected way the Prince shrugged off the attack and even smiled a few minutes after Kang was pounced on by protection officers impressed the world. Just hours after the incident, the Prince gave a relaxed interview to Australian journalists in which he dismissed the scare with humour and modesty.

A Palace insider says: 'It was a massive PR victory for Charles. It showed him, in the most extreme situation, a potentially life-threatening situation, showing the calm and coolness of head he always does. It showed the world conclusively that, in times of crisis, the Prince does not crack under pressure.'

A few days later, Nigel Dempster revealed the story the whole of Britain had been waiting for. MY DUTY BEFORE LOVE read the headline on the front page of the *Mail on Sunday*. In his piece, Dempster wrote: 'Prince Charles has chosen to fulfil his destiny as future king by renouncing his relationship with Mrs Camilla Parker Bowles.

'He has decided to sacrifice his close friendship with the forty-six-year-old mother of two for the sake of his duty to the country.'

Dempster quoted a Cabinet source, who said: 'This decision by the Prince is a clear indication that he takes his future responsibilities very seriously. It is entirely right that he should put his duty first and he should be respected for this decision.'

And a friend of Camilla's was quoted as saying: 'There has been conjecture that Andrew and Camilla will eventually divorce, but only if either of them wanted to marry again, and that is certainly not the situation at the moment.

'Anyone who knows Camilla knows she does not see

herself as the future wife of the Prince of Wales. But he did make a long-term commitment to her which is now over.'

The story concluded: 'In a deeply personal phone call, Charles was recorded telling her [Camilla]: "Your greatest achievement is to love me."

'But one thing, in time, may assuage her grief. The man who admitted that she made him, will one day be king.

'The sacrifice of letting him go may yet be her greatest achievement of all.'

The story was greeted positively by the public. An opinion poll a few days later showed that seventy-four per cent of people believed Charles had made the right decision.

A high-ranking Palace insider was quoted as saying: 'Sir reached his decision with a great deal of thought and difficulty. But his mind is made up. There is a sense of great relief in the Palace. From now on, the country will judge the Prince purely on his merits. And they will discover that he is a very, very fine man indeed, a man who will make a fine and noble king for our nation. He has made the ultimate sacrifice and has paid the ultimate price for his country. And his country will love him for it.'

Privately Charles *did* call Camilla once more. After surviving the shooting incident in Australia, he rang Camilla to assure her he was 'fine' and that the trip had 'gone better than any of us had expected'.

A close aide says: 'It would have been too callous at that stage not to have called her. He knew she would be worried. But the call was only brief. It was too painful to both of them to speak for any length of time in the circumstances. The Prince told Camilla he would not telephone her again for some time.'

The Queen was fully supportive of her son's decision. They met the week after his successful trip to Australia.

A Palace insider says: 'There was no delight from the

Queen about Camilla going, but she was pleased that Charles had chosen duty above love. The Queen has always been remarkably fond of Camilla. She knew about the affair for years and yet always welcomed Camilla to Balmoral or Sandringham. In fact, the Queen was sad for Camilla. But she was proud of Charles for making the most difficult decision of his life. She knew he had proved he was not another Duke of Windsor. When it came to D-Day, Charles made the right decision. The Queen knew he had made a wise choice, and she told him so repeatedly. She knew he was still in love with Camilla, but she respected him more than she had ever done before.'

In January 1994, the way was clear for Charles to continue rebuilding himself in the eyes of the public. The first steps had been hugely successful – now the real work was about to begin.

A Fresh Start

In June 1994, the historic pageantry surrounding the fiftieth anniversary of the Allied D-Day landings on the beaches of Normandy was in full swing.

The Queen, the Queen Mother and Prince Charles all played an active and high-profile role in the numerous memorial services and tributes to those who fell defending the free world. But to the royal family, the D-Day celebrations were the signal for some private celebrations, for, after the most turbulent period the monarchy has had to face in the twentieth century, they were finally on the verge of their own victory.

Prince Charles was celebrating the successful outcome of his own D-Day, Decision Day – to cut free of both Princess Diana and the scandal of his relationship with Camilla Parker Bowles. On the eve of the twenty-fifth anniversary of his investiture as the Prince of Wales, he and his advisers felt more confident than they had in years that nothing would now prevent him from assuming his rightful place on the throne.

A courtier says: 'The D-Day celebrations were a real watershed for everyone at the Palace who'd had such a bumpy ride. The public response was phenomenal and the opinion polls showed, once again, that the majority of people were turning in Charles's favour.

'It was a major turning point for the Palace. After all the upset, heartache and tears, the huge campaign to reinstate Charles as the rightful future monarch in the hearts and minds of the public was being won.'

For Charles believes now more than ever that he *will* be crowned King Charles III on the death of the Queen.

His close friend Nicholas Soames says: 'There was never any question. The Prince will assume his rightful place in history. Being heir to the throne is not an ambition but a duty and one which will befall Charles on a sad moment later in his life. He will inherit the throne, and that is the end of the matter. He is as certain of that now, even more so, than he has ever been before.'

The relationship between Charles and his mother continued to grow closer throughout 1994. Both realized that Diana, for too long, had been allowed to pull the strings. Now, both were beginning to feel in control of their own destinies. Both were determined to safeguard the future of the monarchy and continue to take steps to get the House of Windsor in shape to face the challenges of the twenty-first century.

On 23 June 1994, the Queen approved a cost-cutting plan to take the royal yacht *Britannia* out of service.

It was yet another move to boost the royal family's standing in the eyes of the public. Taking *Britannia* out of service will save the British taxpayer £12 million a year.

A Palace aide says: 'The royal yacht has been a

favourite of the royal family for years. To announce they were giving it up voluntarily, to save money for the country, was a remarkable thing to happen. The Queen has always had a deep attachment to *Britannia*. The vessel has been part of her life since 1953. She perceives it as a graceful symbol of royalty and the nation. It must have been an extremely tough decision for her to take.

'The decision to scrap *Britannia* was one she discussed at length with Charles. It was another example of how aware both of them have become about the way the monarchy is perceived in the country. They both realize that, these days, people will not tolerate what is seen as luxury spending by the royals. That was one of the fundamental reasons the Queen agreed to give up the vessel.

'For many years, the Prince and his mother did not enjoy the closest of relationships. But in recent months, they have enjoyed a very close bond. They speak on the phone almost daily and exchange ideas frequently. The are both working towards the same goals. They have learned a lot from the whole Diana débâcle.

'When at all possible, they meet for lunch at least once a week. A new dialogue has opened up between the Prince and his mother and also between both sets of royal advisers. It's full steam ahead from here on in.

'The Queen is determined the good work that was done to improve Charles's public image should continue. He has her full and unequivocal support in all his goals. He is the rightful heir and the entire Palace machine is now geared towards his succession.'

Another of Charles's closest friends says: 'He sees no reason why he should not become king. He has been groomed for that from birth. He regards that as his ultimate destiny and the real reason for his life.

The man responsible for the massive change in both the Prince's public image, and his own views about himself was his private secretary, Commander Richard Aylard.

Aylard, forty-one, held daily meetings with his 'support' staff and was more accessible to the media than any other of the Prince's advisers. His campaign to rebuild the Prince's image – nicknamed 'the charm offensive' behind Palace doors – was a phenomenal success.

One Fleet Street royal correspondent says: 'It's extraordinary what Richard achieved. He has remoulded the Prince's image and it was a process which continues to this day. The great thing is that, for the first time, there is someone who is willing to speak out with the full authority of the Prince. Commander Aylard became one of the most powerful men at the Palace and certainly one of the most popular men with the media. The biggest change was that Richard knew how to play the publicity game. He knew what to do. He was highly experienced. And he had the full confidence of the entire royal family.'

In March 1994, Commander Aylard appeared on the respected BBC programme *Newsnight*. It was the first time any top-ranking member of the Palace staff had appeared so publicly to defend the Prince.

He said: 'We have decided it is better to go on in a dignified way carrying on with the Prince's public life. It is deeply unpleasant for anyone to have their personal lives published in varying accounts and then dissected in public. I don't want to get into the Prince's present state of mind, but he is certainly not in despair. He is both a very sensitive person and a very determined person.

'That is not always the most comfortable combination because, if you get hurt, and if you are determined, you want to keep going. I can tell you that from my position, he will keep going, even if, from time to time, he gets hurt.'

Aylard's high-profile image only boosted the Prince's own popularity within the press and the country at large. So pleased was Prince Charles by the work Aylard did that he gave him the honour of the Royal Victoria Order in the Queen's birthday honours list in June 1994. The honour is personally bestowed by the Queen.

A Palace insider says: 'It was a clear message from the Palace to the Commander that they are thrilled by what he did. His work was recognized not only by the powers-that-be inside the Palace, but also by anyone who knows what a mammoth task he faced. Commander Aylard was the brains behind a total transformation in the Prince. They both have the most enormous respect for each other. Commander Aylard achieved a tremendous amount of good in building the Prince's image up from a man who was once ridiculed to a man who is now viewed as the rightful future monarch. But the work is continuing. By the time Charles is in a position to ascend to the throne, there will be absolutely no doubt in anyone's mind that he is the right man for the job.'

Aylard built a small circle of experienced men and women around him with the sole purpose of continuing the resurgence in the Prince's image.

Belinda Harley, thirty-six, an Oxford graduate, who runs her own public-relations company, was brought in as an assistant private secretary. She developed a close bond with the Prince. A woman with wit, charm and intelligence in abundance, she worked for years as an adviser to the Prince's Trust before being drafted into his closest inner circle.

A male fan inside the Palace says: 'She's as tough as anything, but she does it all with a smile and bundles of charm. She's a real driving force behind the campaign to revamp the Prince. Because she is a woman, she enjoys a different relationship with the Prince than the stuffy advisers he's used to. When she joined the Palace, it was like a breath of fresh air. She is an ideas woman who is used to making things happen.

'In fact, Belinda and Commander Aylard were instantly nicknamed "The Dream Team". He is down-to-earth, solid, dependable and brilliant and she is flirty, fun and brilliant.'

Belinda was also awarded the Royal Victoria Order in the June 1994 Queen's birthday honours list. Belinda officially left the Prince's staff in July 1994 to return to her PR company. Unofficially, she remains extremely close to the Prince – and still offers wise words of advice to this day.

The Prince also hired two new press secretaries to handle the delicate relationship between himself and the newspapers. Both are hard-working, experienced professionals, well used to handling the most delicate of subjects. Sandie Henney was hired from Scotland Yard; Allan Percival was a government press spokesman for Northern Ireland.

One journalist on the royal patch said: 'For the first time ever, we've got true professionals handling Charles. And the difference it made during the Australian tour in January was staggering. We were getting off-the-record comments and updates all the time.

'Just look at the shooting incident. A few years ago, we would have been given no information. Nothing would have been said. But as it was, we were getting hourly updates from Aylard and Henney. It was great. They know how to deal with the press, how to present Charles in a positive light for once – how to make him human, likeable even.

'They've gone to war on the old image of Charles – and

they're certainly notching up some pretty impressive victories.'

Charles also hired Alexandra Legge-Bourke.

A bubbly, fun-loving twenty-eight-year-old Sloane known universally as 'Tiggy', after the lovable Beatrix Potter character Mrs Tiggywinkle, became the Prince's unofficial social adviser, a mother-type figure to his two young sons – and has developed a close bond of friendship with the Prince.

Officially, she was hired as an £18,000-a-year assistant to Commander Aylard. But within a few short weeks of her appointment in December 1993, it became clear her role was much, much more.

Tiggy, who once ran her own private nursery, had impeccable credentials. Her mother, the Honourable Mrs Elizabeth Legge-Bourke, is a lady-in-waiting to Princess Anne. Her Aunt Victoria is another of Princess Anne's ladies-in-waiting.

Victoria Legge-Burke says: 'Tiggy is the most enchanting young lady that anyone could possibly meet. She comes from a loving, happy family and you cannot help but warm to her. She's got hundreds of friends and I've never met anyone who came across her and didn't fall in love with her. Of course, she is terribly, terribly discreet and loyal.'

An ancestor, the Marquis of Lincolnshire, was George V's Lord Great Chamberlain and an uncle was Page of Honour to the Queen. Tiggy's father William is with the leading City merchant banking firm of Kleinwort Benson and the family owns a vast 1,000-acre estate in Wales.

Tiggy's former headmistress Margaret Parry of Heathfield School says: 'She is a delightful girl, very vivacious, very charming. She is utterly reliable, always on the side of the bright and good.'

Tiggy became exceptionally close to William and Harry. After leaving school at sixteen, she took a nursery teacher training course at the St Nicholas Montessori Centre in London. She then spent a year looking after youngsters at the Little Wandsworth School in Balham, south London, before taking a year off to travel around Australia.

Her former boss at Little Wandsworth, Sophie Irwin, says: 'We were delighted with her. She is a very jolly person who was very good with children. We were very sorry when she left.'

Tiggy soon had her own rooms at St James's Palace and at Highgrove and, according to estate workers, developed an 'extremely good' relationship with the young Princes.

One says: 'William and Harry simply adore her. She is warm and loving and totally solid and stable, unlike their mother. She looked after all aspects of the boys' lives. She packed their cases for school, sewed their name tags into their uniforms. The boys are devoted to her and she is devoted to them. She gave both the Princes and Prince Charles a solid base.

Says one royal adviser: 'Tiggy has put a spring in the step of Prince Charles. She has a bright, positive nature, always upbeat, which is infectious. She is like a ray of sunshine.'

Tiggy encouraged Charles to show the world the close bond he has with his sons. After Tiggy's arrival, Charles was photographed taking the boys fishing, cycling around the estate at Highgrove and even sitting quietly and reading to them.

The Prince said recently: 'I can never remember my father being there for me when I grew up. He never once told me he loved me, he never praised me for anything. It was all very sad. It has taught me I must never be like that with my sons. I always let them know that I love them and I show them I do.'

In February 1994, the Prince took the boys on a solo skiing trip to Klosters, Switzerland, taking Tiggy along to care for his sons.

Again, it was a media triumph. He was pictured as a devoted father, teaching his sons to ski and even holding an impromptu snowball fight with them which ended up with the trio rolling in the snow.

A friend of the Prince's says: 'He was clearly emerging a new man. No one had ever seen him so relaxed, confident and self-assured. He has finally banished all the demons from his life.

'Today, he has listened to the professional advice of his advisers, and their wise words have paid off. Ask anyone in the country how they feel about Charles now and they are sure to say his image has greatly improved in their eyes. A transformation is going on. Most people are now convinced that nothing will stop Charles becoming king.'

But despite the Prince's brilliant efforts at rehabilitating himself, the spectre of Camilla always lurked in the background.

On 15 June 1994, on the eve of a Palace publicity drive to celebrate the twenty-fifth anniversary of Charles's investiture as Prince of Wales, the major ITV network broadcast extracts of the 'Camillagate' tape on air across Britain for the first time.

A courtier says: 'It was the last thing the Prince needed, but he coped with it. He knows the "Camillagate" crisis will never truly go away, but he has proved he has put it successfully in the background and that it has not affected what he sees as his life's work and his destiny in any way.'

Charles has also actively carved out more work for himself.

'He wants to be seen to be *doing* something,' says one aide. 'Of course, he's always been one of the most hard working royals behind the scenes, but now he's putting himself out there, showing people what he's doing.'

Charles streamlined his many charitable interests under the banner of 'The Prince's Trust'. It is a formidable organization with an annual income of £65 million, 500 paid staff and more than 8,500 voluntary staff.

He writes almost weekly to the directors of the various charities in The Prince's Trust. Trust director Tom Shebbeare said: 'There is never a shortage of things to respond to. The Prince takes an enormous and very keen personal interest in what is going on. He is always on the phone or writing letters. He wants to know everything which is happening, no matter how trivial it may appear.'

The Prince is also actively involved in a new role as Britain's 'cultural and commercial ambassador'. State visits are being planned now with the help of the Prime Minister's office for the Prince to take several trips abroad alone to promote British business and enterprise. He has held regular meetings with Cabinet members about how best to 'fly the flag' for British industry abroad. He has personally written 3,000 letters to captains of industry outlining the role he is seeking to play – and asking for their support.

A close aide to the Prince says: 'He writes to industry leaders constantly. Dozens have been invited to a series of private lunches with Charles at the Palace. He is now showing he *has* an active and valuable role to play. He is like a man on a crusade – a crusade to win the hearts of the people and achieve his rightful position in life.

'The whole aim has been to show that the Prince is no

longer drifting. He is a man with a clear focus and a clear goal.

'The biggest change is that the Prince no longer sees kingship as his God-given right. He knows how close he came to having to give up everything he had worked for all his life. He is rejuvenated, reborn. He now works harder than ever but he is more confident and determined than ever. He is like a different person.'

By the summer of 1994, Charles's future was looking rosier than it had for years. Public opinion polls showed his image was higher than it had ever been. Thanks to the wise counselling of men like Commander Richard Aylard, he had successfully countered the devastating years of negative publicity following the breakdown of his marriage and the affair with Camilla. He was a man confident of his future, at ease with his fate – that history has anointed him heir to the throne, a burden he must bear with grace, dignity and fortitude.

Prince Charles was a man convinced of his destiny. He was convinced that his sense of duty would come before all else – for the sake of his family, the Crown and his own happiness.

On 29 June 1994, the Prince and his advisers took the biggest gamble of all in the remoulding of his image.

On a hot summer's evening, 12.7 million viewers across Britain tuned in to watch a two-and-a-half-hour ITV television documentary on the Prince's life: *Charles: The Private Man, The Public Role*, made by the respected broadcaster Jonathan Dimbleby.

Dimbleby and his camera crew had been given unprecedented access to follow the Prince for more than eighteen months, capturing his most intimate thoughts and private times on film.

One of the film crew says: 'We were all astonished by how much access he gave us to all aspects of his life. You could tell it was agony for him sometimes to have us there. But he was determined to show a truer picture of himself to the public.

'A few years ago, a programme like ours would have been unthinkable. But the Prince and his advisers now realize the full power of the media. They knew that if Charles was allowed to come across as himself, the British public would welcome him back into their hearts. It was a risky gamble, but it was a brilliant move. For the first time, the public had a chance to see their future king both at work and in private. And it showed a very different Charles from the one they had imagined.'

Although Dimbleby and producer Christopher Martin had full editorial control of the programme, the Prince was given advance notice of the questions he would be asked. For long periods in the film, the Prince wore a small microphone on his shirt which picked up his every word during both private and public moments.

For days before the programme aired, the country held its breath. On the previous Sunday, a highly-placed source close to the Prince leaked one of the programme's more devastating revelations: that Charles hopes to end the 450-year role of the monarch as Head of the Church of England. He told Dimbleby he would prefer to be the defender of *all* faiths and religions, not just the Protestant Church.

Since Henry VIII became Head of the Church of England in 1531, all British monarchs have sworn at their coronation to: '. . . maintain in the United Kingdom the Protestant Reformed Religion established by law . . .'

The story made the front page of the *Sunday Times*: CHARLES PLANS TO BREAK THE ROYAL LINK WITH CHURCH –

KING SHOULD BE HEAD OF ALL RELIGIONS ran the headline.

The story read: 'The Prince has said he would be happy to be seen as "defender of faith" rather than "defender of *the* faith".'

The Prince was quoted, from the programme, saying: 'I happen to believe that the Catholic subjects of the sovereign are as important [as Protestants], not to mention the Islamic, Hindu and Zoroastrian.'

The statement immediately provoked controversy. Lord Coggan, a former Archbishop of Canterbury, said: 'This is a hornets' nest of problems. If he's saying Christianity is equal with other religions, we should differ profoundly from him. As men, we are all equal before God, but are you talking about religions and saying one is as good as another? I hope he is not saying that.'

The Venerable George Austin, the Archdeacon of York who had so strongly criticized Charles over the 'Camillagate' tapes, was more supportive. He said: 'It is true that the monarch should not be the supreme governor of the Church of England. That's a historical absurdity. But anything else to do with disestablishment is not the concern of the Prince of Wales, it's to do with the Church of England. My feeling is we should have a Church that is established, but doesn't have a monarch as supreme governor.'

While his decision to break with the Church of England caused a sensation, the biggest sensation was still to come. For the Prince had also spoken to Dimbleby about the one subject he had always steadfastly refused to comment on in the past: his relationship with Mrs Camilla Parker Bowles.

On national television, for the first time, Charles would address the question of whether he had ever been unfaithful to Princess Diana. As millions of viewers across

Britain watched on the edge of their seats, Dimbleby cleared his throat and challenged the Prince to 'respond to the most damaging charge' against him.

The broadcaster said: 'You were, because of your relationship with Camilla Parker Bowles, from the beginning persistently unfaithful to your wife and thus caused the breakdown . . .'

The Prince glanced down nervously and then, staring Dimbleby straight in the eye, he finally responded to the question the world had been demanding he answer.

It was to be one of the most sensational confessions of all time . . .

Burying the Hatchet

It was the bombshell the world had been waiting for. Sitting in the sunny lounge of Prince Charles's country home, Highgrove, broadcaster Jonathan Dimbleby asked the future king the 'ultimate' question.

Staring the Prince straight in the eye, Dimbleby said: 'Were you, did you try to be faithful and honourable to your wife when you took on the vow of marriage?'

Without hesitation, Charles replied: 'Yes, absolutely.'

'And you were?'

'Yes . . .' answered Charles. Then he continued: '. . . until it became irretrievably broken down, after us both having tried.'

Dimbleby continued: 'Do you hope the issue will go away?'

Charles answered: 'It would be nice if it did. Other people don't have to go through this when their marriage breaks down. It's the last thing I wanted to happen.'

Then, breaking the tension with a laugh, the Prince added: 'I am not a total idiot. I didn't go into marriage with the intention of this happening. I am not, on the whole, a cynical person. It sounds self-righteous, but I try to get it right and do the right thing by everybody. It has happened – that is that, regrettably.'

For more than two and a half hours, Prince Charles laid bare his life for all to see. He did not avoid a single question, even the most intimate and probing queries about his marriage – and future.

Says one royal insider: 'It was the make-or-break interview. The Prince truly believed that if he was honest and truthful in his answers, the television programme would finally show his subjects he is the right man to become king.

'But it was a gamble. If the programme had backfired, those 150 minutes of television could have cost Charles the lot – his hard-fought-for popularity, his image and even the Crown. It is impossible to overstate the importance of that documentary. You could almost say it was trial by television. If Charles stated his case well and won, his future would be secure. If he failed, his very future would be on the line. It was an astonishingly brave thing to do.'

As millions watched, the future king answered the most intimate questions about his private life for the first time.

Asked by Dimbleby if he thought the marriage breakdown had damaged his image, the Prince replied: 'Well, I don't recommend it to anybody. The breakdown of a marriage is always a difficult thing and creates great unhappiness and consternation and everything else, inevitably . . . I accept that I'm sure there's a certain amount of damage.

'One of the difficulties I find is the predictability of what people will say.

'I'd much rather it had not happened. I am sure my wife would have felt the same. It was not through lack of trying on both parts to ensure it worked. But you can't avoid it.

'I accept there is a certain amount of damage. I mean you can't avoid it with something of this unfortunate nature.'

Perhaps the most telling insight into his innermost thoughts and feelings came when Charles openly discussed his friendship with Camilla for the first time. For it became apparent that, despite the bombshell confession of admitting the affair for the first time, Charles had absolutely no intention of ever giving up his friendship with the woman he has loved for a quarter of a century.

The Prince referred to both his mistress and her husband, Andrew Parker Bowles, as 'dear friends'.

He said: 'Mrs Parker Bowles is a great friend of mine. She's been a friend for a very long time and will continue to be for a very long time. I am terribly lucky to have so many friends who I think are wonderful and make the whole difference to my life which would be intolerable otherwise.

'When a marriage breaks down, awful and miserable as that is, it is inevitable that it's your friends who are so helpful. Otherwise you would go stark staring mad – that's what friends are for.'

Asked about his marriage failure, Charles became noticeably irritated and said: 'Look, come on. It happens to half the country and it happened to me. It is not something I wanted to happen.'

By opening his heart on prime-time television in the most revealing royal close-up ever, Charles pleaded for understanding over his failed marriage.

When Dimbleby probed further about the rumours to the effect that he had been 'persistently unfaithful' with

Camilla, the Prince replied: 'These things are so personal that it is difficult to know how to talk about them. There is no truth in so much of this speculation. Mrs Parker Bowles is a great friend of mine.'

The story made headlines for days.

CHARLES: I HAD AN AFFAIR ran the front-page story in the *Sun*; ITN led its *News at Ten* with the 'astonishing confession'; the *Daily Mail* read: CHARLES: WHEN I WAS UNFAITHFUL and the left-wing *Daily Mirror* newspaper screamed: NOT FIT TO REIGN.

While the Prince never actually named Camilla as his mistress, broadcaster Dimbleby did so in an interview the following day, saying: 'He was unfaithful with someone who has been a long-standing friend and that is Mrs Parker Bowles. I think it is absolutely clear that no-one else was involved.'

Throughout the programme, Charles answered every question fully and frankly.

On the subject of a possible divorce from Diana, his eyes flickered with sadness as he said: 'It is not a consideration at the moment.' But he added: 'That sort of thing is very much in the future. If it happens, then it will happen. The question of divorce is a very personal and private thing between my wife and myself and that's how it will remain.'

Asked if a divorce would be an obstacle to the throne, he replied: 'I don't see why it should be an impediment. All my life I have been brought up to do my utmost and carry out my duty to the country.

'I am not going to say I will not do it. I am not going to live anywhere else and I don't want to.'

He also dismissed as 'extraordinary' any suggestion that he might pass over his chance to reign in favour of his son William.

Defending the role of the monarchy in Britain, the Prince said: 'It would be a great pity to lose it because everything would then be based around politics. This country would lose a great deal. The great thing about the monarchy is its independence, which enables it to function in a relatively free way. It represents the ordinary person's thoughts and feelings without belonging to a particular party.'

But of the 150-minute programme, the five minutes the Prince spent confessing his adultery dominated the headlines – and sparked a widespread controversy.

The Reverend Tony Higton, a leading member of the Church of England's ruling body, the Synod, slammed the Prince as 'unfit to be king'.

He said: 'From what I understand, there does not appear to be any hint of penitence. And that is going to cause him some very serious problems. I therefore do not think he is fit to be Defender of the Faith and Supreme Governor of the Church of England.'

But the Archdeacon of York, George Austin, took a different view. The churchman said: 'I admire the Prince's honesty. He simply confirmed what everyone already knew. He is a Christian and has done something wrong. By making this public statement, he is showing a large degree of regret. I do not believe his future position as king will be affected.

'Nobody wants him to crawl up the Mall from Buckingham Palace to Westminster Abbey on his knees pleading for forgiveness or if they do, they shouldn't. God gave us forgiveness – and it's not for us to question it.'

Prime Minister John Major joined the growing row by insisting Charles's confession 'in no way' affected his position as future king. He said: 'There is no reason why the Prince should not fulfil his duty.'

For the first time, Charles admitted how difficult it must have been for Diana to join the ranks of the royal family.

Referring to the family as 'the organization', he said: 'I do think that those people who marry into my family find it increasingly difficult to do so because of the added pressure, and finding that they're put into positions in the organization which they are simply not trained for and the strains and stresses that become, in some cases, almost intolerable.'

Other parts of the film showed the Prince relaxing with his sons at Balmoral. Dimbleby asked: 'Do you like your children?' to which Charles replied: 'Of course I do. Seeing them develop gives me enormous pleasure, satisfaction and pride. As they grow older, it gets more fun. I like mucking around with them.'

He came across as a loving, doting father. In one scene he sat on a step wearing a kilt watching his son playing football. In another, he tenderly stroked Harry's nose with a handkerchief.

Asked about important values he wished to impart to his sons, he said: 'Good manners. Doing to others as you want them to do to you. It's not a bad way to operate.'

According to those close to Charles, he was 'relieved and upbeat' in the days following the television broadcast. The programme was later broadcast around the globe in countries as far afield as America, Australia, Germany, Japan, Saudi Arabia and The Gambia.

His confessions made headlines in newspapers around the world.

A friend of the Prince's says: He was rejuvenated after the programme aired. It was as if an enormous weight had been lifted from his shoulders. He was pleased with the way the documentary turned out. He felt that even though there had been considerable criticism in some quarters of the press, the British public, while perhaps not condoning his affair could, maybe, understand the reasons behind it better. Don't forget, he was speaking to a nation where one in three marriages ends in divorce. Millions of families go through the same pain as he went through. He felt that the public would understand – and he was right. It was a big gamble to take, but it paid off.'

Constitutional expert Lord St John of Fawsley, a friend of the Prince, said: 'What matters is the truth and the programme was so devastating because we were listening to the simple truth, something you rarely hear in public life.

'The Prince put himself on judgement before the fairest jury in the world, namely the British public. He put everything before them. He relied on their sense of fairness, their sense of fair play and their sense of justice. And his confidence was justified. He was seen for the man his friends have known for years – strong, brave, honest and reliable. A man who will make a magnificent future king.'

Indeed, the television programme proved a master-stroke. A poll in the *Sun* taken the day after the documentary aired showed a massive swing in the Prince's popularity.

In a poll of the same newspaper's readers shortly before the TV programme, sixty-three per cent of people said they thought Charles was *not* fit to be king. But the post-documentary poll showed a dramatic change of heart. Fifty-four per cent of the 6,000 readers polled said that, after hearing Charles confess to the affair, they now believed he was fit to be king.

CHARLES RULES OK read the front page.

A Palace aide says: 'The Prince was thrilled. He read

everything that was written in the newspapers at that time and it soon became clear that the programme had worked very much in his favour.'

A similar poll of 80,000 viewers by the television station GMTV also swung in the Prince's favour. Eighty-five per cent said Charles should reign compared with just forty-six per cent who said they approved of him becoming king prior to the documentary.

The mood was mirrored at Tower Bridge in the heart of London when the Prince went walkabout on his first public engagement after the programme. A large crowd cheered their approval. A royal aide said: 'The Prince's mood was elated. Any doubts he had had about appearing in the television programme evaporated. He knew he had stated his case openly for the first time. And when the British public were left to judge him by his own words and actions, he came out ahead. They saw him at work and at play for the first time – and they liked what they saw. He came across as a man who could be trusted; an honourable man who was prepared to face up to his mistakes but whose sense of duty to the Crown and country was unassailable.'

The Prince's private secretary, Commander Richard Aylard, was thrilled. He said: 'The Prince of Wales has absolutely no regrets about the television show. He went into the project with his eyes open. We think it was a rounded and balanced portrait of a man we know and work for. People are telling us how much they appreciated the intimate portrayal of the Prince.'

Lady Colin Campbell says: 'The television programme was a public-relations masterstroke. I don't think Charles owed the public an apology over his affair, but he gave one, and it won him hearts across the country. He appeared genuinely upset by the marriage breakdown and he came across as a normal husband and father. What was astonishing to everyone who watched the show was how frank and honest he was about his affair. He was fair, calm and honest. And the British public opened their hearts to him.

'It was brilliant. Here was the heir to the throne pointing out that he is just as human as his subjects; admitting his mistakes and putting an end to all the rumour and speculation both about his marriage and his future as king once and for all. By the end of the programme, no-one could be in any doubt that he is the man who *will* be king – and a jolly fine one at that. He showed the side of Charles the public wanted to see – the *true* man behind the image.'

Despite widespread approval for the programme, there was also much criticism of the Prince's decision to open his heart on prime-time television.

The *Daily Mail*'s front-page headline the following morning read: ANOTHER ERROR OF JUDGEMENT? The story said: 'The Prince's aides had been confident that the documentary would rehabilitate his image. Instead, many will feel it portrayed a chronically restless man, well-intentioned but wracked with self-doubt. True, there were touching scenes with his sons William and Harry and glimpses of humour . . . but the programme was inevitably dominated by questions about his marriage, adultery and possible divorce . . . and he looked like a prisoner awaiting judgement.'

But royal biographer Brian Hoey says: 'To be frank, the public debate which began after the documentary aired was totally irrelevant. It doesn't make any difference whether Charles is going to be a good king, a bad king, an evil king or a majestic king. What is clear now is that if he survives his mother, he *will* be king.'

On the day the programme aired, Charles had another brush with danger. Piloting a British Aerospace 146 jet of the Queen's Flight from Aberdeen to Islay, the southernmost isle of the Inner Hebrides in Scotland, he overshot the runway in gusting winds. The Prince was forced to swerve ninety degrees left to avoid a deep ditch at the end of the 1,600-yard runway and the plane finished up nose-down in soft ground with three burst tyres. Neither he nor his ten passengers were injured.

The Prince later told pupils at a school he visited on Islay: 'It wasn't quite a crash. We went off the end of the runway, unfortunately. It is not something I recommend happening all the time – unfortunately it did.'

For Diana and her friends, the Prince's prime-time confession was hailed as a victory for the Princess.

DI TOLD YOU SO! ran the *Sun* headline, which described how the Princess was 'relieved and happy' that her husband had finally admitted his relationship with Camilla. The paper's chief reporter, John Kay, quoted close friends of the Princess as saying she was 'celebrating an enormous sense of victory and relief'.

Her friends spoke of her 'vindication'. One said: 'It proves that everything she said about Camilla Parker Bowles in Andrew Morton's book was true. Her husband *was* having an affair and now he's come right out and admitted it. She felt totally vindicated.'

Indeed, on the very night the programme was broadcast, Diana went out of her way to attract attention. Wearing a plunging off-the-shoulder black cocktail dress, she spectacularly created her own headlines by going to a gala dinner at the Serpentine Gallery in London's Kensington. Sponsored by *Vanity Fair* magazine, the benefit dinner drew 310 guests, including the actress Joan Collins – but all eyes were on Diana.

Royal biographer Brian Hoey said: 'She was annoyed and jealous of all the media coverage Charles was getting because of the documentary. She wanted to show that she'd lost none of her ability to manipulate the press.'

According to those at the gala, Diana smiled and joked the night away. One witness says: 'She was on stunning form. She was either truly relieved or the greatest actress the world has seen. She had a long flirt with the actor Jeremy Irons and flirted and joked all evening. If she was putting on an act, she deserved an Oscar.'

Even the austere *Daily Telegraph* noted: 'She couldn't have chosen a more timely moment to bury the hatchet – in her husband's back.'

But despite Diana's attempts to recapture some of the headlines, the Palace were delighted with the result of the programme.

The Queen gave her full blessing to Charles's comments. A royal insider says: 'It was something the Prince discussed with his mother at length before agreeing to make the television documentary. He felt it was important to answer every question fully and honestly.

'They had a series of meetings throughout the months the TV crew was following the Prince making the show. And they had a final meeting just two days before the programme aired. The Queen watched the programme privately in advance. And she was pleased with the result. The Palace knew that the adultery confession would cause a public storm. But Charles and the Queen were both adamant that he should tell the truth – and allow the British public to be his judge.

'If Charles had refused to answer Dimbleby's questions about his private life, he would have looked ridiculous and people would have been even more angry with him for avoiding the main question. What he did was a remarkably brave thing to do. He faced the question head-on and he answered it honestly. It was a massive gamble, but it paid off. The public in general admired his courage and honesty.'

On 1 July, Charles attended a ceremony to celebrate the twenty-fifth anniversary of his investiture as Prince of Wales at Caernarvon Castle in Wales. Hundreds of wellwishers cheered the Prince as he arrived for the low-key ceremony.

While some members of the local council boycotted the ceremony in protest against the Prince, the Palace was happy at the end of what many described as 'a very long week'. The Prince was cheered by large crowds as he later visited a housing estate, school and council home in the nearby town of Gwynedd.

An insider said: 'The Prince and his advisers knew it was going to be a bumpy ride. Commander Aylard was speaking to the Prince several times a day in the lead up to the documentary being aired and in the days immediately afterwards. But the reaction was, on the whole, extremely positive. The charm offensive had scored its greatest victory.'

For her part, Camilla steadfastly refused to comment on the Prince's confession. Two days before the broadcast, she claimed she knew nothing about the programme's contents and said she would be 'unlikely' to watch it. In fact, she was fully aware of everything Charles was to say. It can be revealed for the first time that on 17 and 18 April, the two days during which Charles's astonishing confession was taped, he repeatedly telephoned Camilla.

A source very close to the couple says: 'They were on the phone constantly; often the first call from Charles to Middlewick House would be as early as seven in the morning. The phone lines were burning up during that forty-eight-hour period.

'Charles asked Camilla's advice on how much he should say. It was Camilla who encouraged him to "come clean" about their relationship. They were talking almost constantly throughout the time he was making his confession. Often, the calls would go well into the night.'

A friend of Camilla's says: 'Of course Camilla knew what Charles was going to say. He would never have made a public confession like that without first discussing it with Camilla. He called her repeatedly throughout the filming of the programme. He asked her advice about how much he should say. In fact, it was Camilla who helped him prepare answers to some of the more probing personal questions. If Camilla had objected to him confirming the affair, the Prince would never have been so frank in his answers. But Camilla knew that Charles needed to make the confession so the whole question of the affair would be ended once and for all. She knew it was the only way he could put the gossip behind him and win back the hearts of the country. Camilla is extremely smart. She actively encouraged the Prince to be candid with Dimbleby. And it was a truly seffless act. Because Camilla knew that once the Prince confirmed the affair, she again would be besieged by the press and again be branded the "other woman". For a woman who guards her private life as fiercely as Camilla, it was a remarkable act of love. For the umpteenth time in her life, she put the Prince's welfare and needs ahead of her own.'

Indeed, once the story broke, Camilla was again under siege at Middlewick House. While her husband remained at work in Aldershot Barracks, Camilla went to ground. The day before the eagerly-awaited broadcast, she and her daughter Laura secretly boarded a flight to Spain to stay at the 2,000-acre private estate of the Marquis of Douro, one of Charles's closest friends, in Grenada.

Prince Charles telephoned her every day, even while he was on an official two-day visit to Northern Ireland. For, despite the official declaration that the affair was at an end at the close of 1993, they were again closer than ever.

A friend says: 'The Prince genuinely tried to cut ties to Camilla when his advisers told him it would be for the best. But she is his greatest friend and by February 1994, they were very much back together again.'

The couple again resumed their lengthy daily phone conversations and began meeting in secret at the 'safe' country homes of friends. Only a handful of people were aware that contact had been resumed.

One says: 'The Prince was determined he would not be "caught out", so to speak. He is an intensely loyal man to his friends and there was no way he could carry on without Camilla's love and support. But less than a dozen people knew he was still seeing her. They began meeting again in safe homes close to their country bases – but it was very much cloak-and-dagger stuff. The charm offensive was in full swing. Camilla and Charles knew they could not risk a backlash if new stories broke that they were back together again.'

And a Palace insider says: 'No-one was supposed to know that Camilla and Charles were close again, but they were.

'The Prince managed to get through a couple of months without any contact with her, but then, despite all the risks to both their reputations, he made the first move to contact her again by telephoning her.

'It is not something one should condemn him for. Camilla is more than just a mistress, she is his best friend.

He needs Camilla's friendship constantly. The Prince simply cannot give up Camilla.

'He is absolutely determined he will be king. But he will not give up Camilla.

'The rest of the royal family always knew he and Camilla are still an item, of course. And they are still extremely fond of Camilla. She has always behaved impeccably. She has never let the side down. And for that reason, she is utterly respected by the royal family.

'While Diana was viewed as a traitor who let the "Firm" down, Camilla is seen as someone who has acted impeccably.

'Camilla, of course, will never let the "Firm" down. She will continue to maintain a dignified silence. That's the difference between Camilla and Diana. Camilla is a real lady. She has class.'

Royal biographer Andrew Morton says: 'It struck everyone in the know as very unlikely that Charles would stop seeing Camilla. I believe they are still in regular contact. He is a man of habit, and old habits die hard.'

After the documentary put Camilla firmly back in the public eye, Charles gave her his full support.

A friend of Camilla's says: 'He is a man who would never abandon a friend, just as Camilla has never abandoned him. When all the fuss blew up around his adultery confession, he was telephoning Camilla constantly

'Throughout that long week when she was in hiding in Spain, the Prince telephoned her at least once a day, sometimes more. As always, despite the intense publicity and speculation, their friendship remained strong.'

Returning from Spain a week later, Camilla remained tight-lipped when bombarded by reporters shouting questions at Gatwick Airport. Looking tanned but tense, Camilla simply smiled at reporters' questions even though a near riot was breaking out around her as photographers jostled for position.

A friend says: 'Camilla was extremely angry about the scenes at the airport. The press pack was jostling and pushing her and her daughter. But even under that enormous pressure, she did not retaliate. You will never see a picture of Camilla screaming at the camera like Diana did. She simply keeps her head – and her dignity. Camilla is a class act. Of course she must feel it inwardly. But she has never been the type to crack under pressure. What makes people who know Camilla so angry is that so much is written about her which is simply not fair. Camilla will never justify any of the gossips by defending herself publicly, it's just not her style. She had never commented on her affair in the past, and she wasn't about to start then.'

After just forty-eight hours at home in Wiltshire with her husband and daughter, Camilla left again to jet off on a family holiday in the south of France.

A friend of Camilla's says: 'It was a tough time for her. She just needed to get away from all the speculation and pressure. Camilla is an intensely private person. For the affair to flare up again must have been torture for her – but, as usual, she bore the pressure with dignity and fortitude.'

While Camilla maintained a discreet silence, other members of her family spoke out.

Her father, Major Bruce Shand, praised the Prince for his 'honesty and courage'. The Major said loyally: 'I was fascinated by what the Prince had to say about all sorts of issues, including the failure of his marriage. I believe he came across as very fair-minded and sincere. I am in no doubt he will make a perfect king.'

Camilla and Charles's great friend Patti Palmer-

Tomkinson added: 'I believe the Prince was incredibly brave. He put much emphasis on honesty and the truth. He is a wonderful, wonderful man – very honest and brave. I saw the man I know.'

Andrew Parker Bowles broke his silence to say: 'Nothing has changed. I don't give a damn about the rumours, about what's being said or about what has happened. I really can't understand what all the fuss is about.'

On 14 July 1994, Camilla turned to her Prince for comfort when her beloved mother Rosalind died after a long illness. At seventy-four years old, Rosalind had suffered from the brittle bone disease osteoporosis for many years.

According to one friend: 'Both Charles and Andrew were tremendous supports for her during those difficult days. Camilla adored her mother; they were extremely close to the end.'

Camilla herself said in a remarkable tribute: 'Both of my parents have been so supportive, indeed, more supportive of me, than parents could be expected to be.' A friend of Camilla's added: 'While she was devastated by her mother's death, she was always tremendously grateful to both her parents for never once wavering in their loyalty for her. To this day, Camilla knows her parents both loved her without question. She is eternally grateful for their love and support.

'When Rosalind died, the Prince was tremendously supportive, calling regularly to make sure Camilla was OK. Her husband was also a terrific rock for her to lean on during those difficult days. It proved to Camilla, once and for all, that the love of her friends and family is unwavering.'

By the end of July 1994, things were looking better than

they had done for years for Charles. Public opinion was more in his favour than it had been in recent times.

Yet there was still another bombshell to come.

While Charles's TV confession of his affair with Camilla had been devastating, the follow-up book by Jonathan Dimbleby, *The Prince of Wales: A Biography*, which was first excerpted in the *Sunday Times* in October 1994, provoked even more controversy.

In the book, Charles delved even deeper into the precise details of his affair with Camilla than he had during the televised interview.

He talked of his 'agony' at being trapped in a loveless marriage. He harshly criticized his father Prince Philip for 'forcing' him into marriage with Diana.

The book also contained excerpts of an extraordinary letter written by the Prince to a friend in which he talked of the collapse of his marriage, saying: 'It has all the ingredients of a Greek tragedy . . . I never thought it would end up like this. How could I have got it all so wrong?'

I NEVER LOVED DIANA, blared the headlines.

The Prince allowed Dimbleby access to his private diaries and 10,000 letters – including dozens of love letters between himself and Camilla.

A source close to the Prince said: 'His judgement failed him at a crucial moment yet again.

'Sir was on a high after the TV broadcast and he naïvely thought the book would simply give people a clearer picture of who he was and the kind of man he is. Unfortunately, he was rather too candid. The book was even more explosive than the TV documentary. It left no-one in any doubt about the strength of his feelings towards Camilla. It blew the lid off the whole affair.'

Privately, Camilla was 'dismayed' at the extent to which Charles revealed details of their relationship.

A friend said: 'She felt he had told too much. She was concerned he had shot himself in the foot by telling all.'

Prince Philip, too, was outraged by Charles's description of him as a cold and uncaring father. According to Charles, his father forced him to marry Diana too early in the relationship. Charles said the press speculation about their budding friendship led his father to demand he propose to Diana or end the relationship to save her reputation. The book quoted Philip as telling Charles, 'It is the only honourable thing to do.'

The Prince, according to Dimbleby, 'felt ill-used but impotent. He interpreted his father's attitude as an ultimatum.'

Charles also told how his father would publicly reduce him to tears with mocking taunts.

The chasm between the two became even deeper. Philip said publicly he had 'never read that turgid book' and added chillingly: 'I have never discussed private matters and neither has the Queen.'

Dimbleby's book portrayed the Prince as 'all too human', according to one of Charles's closest confidants.

He said: 'While the public were sympathetic to Charles's plight, sympathy and respect are two different beasts. People felt sorry for Charles when they read what his book had to say – but airing his dirty linen in public cost him a lot of respect amongst his subjects.'

Indeed, a leading government minister was quoted as saying about the book: 'It could end up being the longest abdication notice ever. Royalty must have mystery as well as majesty. Charles has destroyed the mystery.'

But Charles told friends he had 'no regrets whatsoever' about doing the book.

A friend said: 'He truly felt then, and still does to this day, that coming clean about the affair was the right course of action. The headlines were all blasting out how the Prince never loved Diana when, in fact, the Prince had actually said he did not love Diana at first, but honestly believed he would learn to love her – and would do everything in his powers to make the marriage work.

'But, on the whole, the Prince was pleased with the book. He felt he had been honest with the public.'

Camilla's family, however, were less pleased with the Prince's revelations.

In an unprecedented statement, her brother-in-law Simon Parker Bowles openly criticized Charles for the first time, saying: 'Prince Charles does not have our sympathy at the moment. I'd be more inclined to say "Poor old Camilla".'

Simon accused Charles of being 'mixed-up' and of dropping Camilla 'in a heap' by telling all about their affair.

He said: 'What he has done is wrong and very hurtful.'

For Camilla's husband, the Prince's public confessions of the affair were too much.

A friend of Andrew Parker Bowles said: 'Andrew was beginning to be sick to the stomach of the whole sorry mess. For years, he had stood loyally by in silence while the affair continued. But he felt deeply betrayed by the Prince. He felt that Charles had broken the unwritten code of never talking about the relationship with Camilla.

'Andrew noticeably changed after the TV broadcast and all the publicity surrounding the book. Privately, he was more open in criticizing the Prince to his friends. To put it bluntly, he was hopping mad.

'That was when Andrew decided enough was enough. It was around that time he made up his mind to go for a divorce. The marriage to Camilla was over in all but name. Andrew wanted out of the whole public mess. He's an intensely private man and he found the constant public flare-ups draining. Of course, he was still in love with his wife. You don't spend twenty-one years with someone and have two children together without forging a lifelong bond.

'But Andrew decided towards the end of 1994 that the New Year would be different. He wanted to make a clean break, to seek a divorce and give himself the chance to get on and lead a more private, normal life out of the public spotlight.

'Divorcing Camilla was the only way he could see any chance of a more private future.'

The die was cast.

Yet while Charles, Camilla and Andrew were going through their own upheavals, for Diana things were also not going so smoothly.

Misplaced Loyalties

The woman whose face had adorned a thousand magazine covers glanced furtively around her. Then, without looking back, she quickly slipped into the driver's seat of her green Audi car.

A few moments later, the man walked up to the car and, without even a split-second's hesitation, opened the passenger side door and stepped in. The watching photographer snapped away incredulous at the scene unfolding before his eyes.

Diana, Princess of Wales, had been caught red-handed having a clandestine meeting with a top royal reporter. It was the moment the Palace had been longing for.

Her secret rendezvous with Richard Kay, the handsome and debonair royal correspondent of the *Daily Mail*, in the spring of 1994, put paid to any doubts the Palace or the public had about where Diana's loyalties lay.

A top Palace aide says: 'To say there was dancing in the

corridors of Buckingham Palace when that story appeared would be an understatement. Finally, Diana had been exposed for what she truly was: a woman who ruthlessly manipulated media coverage for her own, selfish ends.'

For years, the Princess had steadfastly denied ever leaking any damaging stories about her husband to the newspapers. Yet the tidal wave of anti-Charles propaganda had continued relentlessly.

At the height of the furore about Andrew Morton's book which portrayed Charles as a heartless womanizer who drove his wife to the brink of suicide, Diana had coolly denied her involvement.

Although refusing to sign a statement distancing herself from the book, Diana nevertheless denied she had spoken directly to the author. Looking the Queen straight in the eye, she said smugly: 'I cannot help what my friends say about the troubles with my marriage. But I can categorically say, hand on heart, that I never once, not ever, spoke to a journalist directly myself.'

Now, on 3 May, her cover had been blown – across the front pages of four million copies of the *Sun.*

Under the headline TWO-FACED DIANA, the *Sun*'s royal reporter Wayne Francis recounted in precise detail how Diana kept her secret rendezvous with Kay, a thirty-eight-year-old bachelor described by friends as enjoying 'a very close friendship indeed' with the Princess. The Princess spent more than an hour locked in conversation with Kay, who was writing yet another 'tell-all' book about the Princess. The meeting took place three days before the *Sun*'s scoop appeared.

According to the report, Diana parked her Audi convertible amid a row of cars near the famous Harrods department store in London's Knightsbridge.

Photographer Glenn Harvey said: 'I saw her there alone

with no detectives or aides at her side and I was intrigued. It was obvious that she was waiting for someone.

'I couldn't figure out what was going on. When I saw what was happening, I was stunned.'

Within minutes of Harvey taking up his position, Kay appeared from around a nearby corner. He walked straight up to Diana's car and quickly slipped into the passenger seat. He appeared to know precisely where the car was – and who its famous driver was.

The pair talked furtively for ten minutes before driving off. A few moments later, the car drew into a more secluded side street and parked again. The pair continued to talk for a further forty-five minutes.

Diana then drove off – dropping Kay off at his newspaper offices in Kensington High Street before returning home to Kensington Palace.

The paper quoted a senior royal aide saying: 'This makes a complete mockery of her protestations about privacy if she is secretly meeting up with people like this. It smacks of hypocrisy that she should complain about press intrusion while orchestrating secret briefings.'

Kay responded to the clandestine meeting being made public by saying gallantly: 'I was tipped off that the Princess was in Knightsbridge and wanted to ask her about her recent trip to Spain.

'She politely refused to answer any questions, but generously offered me a lift. I accepted.' In fact, the Princess had talked to Kay in detail about a recent holiday she had taken in Spain. The exclusive story about her 'nightmare' trip duly appeared in the *Daily Mail*.

One of Charles's inner circle says: 'He was jubilant when the *Sun*'s story appeared. For the first time, the British public could see Diana for what she was. Diana was prepared to tell her side of the story to journalists directly.

'It was a day of much celebration at the Palace. Diana had been exposed as the rat she was.

'Of course, everyone inside the Palace had known for years that the leaks were coming from the Princess. But she adamantly continued to deny it.

'Even when she was caught with her trousers down, so to speak, she claimed she and the journalist were simply "having a friendly chat".'

The very next day, Richard Kay's name appeared on a story about how Diana had felt 'raped' by the topless photographs in Spain. And then later that same week, the *Daily Mail* ran another story about how Diana had 'heroically' helped save a drowning tramp. It was all directly from Diana.

'The Palace knew it was a major victory for them. Diana had managed to fool all of the public some of the time and some of the public *all* of the time for years – but there was no way anyone would believe her protestations now.

'It was clear from the *Sun* story that she had actively participated in all the press attention about the marriage, about Camilla, about everything. And she got too cocky. She was finally caught out. The Palace was quite happy just to sit back and allow Diana to be her own worst enemy. They would allow her to dig her own grave, so to speak.'

Diana's behaviour was becoming increasingly erratic. She was a woman adrift, desperately trying to fill her days after relinquishing her royal duties. On 3 December 1993, Diana made a dramatic statement that she was withdrawing from public life.

In an emotion-packed speech during a lunch at London's Park Lane Hilton for one of her favourite charities, the Headway National Head Injuries

Association, she announced she was withdrawing from public life.

Close to tears, she appealed for 'time and space' after more than thirteen years in the public spotlight. The five-minute speech spelled out her deep unhappiness. She never once mentioned her husband, although she singled out the Queen and Prince Philip to thank them for the support they had given her.

While she said she would continue to act as patron for a handful of her favourite charities, including Birthright, Diana said she would not pencil any official engagements into her diary until at least the summer of 1994.

Part of her statement went as follows: 'A year ago I spoke of my desire to continue with my work unchanged. For the past year, I have continued as before. However, life and circumstances alter and I hope you will forgive me if I use this opportunity to share with you my plans for the future, which now indeed have changed.

'When I started my public life twelve years ago, I understood that the media might be interested in what I did. I realized then that their attention would inevitably focus on both our private and public lives.

'But I was not aware of how overwhelming that attention would become, nor the extent to which it would affect both my public duties and my personal life in a manner that has been hard to bear.

'At the end of this year, when I have completed my diary of official engagements, I will be reducing the extent of the public life I have led so far. I attach great importance to my charity work and I intend to focus on a smaller range of areas in the future. Over the next few months, I will be seeking a more suitable way of combining a meaningful public role with, hopefully, a more private life.

'My first priority will continue to be our children,

William and Harry, who deserve as much love, care and attention as I am able to give, as well as an appreciation of the tradition into which they were born.

'. . . I hope you can find it in your hearts to understand and to give me the time and space that has been lacking in recent years.

'I could not stand here today and make this sort of statement without acknowledging the heartfelt support I have been given by the public in general.

'Your kindness and affection have carried me through some of the most difficult periods. And always your love and care have eased that journey. And for that I thank you from the bottom of my heart.'

Her announcement came just days after the *Sunday Mirror* published photographs of the Princess working out in a gymnasium. The *Sunday Mirror* paid a reported £150,000 for the pictures of Diana, dressed in a leotard, working out on a leg press machine at the LA Fitness Club in London. The photographs were said to have been taken secretly by the club's owner, Bryce Taylor, on a Leica camera hidden in the ceiling above the leg press machine. Diana claimed she had been 'duped' and launched legal action against the newspaper.

But several royal aides showed Diana little sympathy. One said: 'She was so obsessed about publicity. She was someone who, every day, read every single story about herself.

'Her whole philosophy after leaving the immediate royal family was to generate as much negative publicity as possible. She wanted to prove to the powers-that-be inside the Palace that she was still a force to be reckoned with. And she knew she would only continue being a force while her name was constantly in the news. That's why she went out of her way to grab headlines. Her speech about press intrusion was utter nonsense. Diana *loved* publicity.

In fact, Diana never got her day in court over the 'Peeping Tom' gym photos.

In February 1995, it was reported that the Princess had won a huge settlement against the gym owner and Mirror Group Newspapers. The deal was announced just five days before the case was due to open in London's High Court.

Diana said she agreed to the out-of-court settlement for the sake of her sons.

She said: 'I took the legal action for the boys. It is not a question of money. I just want to put a stop to the gross invasion of privacy.'

The agreement also ensured the negatives of the candid snaps were destroyed.

According to Lady Colin Campbell, Diana's master plan to prove to the Palace she was 'indispensable' to the royal family backfired.

She says: 'Her actions after leaving the family were strange, to say the least. She was turning up in the papers as much now as she did before. It seems extraordinarily fortunate that every time the Princess left Kensington Palace, she was photographed walking the streets alone.

'She was effectively frozen out by the Palace. Of course, as the mother of the future king, in public she is accorded the right amount of respect. But in private, the family considered her a Judas. They wanted nothing to do with her. She became a liability. They saw through her act and they never fogave what she did. She thought she was popular and powerful enough to challenge the monarchy. And, by God, she came damn close to fulfilling her dream.

'But the Palace fought back and they beat her at her own game. The sad thing is, that from having so much, Diana had so little by the end.'

Diana's behaviour after relinquishing her royal duties began to concern the Palace. Seasoned royal aides, well used to her 'erratic behaviour' during her marriage, watched aghast as her actions became more and more reckless.

Her first act was to dismiss her private bodyguards. She announced she would only allow her royal protection squad officers to accompany her if she was with her two sons. 'On all other occasions,' she said, 'I wish to be left alone.' It was to be a fateful decision.

One Palace aide says: 'After her announcement that she was withdrawing from public life, Diana's behaviour turned from the bizarre to the ridiculous. She insisted on walking around Kensington High Street and her other favourite haunts on her own and then launched into screaming tirades against photographers when they spotted her.

'There are dozens of pictures of her running down the street with a handbag on her head which are almost farcical. She looks like some soap-opera star rather than the mother of the future King of England.'

Indeed, the Princess's insistence that the Palace should withdraw their royal protection officers actually led to several potentially dangerous moments.

She sparked a security row when she was mobbed by an excitable crowd after a visit to the ballet outside the Royal Opera House in London's Covent Garden.

Photographer Jon Bond said: 'You could just put your hand out and touch her. Any nut in the crowd could have pulled a gun. She was totally exposed.'

Ex-Scotland Yard Commander Terry O'Connell said: 'She was just a sitting duck. She was acting like a woman who seemed intent on setting herself up to be attacked by terrorists, kidnappers or cranks.'

Later, on a private skiing holiday to Lech in Austria, she

'screamed like a banshee' at French photographers as they lined up to take her picture on the slopes.

One said with bemusement: 'Why does she let everyone know where she is going when she is only going to scream at us when we want a picture?'

In fact, Diana had made no secret of her plans to take the skiing holiday. She had even said 'hello' to photographers who waited at the airport for her flight to come in.

'She wanted us to be there,' said another cameraman. 'When we were there, she went nuts. No-one could understand it. But it made for some good pictures and they made the next day's papers so perhaps that was her true intention all the way along.'

In fact, Scotland Yard were so worried about the risks the Princess was placing herself under that they secretly assigned a four-man police squad to tail her without her knowledge. In an operation codenamed 'Pink Panther', the officers were instructed to keep a 'discreet but alert' watch on her during her solo shopping trips and regular lunches with friends.

On one occasion, they watched as Diana 'threw a wobbly' after a photographer snapped her having lunch at exclusive Daphne's restaurant in Knightsbridge with her friend William von Staubenzee, a man wrongly labelled as her new boyfriend.

'To say she became mercurial, is one way of putting it,' said a Palace source.

Even Prince William has suffered from his mother's ill-temper. When he discovered Diana reading a Jackie Collins novel, he cheekily told her 'not to waste her time' on 'such rubbish'.

According to a report in the *Today* newspaper: 'She flew into a rage, saying that his father was filling his head with

Shakespeare. William promptly burst into tears. It was an astonishing outburst at a young child.'

Then, on 1 May 1994, Diana was photographed lounging bare-breasted on Spain's Costa del Sol. She had flown to the Hotel Byblos Andaluz in Malaga with two of her circle of friends, Kate Menzies and Catherine Soames.

When the Princess arrived at the original hotel she was to stay in, she pronounced it 'a flea pit' and hitched a lift from a local hairdresser to the Byblos. Reporters and photographers were everywhere. A fellow guest at the hotel said: 'You could hardly miss them. They were camped out at the hotel entrance, most of them had checked into the same hotel. There were guys lying by the pool with cameras by their side. You'd have had to be blind and dumb not to know the place was crawling with the media.'

Nevertheless, Diana chose to go down to the hotel pool. In full view of dozens of people, including Spanish photographer Juan Carlos Teuma, she slowly and carefully peeled off her bikini top. Teuma snapped happily away. He later said: 'She knew what was going on. She placed the bikini top by her sun-lounger and stood up. She waited just long enough for me to take pictures before she put a towel around her. I know an invitation when I see it.'

When Diana 'learned' of the photographs, she was suitably outraged.

One veteran royal watcher says: 'Her protests had a rather hollow tone. There was no way a woman as used to handling the press as Diana is would have "accidentally" made such a mistake. No, she knew full well what she was letting herself in for when she went topless. The place was crawling with photographers. It seemed extraordinary to everyone that a woman who, only a few months earlier, had been begging for "time and space", had so clearly put herself in a position to capture the headlines.

'The general consensus was that Diana was missing all the attention. She *wanted* to cause a scandal, so, sure enough, she did.'

The offending photographs were later bought by the fiercely pro-royal *Hello!* magazine for an undisclosed sum said to be close to the £500,000 mark. Indeed, it was even suggested that Diana agreed to give the glossy magazine her next 'Royal Exclusive'.

Two weeks later, the Palace pulled another masterstroke when financial records of the Princess's excessive spending habits were revealed. To a public still suffering the hard bite of recession, her lavish spending on manicures, alternative medicine 'therapies', a personal astrologer and hair-stylists was seen as grossly excessive.

It was revealed that Diana's annual 'upkeep' bill was £160,000. In fact, as the *Sun* pointed out, the Princess spent as much on holidays, health cures, astrology and clothes in a *week* as an old age pensioner in Britain received in a *year*. Lavish purchases, such as £728 on sun cream alone, were greeted with growing dismay from the public who once adored her.

The *Sun* reported that Charles was 'furious and incredulous' when he discovered his estranged wife was frittering away £55 a fortnight on such bizarre health cures as colonic irrigation, where the lower intestine is cleaned out with squirts of water – administered through a rubber pipe up the rectum.

Tights and stockings costing £5,000 a year, weekly manicures and pedicures at £322 a time and twice-monthly hair highlighting costing £175 a session added to the enormous list.

It was even revealed that she spent £2,500 a year for weekly sessions with astrologer Debbie Frank.

The decision for the Prince to make public his wife's

enormous personal 'grooming' bills was seen as 'significant' by royal observers. Just weeks before, he had announced a massive cost-cutting exercise to encompass every area of his large Duchy of Cornwall estate. He had agreed to pay taxes for the first time on the estate. And the Princess's records were released as part of a comprehensive audit of the Waleses' household bills – to forward to the Inland Revenue to find out which expenses could qualify for tax relief.

One royal observer said: 'For him to publicly complain about her excessive spending was another shocker for the Princess. He'd been complaining about her spending to her in private for years. He is a very frugal man at heart. He is the type who will happily tell guests dining at Highgrove that the vegetables are from his private garden "and didn't cost a penny".

'He is the sort who posts notes around Highgrove asking people to turn off the lights when they leave the room to conserve energy. He is a man who has always watched the pennies.

'For years he suffered in silence as Diana went on wild spending sprees. They would have frequent rows about money. On one occasion, Diana screamed at him: "Well, you married a clothes horse so you're going to have to pay for me now!"

'But Diana never imagined he'd go public with it. *She* was always the one who went to the newspapers. She was horrified at the furore her bills caused. Of course, the Prince had a legitimate reason for causing the bills to become public. And he was seen in a positive light. The fairy-tale princess image took another blow. And Diana wasn't at all happy about it.

And a Palace aide said: 'She always complained about the old fogeys in the Palace who stopped her doing what she wanted, but, in fact, those old fogeys knew what they were doing. Without their experience and protection, the Princess became a rather sad figure. With the boys away at boarding school, she was left to try and fill her days any way she could. She went to the gym, went shopping, met friends for lunch, played tennis and went swimming. She was bored, world-weary and became like a coiled spring, full of stress and slowly realizing that she had no real role to play any more. She had no job and not that many real friends. Her main problem seemed to be that the friends she *did* have were not giving her the wisest of advice.'

After Charles finally confessed to his affair with Camilla in the Dimbleby documentary at the end of June 1994, Diana again went on a public-relations offensive. She appeared tanned and smiling at the Wimbledon tennis tournament and began flirting with the cameras at every opportunity.

She breached protocol at the British Grand Prix at the Silverstone motor racing track by shaking hands with third-placed driver Jean Alesi during the playing of the National Anthem. Then Diana stood in front of the drivers on the winner's balcony as the 100,000-strong crowd of race fans sang 'God Save the Queen'.

An aide close to Prince Charles says: 'Diana was put out that Prince Charles was getting more attention than her. It was almost amusing to watch her go out of her way to hog the headlines. She hoped the adultery confession would work against Charles, but, in fact, the opposite was true. His popularity level shot through the roof. She was deeply upset by it all.

'The trouble is, Diana did not have a real role to play any more. All she could do is look pretty and smile for the cameras. She was enormously popular among the rank and file of the country. But she needed to find a "proper job" for herself.'

The most dramatic sign of Diana's sadness, frustration and deep-rooted psychological trauma came to light in sensational style on 21 August 1994, when the *News of the World* revealed the Princess had been behind a series of sinister late-night telephone calls to a married art dealer friend.

Dashing Oliver Hoare, a close friend of Prince Charles, acted as a go-between between Diana and her husband as they battled to save their marriage. But, in a sensational scoop, the paper revealed how Hoare and his family had been plagued by phone calls from a clearly tormented Princess.

Under the headline DI'S CRANKY PHONE CALLS TO MARRIED TYCOON, the paper told how the bizarre calls began in September 1992, three months before Di's split with Charles was announced. At their peak, there were as many as twenty calls a week. On one occasion, there were three calls in the space of nine minutes. Each time, the caller would sit silently on the other end of the line – hanging up if Hoare's wife Diane or his children answered the phone.

Hoare's wife became so alarmed at the sinister silent calls that, after a year of enduring the phone pest, Scotland Yard was alerted in October 1993. The wealthy art dealer, who specializes in Islamic art, feared he had become a terrorist target. But when Scotland Yard placed a secret trace on Hoare's phone line, it was discovered that the caller was ringing from Diana's private line at Kensington Palace. Other calls were traced to phone boxes near Kensington Palace and one came from the home of Diana's sister Sarah McCorquodale. One even came from Diana's mobile phone.

When the horrified art dealer was told of the origins of the calls, he immediately ordered the investigation dropped. A police source told the paper: 'His face went as white as a sheet. He never imagined in his wildest dreams that Princess Diana could be making the calls.'

Hoare even confronted Diana when she next called. After he shouted her name into the receiver, the troubled Princess broke down crying and admitted: 'Yes, I'm so sorry. So sorry. I don't know what came over me.'

But the calls started up again within days.

A close friend told the newspaper: 'Diana was captivated by Oliver. He has been a close friend of Charles for more than a decade and when the marriage began falling apart, he offered to act as a go-between. They would talk long into the night about her future. Diana and Oliver formed a close bond.

'He is a very charming, good-looking man who has an intensity about him which women seem to find appealing. They had their differences, but she adored him. He would have had to be made of stone not to be touched by her pain and vulnerability.'

But another friend says: 'Diana developed a crush on Oliver. She developed this obsession about him.'

A senior British government minister was briefed about the incident. He raised the subject with Diana and the calls instantly stopped.

Diana and Hoare rebuilt their friendship. Diana was even photographed driving Hoare into Kensington Palace after a cosy dinner with friends. As her Audi sports car drove through the Palace gates, Di discreetly flipped down the car's sun visors in the hope they would not be spotted.

Psychologist Tony Black says: 'Diana displayed the classic symptoms of a shy, insecure woman desperately seeking a friendly voice on the other end of the phone. She was clearly deeply troubled.'

But another psychologist said: 'She was displaying all

the symptoms of a woman on the verge of a nervous breakdown. It was very sad. She needed help and fast.'

A week after breaking the Hoare story, the *News of the World* revealed Diana's old chum James Hewitt had also been the victim of a mystery caller. The dashing cavalry officer had enjoyed a 'very close' friendship with the Princess when she asked him to help her conquer her fear of horses.

He told the paper he had received ten late-night calls during a three-week period in the summer of 1993, shortly after his friendship with the Princess ended.

He said: 'The phone would ring. I'd pick it up and say, "Hello, hello," but there was nothing at the other end. It would always be me who put the phone down.

'I reckon she phoned other people in the same way.'

Indeed, Camilla, too, had suffered the same sinister phone-call treatment as Hoare and Hewitt but, according to pals, she never reported the hundreds of mystery calls which bombarded her home because she knew instantly that the culprit was Diana.

A close friend says: 'Poor Camilla has been suffering these harassing calls for years. They started shortly after the Prince of Wales's marriage. When Diana discovered the Prince was still calling Camilla after their wedding, she began pressing the redial button on the phone from Highgrove. Of course, Camilla's number would come up. Diana was beside herself. She would ring the number and when Camilla answered, Diana would hang up. When Charles wasn't at home, she would bombard Camilla's home with calls as if in a desperate bid to find out if he was there. The calls would come at all times of the day and night. If Camilla's husband or either of the kids picked up the phone, Diana would slam the receiver down.

'Of course Camilla suspected who it was. When the

calls continued, she even raised the subject with Charles. He was horrified. He tried broaching the subject with Diana and she flew into one of her tantrums, dismissing his accusations as "ridiculous".

'But both Camilla and Charles knew of Diana's mental problems well before they became public. Camilla is so loyal she never reported the harassing calls. She knew it could only embarrass the Prince further and get her embroiled in fresh scandal.

'But when she heard other people associated with Diana had had similar mystery calls over the past few years, it didn't surprise her in the least. In fact, it was almost a relief to find out she wasn't the only one.'

For her part, Diana denied placing the calls to Hoare. On the day before the *News of the World* broke the first story, she again met with her trusted 'friend', the *Daily Mail* journalist Richard Kay.

The pair were secretly photographed meeting in a quiet London square by the *Sun*. Under the headline THE SECRET REN-DI-VOUS, the paper revealed how panic-stricken Diana spent three hours with handsome Kay just hours before the phone-pest scandal erupted.

One local resident who witnessed the meeting said: 'They appeared very close. It definitely looked like a prearranged meeting. It was like watching a spy movie. The Princess was wearing dark clothes and had a baseball hat pulled right down.'

One photograph even showed Diana resting her head intimately against the reporter's shoulder.

The following day, Kay's pro-Diana story appeared across the front page of the *Daily Mail*. WHAT HAVE I DONE TO DESERVE THIS? ran the headline.

In an astonishing interview, Kay revealed how the Princess was close to tears during their meeting as she told him: 'What have I done to deserve this? I feel I am being destroyed. There is absolutely no truth in it.'

She even accused 'sinister forces' of tying to destroy her.

Diana said: 'They are trying to make out I was having an affair with this man or had some sort of fatal attraction. It is simply untrue and so unfair.'

She claimed she had called Hoare and, one occasion, hung up when his wife answered the phone. In a painfully naïve statement, Diana denied making any calls from phone boxes, saying: 'You cannot be serious. I don't even know how to use a parking meter, let alone a phone box.'

To back her story that she knew nothing about the phone calls, she authorized Kay to leak details of her personal diary. She claimed to have been at the hairdressers on one occasion a call was made; at the cinema on another; and having a private dinner another time.

Despite her denials, not one friend came forward to vouch for her 'alibis'.

The whole scandal came as no surprise to those within royal circles.

One former aide said: 'The Princess had been deeply troubled for years. The weird phone calls were just another symptom of her problems. She was a woman desperately searching a role and meaning in life. She had always displayed classic signs of obsessive behaviour. The phone calls were just another example of that.'

In October 1994, Diana suffered another devastating image blow when James Hewitt, the handsome Cavalry officer who had always denied having an affair with her while teaching her and the young Princes to ride, decided to tell all.

In collaboration with author Anna Pasternak, Hewitt

finally confessed to having a torrid five-year affair with Diana.

His tawdry memoir *Princess in Love* claimed Hewitt was Diana's lover from 1986 to 1991.

The British press had a field day.

I TAUGHT DI TO RIDE AND MORE said the *Sun*.

SHE WAS GOING TO LEAVE CHARLES FOR ME blasted the *News of the World*.

Hewitt bragged he had proof of the affair in a series of intimate letters Diana sent to him addressed to 'Winkie' love 'Dibbs' – their pet names for each other.

He even claimed he slept with the Princess in his mother's Devon home.

He said: 'I was *the* man in her life. We were deeply in love. She even contemplated leaving Charles for me.'

Hewitt, who reportedly earned a million pounds from his traitorous confession, bragged: 'I taught Diana to ride and lots more besides.'

The book was ridiculed for its romantic-novel-style sugary prose.

In one passage, Hewitt described how Diana talked about her loveless marriage and said he responded to the Princess's 'cry for help which was like the ghostly cry of a wounded animal'.

It went on in a similar, gut-churning style.

Pasternak wrote: 'Diana stood up and without saying a word stretched out her hand and slowly led James to her bedroom.

'Later, she lay in his arms and wept ... he gently stroked wisps of hair away from her forehead ...'

Yet while Hewitt was branded a 'cad' and a 'traitor', Diana never denied his allegations.

A close friend said: 'To be frank, she couldn't.'

As the scandal erupted, Diana called a crisis summit

with sister-in-law Sarah Ferguson, herself estranged from Prince Andrew, and close girlfriend Catherine Soames.

According to one of her friends: 'Diana was heartbroken by Hewitt's revelations. She told me she never cried as much as she did during those dark days when his book became public.'

And Diana told friends: 'I genuinely helped this man and spent my own money on him. Now he has betrayed me and our special relationship.'

Hewitt fled to France in the wake of the scandal, only to be tracked down by reporters living in a converted pig-sty.

A friend of Diana's said: 'It seemed appropriate that the swine would turn up living in a place fit for pigs. He was a dirty rotter. He was the one who shattered Diana's squeaky-clean image for ever.

'Up until that point, everyone had always believed it was only Charles who had cheated during their marriage. Now Diana was exposed as an adulteress as well. She privately told friends she would have sent Hewitt to the Tower of London as a traitor if she had more power.'

In February 1995, Diana was plunged into more controversy when Oliver Hoare, the married father-of-three to whom she had denied making late-night phone calls just a few months earlier, was revealed as being yet another of her lovers.

Hoare's chauffeur Barry Hodge told the *News of the World* newspaper how his boss had begun an affair with Diana in 1991, shortly after she had dumped James Hewitt. Hodge claimed Hoare and Diana had been meeting three or four times a week at the safe houses of friends. He also told of how be overheard his boss and Diana talking passionately on the phone.

Hodge said: 'I could always tell when he was speaking

to the Princess. He'd always say, "Big, big kiss" when he ended a call to her. He could get very soppy.

'It was the way someone would talk to a wife or a girlfriend, except he never did talk to his wife that way. There was an intensity about the calls to and from the Princess that was a bit embarrassing.

'It was "darling" this and "darling" that and lots of passionate-sounding whispering.

'Sometimes she could phone more than twenty times a day while we were in the car driving around London.'

Hodge also claimed Hoare left his wife for two months – but later returned to the family home because he could not live without his 'creature comforts'.

A few days later, it was revealed that Hoare had left passionate love messages for Diana on a royal pager.

One message read: 'Longing to hear you and love you madly.'

Another said: 'Thinking of you every minute.'

And yet another gushed: 'Please call. I can't reach you and have to get out soon. All my love . . .'

The revelations ended Hoare's marriage, with his wife Diane filing for divorce.

Diana again refused to comment publicly about the affair.

But a friend says: 'It was a second, shattering blow. Diana knew her public image was rapidly becoming tarnished. Diana had always been the master of manipulating the press. Yet, suddenly the press were turning on her. She didn't understand it and she liked it even less. The image of the fairy-tale princess had been shattered.'

Another Marriage Ends

It was the scoop of the year.

On the afternoon of Monday, 9 January 1995, the *Sun*'s royal reporter Wayne Francis received a phone call from one of his most reliable sources

In one brief sentence, Francis was told the marriage of Camilla Parker Bowles and her husband Andrew was over – and the divorce announcement was to be officially issued the following morning.

Francis says: 'It was pretty much a bolt from the blue. Everyone knew the Parker Bowleses' marriage had been a sham for years. But it still came as a complete surprise to most people when they decided to divorce. It was something not even their closest friends had expected.

'For years, Andrew Parker Bowles had stoically put up with his wife's affair. But Prince Charles's public confession of his long love affair with Camilla proved to be the straw which broke the camel's back.

'That previous weekend, Camilla and Andrew had

privately confided to a handful of friends that the divorce announcement was imminent. We got the call, checked it out and had it confirmed 100 per cent from impeccable sources. We decided to run with the story'

The following morning, the *Sun*'s front-page headline said it all – CAMILLA DIVORCE.

It was a story which sent shockwaves through the country. Within hours of the *Sun* hitting the news stands, the Parker Bowleses released a statement through their lawyers confirming the split.

As one friend of the couple said: 'It was a real bombshell. Everyone expected they would stay together. Andrew had put up with Camilla's affair for so many years; no-one could understand why things would so suddenly change.'

What had changed was that Andrew Parker Bowles was hopping mad.

A friend says: 'When Prince Charles went on television and told the world about the affair and then repeated it in his book, it marked the breaking point for Andrew. Quite simply, he was fed-up to the back teeth with "the whole bloody mess" as he called it.

'Andrew decided to stop living a lie. He was sick of the constant jibes, he was fed-up with his privacy being constantly invaded. He decided "enough was enough".'

The joint statement from the couple via their lawyers was brief and to the point:

> 'The decision to seek an end to our marriage was taken jointly and is a private matter. But, as we have no expectation that our privacy will be respected, we issue this statement in the hope that it will ensure that our family and friends are saved from harassment.

'Most especially, we ask that our children, who remain our principal concern and responsibility, be left alone to pursue their studies at what is clearly a difficult time for them.

'Throughout our marriage we have always tended to follow rather different interests, but in recent years we have led completely separate lives. We have grown apart to such an extent that, with the exception of our children and a lasting friendship, there is little of common interest between us, and we have therefore decided to seek divorce.'

The story made headlines around the world for it had far-reaching implications for the monarchy itself. With Camilla free to marry, was it conceivable that Charles would now divorce Diana and wed the true love of his life?

In time, that question would become irrelevant.

For his part, Andrew Parker Bowles said simply: 'I cannot go on living someone else's life. It's time to move on.'

Prince Charles was told of the divorce announcement while he was enjoying a skiing holiday in the Swiss Alps. Naturally, the call was made by Camilla.

A close source said: 'Of course Camilla told him in advance, she tells him everything as he tells her everything. The Prince was concerned for Camilla and her family but he greeted the news as no surprise. He just gave her his full and unequivocal support, as always.'

Andrew Parker Bowles had given some indication of his dissatisfaction with his life a few weeks before the divorce announcement, when he spoke to reporters on his retirement from the army after thirty-seven years' service.

Asked how he was feeling, he replied glumly: 'Things can only get better, can't they?'

A friend says: 'Andrew just got to the point where he wanted to make a fresh start. He retired from the army still a relatively young man and he wanted the freedom to enjoy his retirement out of the constant glare of publicity surrounding Camilla's affair with Charles. He wants to be able to see people and live life without the constant spectre of Charles and Camilla hanging over his head. The truth of the matter was that he became sick and tired of the constant stories in the press. Every time a fresh scandal broke, he was thrust into the spotlight against his will.

'Another factor was that the Parker Bowleses' son Tom was now twenty and away at university. Their daughter Laura was sixteen and at boarding school. The children were old enough to deal with the split.'

Yet another factor cited by Andrew's closest friends was the retired brigadier's growing friendship with divorced mother-of-three Rosemary Pitman, fifty-four.

The friend added: 'He felt the time was right on all counts to end the sham marriage to Camilla.'

The divorce announcement took Princess Diana completely by surprise.

A source close to Diana says: 'The first she knew about it was when she turned on the television and saw the Sun's front page emblazoned all over the screen.

To be honest, it just confirmed her belief that she was being frozen out of the Royal Family. Prince Charles had obviously known about the impending announcement for days, but, yet again, Diana was purposely kept in the dark.

'Diana greeted the announcement with nothing more than a wry smile. She had known about Camilla for too long by then to feel any resentment or jealousy towards her.

'But Camilla's divorce did make Diana more determined to thrash out her own divorce settlement properly. The one thing Diana was adamant about was that Camilla will not become some kind of stepmother figure to her sons.

In fact, Diana once cancelled a planned trip by William and Harry to Sandringham to see their father because she knew Camilla was there.'

According to courtiers close to the Queen, the monarch gave Charles her approval to continue seeing Camilla.

One said: 'Of course Charles told his mother about Camilla's divorce in advance. The Queen's attitude was pretty much "I approve of your relationship; always have done, always will."

'Nothing has changed the Queen's opinion of Camilla. She still adores her. The fact that Camilla is a divorcee made no difference to the Queen. She still respects and admires Camilla enormously for the way she has handled herself through all the ups and downs of the past few years. Camilla has never spoken out, never breached royal protocol. The Queen admires her strength of character enormously.'

In fact, as more details of Camilla's divorce became public, it was clear she and Andrew had been living a lie for at least the last three years of their marriage.

On 19 January the couple were absent from a dingy courtroom in London's Somerset House as their decree nisi was granted. The £40 decree took just three minutes to be granted. According to court documents filed by the couple, Andrew Parker Bowles admitted spending just ninety nights at the family home in Corsham, Wiltshire in the previous three years.

In typical style, Andrew played the gentleman to the end – allowing Camilla to be the petitioner in the divorce and citing 'irretrievable differences' for the split, *not* his wife's admitted adultery.

In her written statement to the judge, Camilla said: 'The respondent and I, although both having our place of residence as Middlewick House, have led separate lives through the said period. By February 1992, at the latest, it had become clear to both of us that the marriage was finished.'

According to friends of Camilla, Charles called her within hours of the divorce decree becoming official.

One said: 'Even though Camilla had accepted her husband's wish for a divorce, it was still an immensely sad day for her. Despite all that had gone before, she remained enormously close to her husband. After twenty-one years of marriage, of course she felt immense sadness.

'She needed the support of her Prince even more on that difficult day – and she had it. The Prince called her several times that day to give her his full support.

'That's the strength of Camilla and Charles: they have always been there for each other. Camilla's divorce was no different.

'In fact, Camilla coped well with the pressures of the divorce. She remained her usual self. She has a fantastic capacity to keep her sense of humour through even the darkest of days. Her close circle of friends rallied round and remained loyal and protective.

'And, of course, the relationship between Camilla and Charles did not alter one jot after the announcement.

'They will be great friends until the day they die. The divorce made no difference whatsoever to their relationship.'

Another friend revealed how, while Camilla and her husband admitted publicly living apart for three years, they had not shared a bed for at least a decade.

The friend said: 'Basically, the Prince didn't want to

share his mistress with anyone, not even her husband.

'Andrew was never allowed back into the marital four-poster bed after Charles and Camilla's affair resumed shortly after the birth of Prince Harry.

'When he did sleep at home, he stayed in the spartan spare bedroom down the corridor from Camilla.

'Andrew put up with it for lots of reasons, but mostly because of his loyalty to the Crown. He would have petitioned for divorce sooner, but Prince Charles felt an earlier divorce would have damaged the monarchy.

'So Andrew agreed to continue with the lie for as long as he could stomach it.

'The marriage rumbled along for years, but it was hollow. They were going nowhere. When Andrew started asking himself what the future held, he realized there was no future with Camilla – so he decided to end it.'

Six weeks and one day after the decree nisi was granted, Andrew and Camilla's decree absolute became final. For the first time in nearly a quarter of a century, Camilla was finally free to be with the one great love of her life.

Yet, ironically while she knew they would never be apart, she also knew they would never be allowed to be truly together.

Free At Last

It was the watershed which, finally, allowed the truth to be told.

Once Camilla's divorce became final, the full details of her torrid relationship with her Prince began to emerge. Many of those who had remained steadfastly loyal and silent throughout the long years of rumour and speculation felt free to paint a truer portrait of the astonishing lengths Camilla and her princely lover would go to in order to enjoy their secret trysts.

One of the first to break his silence was Prince Charles's own valet, Ken Stronach.

Stronach, who had been one of the Prince's most loyal and trusted servants for fifteen years, told how his master would make love to Camilla in the bushes of his Highgrove mansion while Diana slept upstairs.

In an interview with the *News of the World*, Stronach, a fifty-year-old ex-Marine who had become one of the

Prince's closest confidants, revealed that Charles was so besotted by Camilla that he has kept a framed photograph of her on his bedside table for years.

The picture, published across the pages of the newspaper, showed a smiling Camilla sitting on a bench outside the Queen Mother's Scottish estate, Birkhall, with Prince William in the background romping with his father's Jack Russell terrier.

A family friend says: 'That picture was extraordinary. What it showed was that the Queen Mother has given her full approval for Camilla and Charles to be together. Her attitude is "What is good for Charles is good for the family."

'Everybody has known the true situation between Charles and Camilla for years and they have all accepted it.

'Now that Camilla is divorced, there is no reason for them to hide.'

Trusted valet Stronach revealed how one of his most secret duties was to scrub grass stains off Charles's pyjamas after his master's late-night romps with Camilla in the grounds of his country home.

Stronach said: 'There was mud and muck everywhere. They'd obviously been doing it in the open air.'

Stronach said the open-air trysts between Charles and his mistress would take place when Diana spent the weekend at Highgrove.

The paper reported: 'The ritual followed a familiar pattern. When Diana was staying at Highgrove, Camilla knew she would not be welcome, so she and Charles had to meet in the huge gardens.'

Stronach claimed Camilla would often spend the night at the mansion when Diana was in London. She would be given a guest bedroom to stop the servants gossiping, but would sneak into Charles's bedroom in the middle of the night.

The late-night rendezvous posed an enormous security risk for the future King. His bedroom was wired up to an elaborate, high-tech security system which, when turned on, would alert the Prince's armed guards to any intruder in his room within seconds. But when he was expecting a visit from Camilla, the Prince would disarm the system.

Stronach said: 'It was a big risk, a stupid thing to do. But he's blind to everything where the lady is concerned.'

The valet would go to extraordinary lengths to keep the affair secret. Used pillows would be placed in Camilla's bed to make it appear she had spent the night there. When Charles sneaked out to visit Camilla at her house nearby, the valet would circle TV programmes in a television magazine to make it appear the Prince had spent a quiet night at home but, he added: 'It didn't fool anyone.'

Stronach said: 'We were told to treat Camilla as if she was mistress of the house. It was as if Princess Diana had never existed.'

The valet told of Diana taunting her husband from room to room around Highgrove. When Charles exploded: 'How dare you talk to me like that! Do you realize who I am?' the Princess allegedly retorted: 'You are a fucking animal.'

Charles, at the end of his tether, hurled a heavy boot jack at the wall as his wife walked out.

Stronach told the newspaper's royal reporter Clive Goodman that he had decided to speak out because of Charles's own public confession of the Camilla affair.

Stronach said: 'All through my time with him, we've all been told not to speak to anyone about anything. We all kept the secrets. Then he does a TV show and book telling the world what we spent years hiding. I feel let down.'

The Prince, who was with Stronach at Balmoral Castle in Scotland when the valet's account appeared, was 'outraged' by his servant's blatant disloyalty.

Stronach resigned from his £12,000-a-year post two weeks after his story appeared, admitting 'gross misconduct'.

Yet others close to the royal circle were willing to reveal even more details about the twenty-five-year romance between Charles and Camilla.

One source close to Camilla says: 'Now the affair is out in the open, the public have the right to know what has been going on.'

The insider told how Charles would visit Camilla up to *four* times a week.

The besotted Prince would arrive under cover of darkness at Camilla's country home for trysts lasting until dawn. On Sunday evenings, he would sometimes turn up just minutes after Andrew Parker Bowles had left to return to his job in London.

Staff at Camilla's home joked that Charles had such a familiar routine, they could 'set their watches' by him.

One said: 'He'd arrive on Sundays as regular as clockwork. Often he came on Thursdays and sometimes on Wednesdays and Tuesdays too.'

Charles went to Camilla's home nearly every Sunday for five years between 1989 and 1994. Each time, he would arrive after night had fallen. The source added: 'In the summer he would turn up between 9pm and 10pm and in the winter as early as 7pm.

'Charles was known as the Prince of Darkness because he never turned up in broad daylight.'

Charles would park his estate car at the back of the

house next to Camilla's own green Subaru. The Prince and Camilla would sit at the kitchen table to enjoy a cosy supper of chicken salad followed by strawberries and cream from Sainsbury's supermarket.

Then, glasses of wine in hand, they would slip up to Camilla's bedroom. There, they would enjoy passionate clinches for hours in a magnificent four-poster bed, bathed by the glow of candles.

Just before day began to break, Charles would emerge from Camilla's bedroom and the royal estate car would glide slowly and quietly down the drive.

The source said: 'After Charles had been, there were often two empty wine glasses left on the table beside Camilla's bed.

'There would also be half-melted candles standing around the room. Whenever Charles was due to pay a visit, the household would know. Camilla virtually advertised it by blacking out the house.

'Normally it is a blaze of light until late at night. But when Charles was due, she would switch off all the outside security lights, close the shutters downstairs and draw all the curtains.

'It was a standing joke among the staff, who used to call it "the blackout".

'An hour later, Charles would turn up in a car. In the morning there would be two plates in the kitchen with the remains of their supper. The only time Camilla ever made a meal was for Charles. She didn't even make her own breakfast.'

Staff were amazed at the lengths Camilla would go to in order to keep dates with her lover.

A friend of the Parker Bowleses said: 'I remember in the summer of 1989 Camilla was meant to join Andrew for a London party for his senior officer.

'It was a privilege to be invited and Andrew was very excited. But just a few hours before the dinner, Camilla phoned Andrew to say she had been struck down by 'flu and was too ill to attend.

'Andrew was livid. He told me he ordered her to ring the officer's wife herself to make her own bloody excuses.'

The reason for the ''flu attack' was that Camilla had already made secret plans to meet Charles that night.

An insider said: 'Camilla had complained all day she had 'flu. She had shivers and shakes and her voice was a whisper. That afternoon, she took to her bed, insisting she should be left on her own.

'But a few hours later, Charles's car was seen coming up the drive.

'On another occasion, during Ascot week in 1990, Camilla's mother was taken ill. She was rushed to the hospital. Camilla's sister had been calling the house frantically all day trying to get hold of her.

'When Camilla came home at 6pm, hot and flushed from her day at the races, the staff told her the bad news. Camilla called her sister back immediately and spoke to her about the family crisis. But when she walked back to the kitchen, she was amazingly cool and composed. She announced she was not going to drive to Suffolk to see her mother because there was little she could do at that late hour.

'A few hours later, Charles turned up. Then it all became clear. She had delayed her visit to see him.

'I remember another time when she and Andrew were due to stay overnight with friends at Newmarket in Suffolk. Andrew was travelling up from London and Camilla was due to catch the train from Wiltshire. But she never made it.

'That afternoon, she called Andrew in London and told

him she had a mystery virus. She was coughing and spluttering all over the place and he agreed to go alone.

'Camilla took to her bed once more. Everyone felt sorry for her and then, at around 9pm, Prince Charles's car arrived once more.

'Next morning, two dirty dishes were lying on the kitchen table with two empty wine glasses. No attempt at all had been made to clean up or cover her tracks.'

And another friend said: 'Despite the affair, Andrew Parker Bowles tried to be cordial towards the Prince. There was one time when Camilla hosted a lavish dinner party at home in March 1991 to which the Prince was invited. The seating arrangements were amazing. Camilla was next to Charles at one end of the table while at the other end of this long table was her husband.

'Throughout the meal, Andrew and Charles appeared on civil terms. But all the staff are pretty sure Andrew knew exactly what was going on. He was just too much of a gentleman to say anything.'

And a local poacher once spotted Charles and Camilla enjoying an intimate supper on the darkened terrace of her home.

He said: 'It was like something straight out of a love film. Camilla looked absolutely stunning. The candlelight flickered on her face and she looked years younger than normal.

'I couldn't believe it. I was out hunting for rabbits and I ended up catching the future King red-handed with his mistress.

'The house was in darkness and the only light came from the candle on the table. They were chatting and laughing and I saw Camilla lean towards him. I thought they were going to kiss, but instead she must have told him a joke because I heard him laughing out loud.

'The Prince was dressed very casually. He looked very relaxed. It was clear they were both head over heels in love with each other – even to me.'

And another source close to Camilla said: 'They would love to walk in the night through the garden. They would walk so close together that their shoulders touched.

'It was the way young lovers walk together. They were oblivious to everything around them. Camilla sometimes pointed to the plants and Charles would lean down to inspect them. They looked like any other couple in love – without a care in the world.'

On nights when Charles was to visit, Camilla would spend hours getting the house – and herself – ready.

A friend said: 'Camilla would fuss around for ages making sure the house was perfect and then she would have a long soak in the bath. She would take ages to get ready for him. Camilla has this public image of being dumpy and dowdy but she really made the effort to dress up for her Prince.

'She has good, shapely legs and loved to show them off to Charles. She would spend the day flopping around in a pair of scruffy jeans, but when Charles was due, she would transform herself.

'There were two outfits the Prince particularly liked. One was a little black dress. It had a scooped neckline and ended about an inch above Camilla's knees. The other favourite was very striking. It was a figure-hugging, military-red number. It showed off her tiny waist and lovely bottom to perfection. It was a calf-length dress with a kind of sexy come-hither slit at the side.

'Camilla always wore flat shoes when she was with Charles. He's quite a short fellow, around 5ft 8in. She's around the same height and she didn't want to tower over him.'

Charles became so open about his visits to Camilla's home that he often waved to locals as he sped by in his car.

One elderly villager said: 'I remember him going past me in his big estate car and raising his hand with a smile. I was so shocked I nearly fell off my bike!'

The only time Charles kept away from Camilla's house was when Camilla's children Tom and Laura were home during the school holidays.

A family friend said: 'He never showed his face during the school breaks.

'We referred to that time as "the closed season".'

Another friend revealed how Camilla only lost her temper once when the *Sun* newspaper revealed how Diana had nicknamed her 'The Rottweiler'.

'She was boiling mad and furious as hell,' said the pal. She was screaming abuse at Diana. She raced into the kitchen and grabbed the paper from the cook's hands. She looked at the headline and stomped out.'

A wealthy friend added: 'She called me up that day. She could barely get the words out fast enough. I'd never heard Camilla so outraged. She felt powerless and helpless. There was no way she could strike back at Diana. She couldn't call up the newspaper and make a fuss. It would have been an admission of the affair. She was outraged but unable to hit back.'

Another friend from Camilla's inner circle revealed: 'Camilla was always secretly obsessed by Diana. She would read every word ever written about the Princess. She would scour the newspapers and magazines looking for stories about Diana. When one newspaper compared her unfavourably to Diana, Camilla cancelled it instantly.

'She cancelled another paper after one of Prince Charles's visits. A detective had been sitting in the playroom as usual waiting for Charles and Camilla to finish their business upstairs. He flicked through one of the papers and left it open at an article that was horrible about Camilla.

'She found it when she popped into the playroom to get a video. She was livid and said she wouldn't have the paper in the house again.'

Camilla's obsession with her rival was so great she even began to wear identical outfits to Diana.

Another source said: 'I once saw Camilla in the garden with Charles. She was wearing a bright red sweater and black-and-white checked skirt. A few days before, I had seen a newspaper with a picture of Diana in it wearing the identical outfit.

'Camilla loathed Diana but she admired her style.

'There was another occasion, only recently, when the papers revealed Diana had been making crank calls to her married art-dealer friend.

'One of the guests having dinner at Camilla's house defended Di, saying she would never have made the calls.

'Camilla immediately leaned forward and said: "Don't be so ridiculous. That's *exactly* the kind of woman she is. She drove that poor man's wife out of her mind!"

'Of course, Camilla had been getting weird calls for years.

'The whole table went silent for a few seconds.

'Camilla realized she had gone too far because she tried to make a joke of it by saying:
"Sorry to snap, it must be my rottweiler teeth!"

Friends of Charles also revealed the depths of the affair.

Just days after Camilla's divorce was announced, one said: 'I feel like I can tell the truth now because there's nothing for anyone to lose any more.

'I know Charles called Camilla every day. I heard it

from the horse's mouth, so to speak. He is so dependent on her, he can't get through the day without ringing her at least once. He still continues to call her daily even now.

'Most days, he calls her first thing in the morning and last thing at night.'

And another insider said: 'Charles would call Camilla's house constantly. If one of the staff picked up the phone he would never refer to Camilla by name, he would simply say something like "Is she there?" in an apologetic tone.

'The staff would go off to find her, but no-one was supposed to mention Charles by name.'

Charles even rang up Camilla when he was celebrating his tenth wedding anniversary to Diana in July 1991.

The insider said: 'Camilla was about to sit down to dinner with her husband. When a staff member told the Prince she was sitting with her husband at the table, he said: "Oh really, don't disturb her, I'll call back."

'Out of mischief, the worker offered to take a message, but he said: "No, no, that won't be necessary." He was very hasty but then his manner changed and he said more calmly: "Don't worry, I'll call back later."

'Sure enough, he did. Camilla went off to her private room to take his call.'

When she was not with her lover, Camilla would ease her loneliness by burying herself in romantic novels. She would spend hours curled up on the sofa devouring her favourite books by Catherine Cookson, endless cigarettes burning in an ashtray beside her.

A frequent visitor to her house said: 'Camilla rarely lifted a finger to help the staff keep her house in order until Charles was expected. Most of the time she would just lounge around reading these novels. They helped pass the time and ease her heartache while she was waiting for the Prince to show up.

CAMILLA AND CHARLES – THE LOVE STORY

For most of Charles's and Camilla's close circle, her divorce marked another chapter in one of the most incredible love stories of all time.

One says: 'What is so amazing, and at the same time so ultimately tragic, is that this affair has cost everyone so dear.

'It had cost Charles his marriage, his reputation and almost the monarchy itself.

'It had cost Diana her happiness and, ultimately, led her to embark on the affair with Dodi Fayed that would cost her her life.

'It had cost Andrew Parker Bowles his marriage.

'And it has cost Camilla everything. She lost her marriage, her freedom, her private life. She has been ridiculed and been forced to endure more negative publicity than a woman should have to.

'Yet what shines through it all, even now, is that Charles and Camilla have been prepared to give up everything to sustain the relationship they have.

'The power of the love they share cannot be measured. It has survived the test of time; it has survived all the press attention; it has survived through all the heartache and pain.

'Whatever people think about the rights and wrongs of the situation, no-one can deny the bond of love Charles and Camilla share.

'Love is the one thing which sustains both of them. It gives them the strength to cope with whatever heartache and agony life throws at them.

'When it comes down to it, both of them have realized that this incredible passion they feel for each other will never die.

'Someone said to me the other day that they hope, one day, people will look back on Charles and Camilla and say: "Gosh, they really did love each other, didn't they?"

'I like to think of it that way. Because, after all is said and done, that is the truth – and that is the ultimate tragedy.'

Diana the Outsider

For the 'mistress of media manipulation', as Charles's circle had come to call Diana, it was a master stroke. Still smarting from his public comments to Jonathan Dimbleby which confirmed his affair with Camilla, Diana secretly began planning her own, very public, televised response. Telling no one at the palace, she furtively met with BBC reporter Martin Bashir. Using compact cameras smuggled into Kensington Palace, Bashir taped a devastating *Panorama* interview with Diana that aired in November 1995.

Diana claimed her responses were all 'unprompted' and 'from the heart'. In fact, a close associate of the Princess now claims she received a list of questions in advance. The female friend says: 'Do you honestly think she would have gone in front of the cameras without knowing what was coming? Nothing was left to chance. Diana knew the questions in advance and she rehearsed her responses in front of a mirror. She even practised with several types of make-up to choose the combination which made her look the most fragile and vulnerable.'

Dressed demurely, her face made-up discreetly apart from heavily-lined eyes and white face powder, it was Diana at her most devastating. Millions of television viewers – including Charles and Camilla – sat in stunned silence as she spoke openly of the Palace campaign to portray her as a psychologically damaged loony. She confirmed her affair with James Hewitt, whispering 'Yes, I adored him. Yes, I was in love with him. But I was very let down.' When asked if she thought she would ever be Queen, she faltered and said she would like to be known as 'the queen of people's hearts.'

Diana poured out her hatred and venom for Charles. She pronounced that she was unsure whether Charles would ever be King. Of their failed relationship, she said: 'Well, there were three of us in that marriage, so it was a bit crowded' – a direct swipe at Camilla's role in the break-up.

Her attack on Charles continued: 'Friends of my husband's side were indicating that I was unstable, sick and should be put in a home of sort. I was almost an embarrassment.'

When asked her thoughts about a divorce, Diana replied clearly: 'I don't want a divorce but obviously we need clarity.' She talked of her 'deep, deep, profound sadness. Because we had struggled to keep it [the marriage] going but obviously we'd run out of steam. I come from a divorced background and I didn't want to go into that one again.'

For the Queen, the charade of trying to keep the 'fairytale marriage' going was over. She immediately wrote two letters; one to Charles, the other to Diana, expressing her frustration and spelling out her 'desire that you both make plans for an early divorce.' It was not a request – but an order.

A friend who spoke to Camilla shortly after Charles read her his mother's one-page letter said: 'Camilla had almost a sense of relief that someone had finally made a move to end the lie. She told me it was a 'very loving letter from a mother to a son – but with steely undertones.'

The Princess was at her lowest ebb. Details of her latest 'fling', with rugby player Will Carling, were all over the newspapers. She began taking sleeping pills. She felt hounded by the ever-present paparazzi. Prince William, then just 13 and at Eton, told his mother during a tearful phone call: 'Why did you have to make that awful show?'

Diana issued a statement: 'The Princess of Wales has agreed to Prince Charles's request for a divorce. The Princess will continue to be involved in all decisions relating to the children and will remain at Kensington Palace, with offices in St James's Palace. The Princess of Wales will retain the title and be known as Diana, Princess of Wales.'

The divorce negotiations began in earnest. Diana had a tense 30-minute meeting with the Queen in which the central issue was whether Diana would retain her HRH title. The Queen and Prince Phillip were adamant that the woman who had done more to rock the Royal Family to its foundations that anyone in history, would not. Diana fled the meeting in tears.

She heard from her husband – via letter. The three-paragraph missive told Diana he would agree to the early divorce. Diana later said: 'It was cold and unemotional. Just like Charles.'

On 28 August 1996, the divorce was finalised. Diana remained at Kensington Palace and received a lump sum cash settlement of £17 million and £400,000 a year to maintain her offices. She was stripped of the title Her Royal Highness. That meant Diana's name no longer appeared in Court Circular announcements, and she was no longer a bone fide member of 'the Firm'. The outsider was now firmly outside the camp.

Defiant, she struggled to forge a new identity. She met with Prime Minister Tony Blair to discuss taking a permanent 'ambassador' role for Britain; she selected just a handful of charities to concentrate her attentions on. She became a prominent and outspoken campaigner to focus public attention on the devastation caused by landmines. She enjoyed a 'deep and profound' relationship with Pakistani heart surgeon Hasnat Khan, whom she had first met just 11 weeks before the *Panorama* interview. A friend said: 'Diana was shattered by the divorce. It was what she had always tried to avoid. When it happened, she was torn apart. But by then, she was also a stronger woman. She knew that in order to thrive, she had to survive and carve out a new niche for herself. She started slowly rebuilding her life.'

For Charles and Camilla, the divorce also marked a watershed.

'Finally,' said Charles: 'we can start to plan for the future.'

New Faces

It was to be a 'fresh start in a fresh place'. For Camilla, the turmoil of her own divorce and the screaming headlines over Charles's marital crisis, had left her exhausted. She would later describe the period between the two divorces as 'the most turbulent of my life'.

In May 1995, Camilla moved out of her marital home, Middlewick House, which was sold to Pink Floyd drummer Nick Mason for £1.3 million. She and Andrew split the proceeds evenly down the middle. Her new home, a place even today she calls 'my sanctuary', was £850,000 Ray Mill House, a Regency mansion set in 17 rolling acres of Wiltshire countryside only 16 miles from Highgrove, Charles's country home.

Ray Mill House, in the village of Lacock, near Chippenham, Wiltshire, was perfect for Camilla, with stabling for her beloved hunters, a secluded garden and a private drive to keep out the uninvited. Art historian

Worthy Gilson and his wife Gill sold their home of 20 years to Camilla. Mr Gilson said: 'We are delighted that Mrs Parker Bowles and her family have chosen Ray Mill House as their new home. We were determined that it should go to someone who knows and cares about animals and has an appreciation of the countryside. We wish her the same peace and happiness we have enjoyed here.'

Camilla's horses were 'boarded' at Prince Charles's estate during her move. Charles also helped her with moving costs, even 'donating' a priceless antique Louis XIV chair to her as a house-warming gift. He also gave her a silver photo frame containing a black-and-white photograph of her father. The night Camilla finally took residence at Ray Mill House, her lover was her first visitor. The two celebrated with 'monster' gin and tonics and later sat out under the stars talking about their future – on two simple wooden deckchairs.

The move to a new home marked the most important transition in Camilla's life – from loyal, but unhappy, wife and mother to her new role as a single, independent woman; a woman stepping more and more publicly – and comfortably – into her role as mistress to the future king.

A friend said: 'Once her divorce was final and once Charles was "free", they settled into an easy domesticity. Weekends were sacrosanct. They spent every weekend together. For the first time, Camilla and Charles were both single and free to be "open" in their relationship'.

Well, open to a degree. The couple could still not be seen openly together, but careful steps were taken to 'introduce' Camilla gradually to the public. In September 1995, she stepped out of the shadows to pose for photographers at a party to raise finds for the National Osteoporosis Society, the brittle bone disease which claimed the life of her 74-year-old mother Rosalind in

1994. Her grandmother was also a sufferer. Camilla accepted the job of Patron of the Society.

Charles then announced he would 'officially host' Camilla's fiftieth birthday party, a black-tie event at Highgrove for 150 of their closest friends, on 17 July 1997. Guests would include Camilla's father, Major Bruce Shand, and, rather bizarrely, her former husband Andrew and his new wife Rosemary. In fact, Andrew and Camilla enjoyed what she would tell friends was 'the best divorce ever'. Amicable and civil for the sake of their children, there were no regrets or recriminations. Camilla told a friend just a few months ago: 'Andrew was always my best friend, apart from Charles. When we split, it was heartbreaking, but we decided to do it with dignity. He is still one of the few people I trust implicitly and whom I know I can turn to, no matter what. I am happy he has found contentment in his private life. I just wish I could find peace in mine.'

At the time of the birthday party, Andrew Parker Bowles told Sarah Oliver of the *Mail on Sunday*: 'Camilla is adamant she has no desire to become Queen and will refuse it at any cost. She knows that might prevent her marrying the Prince but she is willing to forgo a wedding to avoid having to take the title and the throne.'

Within the couple's close circle, concerns were growing that Charles was trying to 'force' Camilla into a public role too soon. Charles Benson, Camilla's lifelong racing friend, told Oliver: 'I know for a fact that there are those among their closest friends who feel they are being used as part of a pro-Camilla propaganda campaign and, because of that, some of them have turned down invitations to the party.'

Meanwhile, Prime Minister Tony Blair, on the advice of Charles's 'spin doctors' at the Palace, began drawing up plans of what should happen, in the eventuality that the future King should choose to marry his divorced lover. In July 1997, the Prime Minister's private secretary, Alex Allan, prepared a detailed memo outlining the constitutional ramifications of Charles taking Camilla as his Queen.

It was the most significant development in the couple's three-decade relationship to date. For the first time, a government official was directly involved in preparing a 'battle plan' should the Prince of Wales decided that his 'non-negotiable' relationship with Camilla would, inevitably, lead to the altar. Prime Minister Blair took a 'huge personal interest' in the plan. He had several private meetings with Charles in which the two men talked candidly of the political – and constitutional – crisis any remarriage would provoke.

Allan's document – the contents of which are revealed for the first time – ruled out any heirs of Camilla and Charles from succeeding to the throne; a remote possibility anyway, given the couple's ages. The document put forward the idea of a civil marriage for Charles, but without Camilla becoming Princess of Wales. Instead, she would become his 'consort' and would be referred to as such, rather than the title of Queen. The marriage would be blessed by the church but Charles would have to renounce his position as the head of the Church of England.

The pieces were being put into place. Charles, for the first time in years, was feeling confident and at ease. He was gradually being allowed to have Camilla, the one true love of his life, play a more active part in his life. She became a regular visitor to his apartment at St James's. She was the chatelaine of Highgrove. Within their inner circle, Camilla was already Charles's *de facto* 'wife'. Diana was still a problem, but even her venom was subsiding.

Charles told a close aide: 'I honestly feel upbeat and positive about the future for the first time. This is the closest to stability I have felt. For the first time in my life, I am beginning to believe I can have it all; I can be at peace.'

How prophetic and poignant his words were to be. Within weeks, the monarchy was to be plunged into its greatest crisis ever. Charles and Camilla were to see their relationship 'regress to the dark ages' and Britain was to enter a period of turmoil unparalleled in modern times.

For Diana, the summer of 1997 was also a period of transition. She was a woman adrift and alone. Her surgeon lover Hasnat Khan had accused her of leaking details of their relationship to the press. Tearfully, she had ended their affair. In early July, she received a call from Mohamed Al Fayed, the controversial owner of Harrods. He invited Diana and her sons to spend a holiday aboard his private yacht in St Tropez. Diana, desperate for a break with her boys and fully aware of the orchestrated Camilla and Charles campaign in London, jumped at the chance. She told her good friend Annabel Goldsmith: 'What do I have to lose?'

The subsequent furore over Diana's holiday photographs caused headlines around the world.

En route to Al Fayed's holiday home in the South of France, a relaxed Diana took time to poke fun at her chubby Egyptian host, pointing to the vulgar upholstery on Al Fayed's private Gulfstream IV jet, Diana giggled to her good friend and travelling companion Rosa Monckton: 'Look at this, isn't it awful?'

Al Fayed, a controversial figure who had been repeatedly denied British citizenship because of business and political deals, was in heaven. To him, having Diana and her sons as summer guests was 'a poke in the eye to the establishment'. He was determined to introduce the lonely and vulnerable Princess to his eldest son Dodi, a playboy with a reputation for loving – and leaving – women, and who was also alleged to fuel a persistent cocaine habit. Dodi, who dabbled as a producer in Hollywood, was best known in Los Angeles for his love of the high life, fast women and his ability to 'trash' expensive rented houses.

While many have speculated on the precise nature of the relationship between Dodi and Diana, her closest friends, even today, insist it was nothing more than a summer fling. On the holiday with her sons, Diana was a woman lapping up the sun – and the attention. A friend said: 'She had finally found someone with the money to provide for her lifestyle. Al Fayed was amusing and he was rich. Dodi was handsome and fun. This was not a major romance, this was a summer affair with Diana having fun and sticking two fingers up at Charles and Camilla who were orchestrating Camilla's first forays into society back home in England. For Diana, the summer with the Al Fayeds was nothing more than a fun, frivolous escape. Mohamed Al Fayed had the money she thought would protect her. How wrong that would prove to be.'

Diana cavorted happily for the assembled press in a sexy leopard-skin swimsuit. At one point, she jumped into a speedboat and raced across to a boat containing British photographers. When she asked 'how long' the incessant press attention would last, one royal correspondent on board began berating her. A witness said: 'It was almost embarrassing. He tore her off a strip for leading us on and wanting everything her own way. It was the worst tongue-lashing I'd ever heard a member of the press give her. Diana had tears in her eyes.'

As she sped off, Diana said: 'You're all going to get a big surprise with the next thing I do.'

Diana's 'holiday' had the desired effect. Camilla's birthday party was all but overshadowed by her frolics on the French Riviera. By this time, Dodi Fayed and his fiancée, a beautiful but hardly intellectual model called Kelly Fisher, were also on the scene.

Dodi 'harboured' his fiancée on one boat. Diana and the rest of his family were on another. The playboy Egyptian whizzed between the two, cheating on both women with the other. A tearful Kelly Fisher would later tell me: 'I had no idea Diana was there. I thought Dodi was going to see his father. I couldn't understand why he didn't want me to come with him. But he kept reassuring me it was because he wanted to discuss 'family stuff' with his dad. I had no idea he was seeing – and making love – to Diana at the same time he was making love to me. He made love to me without using protection. I often wondered if he did the same with her. He was reckless. And he was a liar. He broke my heart and I fully believe he would have broken hers.'

For Diana and Dodi, in the throes of a summer fling, life had never seemed sweeter. After their first holiday, Diana flew to Milan for a star-studded memorial service for the designer Gianni Versace who had been gunned down by psychopath Andrew Cunanan on the steps of his Miami mansion. She went immediately from the service to Paris for a romantic weekend with Dodi at the Ritz – the hotel owned by his father. The following day, Dodi escorted Diana to the villa of the exiled Duke and Duchess of Windsor on the outskirts of Paris. Dodi's father had bought the villa on the death of the Duchess in 1986. As they walked around the opulent rooms, where Wallis Simpson had played 'queen in exile' to the abdicated king,

Diana became overcome with emotion. At one point she stopped, with tears in her eyes, and said: 'I always thought I would be Queen, but now I will have to live my life in exile. I am the most famous woman in the world and yet I feel so lonely. I have never had a "home".'

Mohamed Al Fayed would later claim he offered the Windsor house to Dodi and Diana. Of the suggestion that Diana would have one day married Dodi, one of her friends says simply: 'Preposterous. She was having a fling with him. You have to understand she was at a very delicate place in her life. She had just gone through a divorce she did not want, she knew Charles was entertaining Camilla at Highgrove and Diana was in a state. She wanted the world to think she was madly in love with Dodi, but that was not love. She was still missing Hasnat Khan and, to a certain degree, she was still missing Charles. The ultimate irony is that Diana never stopped loving Charles. People talk about the loves in her life, and there were several, but he was the true love. She always thought – right to the end – that one day they would be together again.'

Later that week, Diana said 'goodbye' to her sons, who were to go hunting with their father at Balmoral, and returned to Al Fayed's yacht, *Jonikal*, sailing from Nice to Sardinia.

While Dodi's ex-fiancée now bitterly described him as 'less than adequate' and 'pathetic' in bed, Diana seemed content. She told one girlfriend their lovemaking sessions were 'the best I have ever had'.

Blurry photographs of Diana and Dodi kissing – taken by a photographer who had been 'tipped off' by the Princess – caused a frenzy around the world. The woman who had repeatedly complained about press intrusion was fanning the flames. The couple lounged side-by-side on the deck. Diana allowed Dodi to push back her wet hair.

For Charles and Camilla back in Balmoral watching the unfurling headlines day after day, the situation was untenable. A friend of Camilla's said: 'Charles was dumbfounded. His main reaction was 'Why him?' He was genuinely perplexed. And he was embarrassed for the boys. He banned the tabloids from Balmoral. He didn't want William and Harry seeing their mother cavorting with her slightly dodgy playboy lover all over the front pages.'

Diana returned to London but was anxious to return to her new love. She told one friend: 'He is so passionate. He makes me feel alive.' On 21 August, Diana and Dodi flew to Nice. The couple played aboard the *Jonikal*, and Dodi picked up a £125,000 diamond ring from the Monaco jeweller's Alberto Repossi, later wrongly called an engagement ring. In fact, said Kelly Fisher, his one-time fiancée: 'He gave all his women jewels. I don't think Diana was anything that special to him. He was having that relationship for his father. Dodi was in love with me; I will never stop believing that. But how can anyone compete with the Princess of Wales?'

When Fisher tried to contact her one-time fiancé, Dodi's father intercepted the calls. The tearful model told me: 'He screamed abuse at me. He said terrible things. This was a man who, at one stage, was going to be my future father-in-law. But he changed beyond all recognition once Dodi and Diana got together. I think more than anything Mohamed wanted them to get married. It would have been his ultimate revenge against the British Establishment that he felt had always snubbed him and treated him badly. But it was just not meant to be.'

On 30 August, Diana and Dodi flew to Paris. That afternoon, Diana talked to one of her closest girlfriends, Annabel Goldsmith, telling her: 'Don't worry. I'm having a wonderful time, but the last thing I need is a new marriage. I need it like a bad rash on my face.'

Speaking to another friend, the respected royal reporter Richard Kay at the *Daily Mail*, she said: 'I have decided I am going to radically change my life. I am going to complete my obligations to my charities and to the anti-personnel landmine cause, but in November I want to completely withdraw from formal public life.'

Like Diana, Charles and Camilla were contemplating the future. Charles was genuinely concerned for his wife's wellbeing. A senior courtier said: 'When he saw her frolicking with Dodi on the yacht, he was worried. Diana had refused all official protection from the Palace. The Prince of Wales voiced his concern about her safety and wellbeing to more than one person during that time. But he didn't want any more rows. They had reached a kind of impasse in their relationship. For the first time in years, Diana was not obsessing about Camilla. Charles was preparing to talk to her when she got back to England. He wanted to speak to her about getting at least one protection officer alongside her. He just had this 'feeling' about the Al Fayeds and the world she was getting involved with.'

That night, Dodi and Diana had dinner in a private suite at the Ritz Hotel in Paris.

Charles would never have the chance to speak to his ex-wife again.

A Tragic End

When the call came, it was abrupt – and unbelievable. Asleep in Balmoral at 1.00am in the morning, Prince Charles, a notoriously heavy sleeper, fumbled for the receiver after several rings. On the other end of the line was the familiar voice of Robin Janvrin, the Queen's deputy private secretary. But the normally unflappable Janvrin was fighting to control the obvious fear and anguish in his voice: 'Sir, there has been a serious car accident in Paris. Dodi is dead and the Princess of Wales has been injured.'

Charles immediately sat bolt upright. He grilled Janvrin about the few details that he knew: 'Is Diana OK?' implored the Prince.

'We believe so, Sir,' came the reply: 'We really do not know.'

Shaken with disbelief, Charles immediately called Camilla who was fast asleep at home in Wiltshire. For the rest of the night, the pair spoke every few minutes. At first, the news reports seemed good – Diana was suffering from broken bones, but was otherwise all right. One erroneous agency report even claimed she had walked unharmed away from the wreck of the Mercedes. Finally, when news came through at 3.30am British time that Diana had died of her injuries, the Prince sobbed openly on the phone to his lover, crying: 'Why, why, why?'

Camilla's first reaction, she later told a friend, was: 'Poor William and Harry. What are we going to tell them?' The couple spoke for three hours until, finally, at 6.45am, Charles walked into William's room and gently shook his son and heir awake to tell him the terrible news. The two, clutching each other, then walked into Harry's room and broke the news to him. The three hugged each other and sobbed.

Later, along with the rest of the world, the Prince would learn how drunken Ritz chauffeur Henri Paul, a depressive with a history of alcoholism and drug dependency, stepped behind the wheel of a jet-black Mercedes S280 and drove Diana and Dodi to their deaths in a Paris underpass. Bodyguard Trevor Rees-Jones, employed by Dodi's father Mohamed Al Fayed, was the only passenger wearing his seatbelt. He sustained horrific injuries – but survived.

At 12.20am on the morning of 31 August 1997, the Mercedes approached the Alma Tunnel in Paris at a speed witnesses later estimated at 110 mph. Driver Henri Paul, his reflexes numbed by drinks he had consumed in the Ritz hotel bar while waiting for his famous passengers, clipped the thirteenth pillar of the bridge. The car spun round a full 180 degrees and slammed into the tunnel wall.

Dodi and Henri Paul died instantly. Diana, whose gold

earring was ripped off and was later found embedded in the dashboard due to the force of the crash, was found facing backwards on the floor between the back and front seats. Externally, she showed little sign of injury. Internally, she was bleeding to death. A witness at the scene, motorcyclist Eric Petel, would later recall: 'Her eyelids were fluttering but she didn't open her eyes. I asked her if she was OK and she didn't answer me.'

In fact, Diana never said another word. While Dodi's father later claimed she had whispered some final words about her boys to a nurse at La Pitié-Salpêtrière hospital, that was simply not true.

Charles accompanied Diana's two sisters to France to collect her body. He asked to see Diana alone. He emerged from the hospital room, where Diana was lying in a dress borrowed from the wife of the British ambassador to France, red-eyed and shaking. He would later tell Camilla that seeing Diana's lifeless body 'was the worst sight I have ever had to bear witness to. I could only think of the girl I had first met, not the woman she became and not the problems we had been through. I wept for her – and I wept for our boys.'

The worldwide outpouring of grief for the woman Prime Minister Tony Blair dubbed 'the People's Princess' was immediate – and profound. While the Royal Family remained at Balmoral, mourners gathered in their thousands to lay flowers outside Diana's home, Kensington Palace. On the morning of her death, Diana's sons, ex-husband and former in-laws sat stoically through a morning service in Scotland at which Diana's name was not even mentioned – on the advice of the Queen. She would later argue privately that she thought it 'better for the boys'.

The Queen's refusal to fly the flag above Buckingham

Palace (she used the excuse that the flag is only flown when the monarch is in residence) caused a national outcry.

Behind the scenes, with the ultimate of ironies, it was Charles – with the constant support and advice of Camilla – who argued that Diana should be given a 'fitting' funeral. The Queen and Prince Phillip were adamant that the woman who had caused so much harm to the Royal Family in life should not be restored to royal status in death. The Queen's outward lack of emotion caused near rebellion among her subjects. The tabloid press was unanimous in their daily tirade against the Royals. The *Sun* asked: 'Where is our Queen? Where is her flag?' Eventually, when she returned to London, the Queen *did* fly the flag – at full mast.

Three days after Diana's death, Charles had an angry meeting with his mother. He demanded Diana be buried with full honours in a State funeral. He also implored her to make a public statement immediately. A courtier said: 'Charles has been criticized in the past with not being in tune with the nation. But in this case, he understood. The country, and the world, was in deep shock. It would only have taken a tiny spark to cause revolution on the streets. The people were disgusted by the Queen's lack of obvious grief and they demanded more. Charles realised this and he implored her to go on television to make a public statement, which she did.'

In a broadcast watched by 26 million of her subjects, the Queen said: 'I want to pay tribute to Diana. She was an exceptional and gifted human being. In good times and bad, she never lost her capacity to smile and laugh, to inspire others with her warmth and kindness. I admired and respected her for her energy and commitment to others, especially for her devotion to her two boys. No one who knew Diana will ever forget her. Millions of others who never met her, but felt they knew her, will remember her.'

Afterwards, the teetotal Queen allowed herself a stiff sherry. The woman who had almost destroyed her family was now gone for ever, but the repercussions were monumental. For the first time, senior courtiers were admitting that 'the Firm' had got it badly wrong. One said: 'The Queen just did not realise the depth of feeling the people had for Diana. It was almost like mass hysteria on the streets in the days after she died. Her Majesty was reluctant to get involved but even she realised she had to say something. It was a remarkable performance. She could not stand Diana towards the end.'

Charles was consumed by what one friend described as 'a haunting sense of guilt'. The friend added: 'He was in deep shock. His main concern was for the children. They were at such a vulnerable age to lose their mother. Not for the first time, he felt guilt. Charles is a very sensitive man and even though Diana was rebuilding her life, he kept asking himself whether, if he had handled things differently, she might not have ended up in the arms of a playboy, a decision which ultimately led to her death.'

Another courtier who was close to Charles during the dark days after Diana's death said: 'He spent many, many hours just walking alone in the garden. He was very tearful. He barely ate or slept. His grief was genuine. Many people say Charles never loved Diana, but anyone who saw him then would have been in no doubt. This was a man in deep grief for a woman he truly cared deeply about.'

Charles's 'other woman' stayed away. While the two spoke constantly, Camilla remained out of sight in Wiltshire. She offered her lover advice, love and support as she had so many times in the past, but privately, she feared for her own safety.

A friend now says: 'In those first few days after the Diana tragedy, Camilla was genuinely concerned about her safety. The mood of the country was turning uglier by the day and Camilla was seen by many as the cause of Diana's deepest misery. Camilla actually increased her security and there were police officers from the local constabulary on guard at her mansion every night.'

There were also members of the royal protection squad. A source says: 'Charles was aware of the possible danger to Camilla. At least two royal protection officers were dispatched to her home. Camilla was getting hate mail and death threats. It was a very frightening time.'

For Charles, a man his sons adoringly call 'Papa', it was William and Harry who came first, above even his one true love, in the dark days after the Paris crash. He spent hour after hour counselling his sons, talking to them about their mother and going through family albums packed with photographs of happier times. When they wept, he hugged them. When they asked questions about Diana, he answered them in the most honest way possible. Alone at night, in his own room, he would weep down the phone to Camilla. A friend would later say: 'He was torn apart. He felt alone. He felt desperately guilty. He felt bereft. He felt scared. Yet again, Camilla was the one person in the world he could truly confide in. She was there when he needed her most.'

At Diana's funeral, Charles, William, Harry, Prince Phillip and Diana's brother Earl Spencer, marched behind the funeral cortége as it wound its way through the streets of London towards Westminster Abbey. As they passed Buckingham Palace, the Queen, stony faced, bowed her head. It was the first time in living memory anyone could recall the monarch bowing. Diana was no longer even a royal, having been stripped of her HRH title. The gesture was not lost on anyone. Queen Elizabeth was, finally, showing her respect to a woman who, in death, was still a profound threat.

Diana was buried on an island where she had played as a child at the family home, Althorp. To this day, Charles has yet to visit her unmarked grave. Her sons have visited occasionally. For Charles, paying pilgrimage to a place in the ground is meaningless. He said recently: 'I think about Diana often and she is ever-present in the lives of myself and the boys. I would prefer to focus on the good times and the future. I do not wish to dwell on the past.'

For Diana's brother, the snub is an ongoing attack against his sister. In July 2001, speaking on BBC Radio 5 Live, he blasted Prince Charles saying he had 'an open invitation' to visit the grave – but had yet to do so. The Earl said angrily: 'It's an ex-wife from his point of view, so maybe that's how he views it. He recently said he wished to draw a line under the whole episode and let Diana rest in peace and maybe he views not going there as part of that process.'

Public Approval

With a nation, and two young boys, raw with grief over Diana's death, Charles and Camilla were forced back into the shadows. While their relationship never faltered – indeed, the Princess's death served only to bring them closer, in public at least – the couple were never seen together. 'It could not be,' Camilla told a family member, 'they would never have forgiven us.'

As soon as Diana died, Charles immediately cancelled plans to accompany Camilla to a ball in aid of the National Osteoporosis Society in September 1997. She would later explain: 'There was simply no way we could be seen together. The grieving process for Diana had to run its natural course.'

In private, however, Diana's death allowed Charles and Camilla to begin living as husband and wife. By March 1998, Richard Kay in the *Daily Mail* was reporting that Camilla was staying at St James's Palace as often as three times a week – though always when William and Harry were away at school. They continued to meet at Highgrove most weekends, except on those weekends when Charles stayed in London to be with his sons.

The press was fed small snippets of information about the ongoing relationship. 'Charles has vowed never to marry Camilla, they just wish to lead a "normal" life in private,' was one line which regularly emerged from St James's Palace in the months after Diana's demise. 'Charles is devoted to his sons, Camilla is very much in the background,' was another. In fact, nothing could be further from the truth.

With Diana off the world stage, Charles began looking to the future, a future he then believed – and still does – will see him walking through life with the woman he loves.

The most pivotal person in the 'rehabilitation of Camilla' was to be Mark Bolland, a former director of the Press Complaints Commission who became Charles's first ever 'spin doctor'.

While Bolland was given the official title of deputy private secretary, his role was more clear – to devise a plan to bring Camilla Parker Bowles out of the shadows and to make the most hated woman in Britain an acceptable consort for the future king.

Charles's loyal private secretary Richard Aylard was let go in 1996. Senior aide Stephen Lamport replaced him, together with Elizabeth Buchanan, Charles's assistant private secretary and Colleen Harris, his press secretary. 'Operation PB', as it was known behind the walls of St James's Palace, was mapped out.

A senior aide said: 'The master plan was to gradually ingratiate Camilla into the public consciousness. Charles has always said his relationship with Camilla is 'non-negotiable'. Even after Diana's death, his feelings did not waver. There was considerable pressure from certain quarters at the Palace after the Princess died for Charles to go public and renounce Mrs Parker Bowles. But when the subject was broached, he went nuts. He literally shouted out loud that it was not going to happen. Regardless of everything that has been said about them, they are devoted to each other and times of crises serve only to make them stronger.'

Operation PB, as devised by Bolland and Lamport, was simple, but brilliant. The ultimate goal was to make Charles more popular and Camilla more acceptable to the public, with the ultimate aim of getting the public to approve the couple's final goal – to marry.

Through his role at The Press Complaints Commission, Bolland knew every major Fleet Street editor and was on good terms with most. He began to give regular 'briefings' to the editors of Fleet Street's notoriously tough tabloids. One editor now admits: 'It was the first time someone in Charles's camp had taken the initiative. Diana always knew the power of the press and would often call up favourite journalists like Richard Kay of the *Mail* herself. She knew how to 'spin' her side of the story. But Buckingham Palace had always resisted that approach. The Queen's advisers might talk to the *Telegraph* or the *Times*, but that was about as far as they would sink. What made Bolland unique, and very clever, was that he became friends with the editors of the *Sun* and the *Mirror*; he regularly briefed the middle-market editors of the *Mail* and the *Mail on Sunday*. He understood where the true power lay and who was really setting the agenda. And he favoured those editors who carried weight in terms of circulation and reaching the most amount of people. Mark Bolland is brilliantly astute. He did a fantastic job of rehabilitating Camilla. Within 18 months of Diana's crash,

Charles and Camilla were being talked about as a couple – and there were very few objections.'

At first, Operation PB was low key. When a member of Camilla's staff was fired for leaking information to the press, the official statement came from Charles's office at St James's – a tiny, but significant public step towards showing Camilla to be very much part of Charles's life.

She began sitting in on his all-important twice-yearly 'diary meetings', the forward-planning strategy meetings which map out the Prince's daily schedule for the next six months. At first, Camilla sat quietly in the corner while Charles and his aides weighed up the pros and cons of the thousands of invitations he receives. But, slowly, she began taking a more active role, encouraging him to accept causes close to both their hearts – and to decline invitations which would take him away from both her and his boys for too long a period.

An aide said: 'Camilla gained a lot of respect at the Palace. Many people were naturally leery of her at first. But she behaved with great grace and dignity and it was obvious that Charles placed great stead in her opinion and that she put his welfare first. She really impressed us all. You have to remember, Diana and Charles were always at war. That caused great tension and problems for their staff. To say we fell in love with Camilla is probably too strong a term. But we all certainly grew to admire and respect her. She is a very smart and likeable woman.'

In July 1998, it was carefully 'leaked' that Camilla had, for the first time, met Prince William. According to the breathless reports in the press, William 'popped home' to St James's unexpectedly for a change of clothes en route to a cinema trip with friends to London – only to find his father's mistress also in residence. When Charles gave his son the option *not* to meet Camilla, William declined. The three were said to have enjoyed a 'convivial' meeting for 30 minutes during which they had 'a cordial and general discussion about all manner of things'. Afterwards, a relieved Camilla is said to have demanded 'a stiff vodka and tonic'. The stories further claimed that William and Camilla went on to enjoy another meeting – tea alone together – and yet a third liaison at a lunch organised by Charles where William sat opposite his father's lover.

The story was carefully planted to show the public that William had no objection to his father living with his mistress less than a year after Diana's death. A spokesman for the Prince of Wales confirmed: 'Yes, Prince William and Mrs Parker Bowles have met. Meetings between the children and Mrs Parker Bowles are a private family matter which we are not prepared to discuss and we wish, for their sakes, the media would leave this very personal matter alone.'

In fact, the story was not totally accurate. William *had* met Camilla before, at Highgrove, at least two years prior to the St James's meeting. The first meeting between the future King and his father's mistress took place in the garden of Highgrove during a family picnic. In fact, Charles has a photograph of William and Camilla, taken at Highgrove, by his bed in St James's Palace. An aide says: 'The idea that William only met Camilla as late as 1998 is preposterous. He knew of Camilla's existence way before then. When Charles and Diana were splitting up, Diana talked to him about Camilla, and so did Charles. William is a bright boy and he met Camilla on several occasions before the public was 'officially' informed of their meeting. The leak was carefully planned to show the public that Diana's eldest son approved of the union. And if he did, who were they to object? Of course, William and Camilla had met before. It is ridiculous to suggest otherwise.'

Camilla's first 'big' public test came in November 1998 when she hosted Charles's official fiftieth birthday party at Highgrove – with his two sons as honoured guests. Camilla's ex-husband Andrew and their two children, Tom and Laura, were also guests of honour at the top table. A few days' earlier, she had taken her first faltering steps into the spotlight at a smaller function to start the Prince's birthday celebrations at Hampton Court. While Camilla did not side beside her lover, Charles publicly acknowledged her presence saying: 'We have killed a lot of birds with one stone tonight.' There was one grand gesture which only became apparent afterwards. The stunning necklace worn by Camilla that night was given to her by Charles – and had once belonged to her great-grandmother, Alice Keppel, the mistress of Edward VII.

After years of hiding their love from the world, the couple finally 'came out' at Charles's lavish birthday bash and danced cheek to cheek in an unprecedented display of intimacy. Though the cameras were not allowed inside the event, waiting press captured images of Camilla arriving at Highgrove, looking to the entire world like the radiant hostess. No expense was spared. Camilla hired a New Orleans jazz band to pay Charles's favourite music. A grubby William was photographed arriving from an Eton school army cadet outing. He later changed into a lounge suit.

With Camilla watching proudly, it was William who gave the birthday toast to his father – a brief speech which, indeed, he had practised with Camilla in a back room shortly after he had arrived at the party.

The 342 guests included several members of the Royal Family – Princess Margaret, the Duke and Duchess of Kent, the Duke and Duchess of Gloucester and Princess Michael of Kent. Foreign dignitaries included King Juan

Carlos and Queen Sofia of Spain, King Harald of Norway and ex-King Constantine of Greece.

To all, Camilla was every inch the 'perfect hostess', resplendent in a deep-green velvet dress with a blue jacket over it and a stunning aquamarine and diamond necklace around her neck, a family heirloom. Her normally windswept hair was coiffed and groomed, styled by Mayfair hairdresser Jo Hansford. She was totally at ease alongside the crowned heads of Europe and the nobility of Britain. Charles rarely left her side all evening. The two were seated together at the top table. As they greeted guests entering Highgrove's main function room, the Orchard Room, Camilla stood alongside her lover, shaking each person's hand. After the party, the Duchess of Kent admitted: 'Prince Charles and Camilla were very happy together. It was an absolutely stunning evening. The food was wonderful and everyone had a marvellous time.'

The Prince had asked every guest to give him a plant as a birthday gift. The soft scent of roses filled the air. Camilla's gift to her lover – presented in the garden two hours before the first guest arrived – was a specially commissioned sculpture. The Highgrove staff gave him a new greenhouse.

The four-course banquet was prepared by celebrity chef Anton Mosimann with smoked salmon from the Queen's Scottish estates, followed by lamb from the Duchy of Cornwall with organic vegetables from the gardens of Highgrove. Vegetarians were offered a special vegetarian dish, a favourite of the Prince. The evening ended with a lavish chocolate birthday cake being wheeled in with everyone standing to serenade the Prince in a rousing chorus of 'Happy Birthday'. In full view of the cheering crowd, Prince Charles put his arms around Camilla and gave her a kiss. As a 'birthday surprise', Camilla arranged for impressionist Rory Bremner, a favourite of both, to perform a series of skits including his devastating impersonation of Charles.

The only sour note of the evening was the absence of the Queen, but she had made it clear to her son that she could not be seen at a party with Camilla. The Queen held a smaller lunch party for him at Buckingham Palace. Prince Phillip also refused to attend, telling one aide: 'I will not and cannot endorse a relationship which I do not approve of.'

Charles and Camilla took one spin on the dance floor before leaving the disco to their children. Prince William and Harry danced alongside Laura and Tom Parker Bowles and Lady Gabriella Windsor, Prince Michael of Kent's stunning 19-year-old daughter. As the rest of the guests left beaming at 2.00am, there was one who noticeably did not. Camilla spent the night at Highgrove. It was yet another public sign that she was very much the Prince's consort.

The next phase of Operation PB took place just two months later, in January 1999. While Camilla and Charles had enjoyed 'a quiet Christmas' together, they still had to overcome a significant barrier – to be photographed together 'officially' for the first time. Over the years, the only photograph of the two in he same frame was the famous, unposed shot of the two as youngsters standing by a tree on a damp polo field in 1975. It was time for them to appear side-by-side in public.

The scene lasted just seconds, but the build-up had been felt around the world for days. The occasion was the birthday party of Camilla's sister Annabel Elliot, at the Ritz Hotel in London where Alice Keppel had lived during her affair with King Edward VII over a century earlier.

The Palace 'discreetly' let it be known that the Prince and Camilla would agree to be photographed leaving the event together. For days, photographers from around the world camped out on the hotel's doorstep. Police cordoned off streets around the event and held back the media scrum. The couple arrived at the party separately, both giving big smiles for the hysterical cameramen. Camilla, wearing a black dress and a jewelled necklace, a present from ex-husband Andrew Parker Bowles, drove up with her two children. The Prince arrived a full two hours later on foot.

Inside, one witness said Charles 'seemed at ease, if slightly nervous. He had a stiff whisky right before he prepared to leave.' At exactly midnight, Charles, slightly ahead of Camilla, walked out, gently touching her arm in support, and steered her towards a waiting limousine.

It was the biggest royal photo opportunity in years, comparable to the engagement of Charles and Diana. The picture went around the world. One public relations' expert put the value of the picture, in terms of positive press for Charles and Camilla, at over £1 million pounds. After years of furtively hiding from the cameras, the endless game of cat and mouse was over. Charles and Camilla were 'out'.

Once Operation PB was fully underway, it seemed there was no stopping the Prince's desire to be seen out and about with his love. A senior aide said: 'After so many years of subterfuge, it was such a relief for both of them just to be able to do 'normal' things without constantly looking over their shoulders.'

In April, the pair went to the Lyric Theatre in London together to watch the musical comedy *Animal Crackers*.

Arriving together, Camilla was clapped by onlookers as she walked into the theatre a few steps ahead of the Prince. They later went to a Royal Shakespeare Company performance of *A Midsummer's Night's Dream* and to a recital at the Royal Festival Hall. 'Life,' said Camilla later: 'started to feel normal at long last.'

Meanwhile the couple's children were growing increasingly close. William and Tom and Laura became regulars at the Chelsea restaurant Foxtrot Oscar and spent regular weekends together at Highgrove with Camilla and Charles. William viewed Tom as 'an older brother figure', confiding in him about everything from his plans for university to his first romances. A friend of Tom's said: 'The fact that the children get on so well has been a huge boon to their parents. It would have been much more difficult for Charles and Camilla if they had not. Both of them are rather proud that their children have hit it off so well. Tom is a great source of fun for William because he is so unstuffy.' And, some might say, reckless.

In May 1999 Tom Parker Bowles was caught offering to supply cocaine to an undercover reporter at the Cannes Film Festival. Tom was reported as saying: 'Do you want some charlie [cocaine]? I've got my own.' The revelation that Tom had snorted cocaine 'devastated' Camilla. Tom was immediately ordered home. After a heart-to-heart with his mother, he agreed to stop taking drugs immediately. Tom later gave up his PR job and started his own upmarket internet company. A friend of Camilla's said: 'Charles was supportive throughout the whole saga. Tom has cleaned up his act now and is still close to William. There was never any suggestion that he would be kept out of the royal circle. But Charles did sit William down for a serious talk about drugs. So many young people, especially those within the circles William moves in while in London, have experimented with the drug. William is a sensible lad, but the temptations are obviously all around him. Charles is exceptionally close to William. He trusts him not to let him down.'

An official statement from St James's Palace said: 'Prince Charles and Mrs Parker Bowles are primarily concerned with the welfare of all the children – William, Harry, Tom and Laura. They are all part of the extended family. An open mind is kept about all methods of support and all routes of help that are available.'

An unnamed friend of Tom Parker Bowles was quoted extensively in the British press saying: 'Tom's life has been on a roller-coaster ever since his mum and Prince Charles went public. He gets all of the hassle of being a royal, but none of the perks.'

Tara Palmer-Tomkinson, another member of Charles's circle, whose mother Patti was injured in the Klosters ski accident which also nearly claimed Charles's life, became another high-profile drug 'casualty' when she checked into an American drug rehab clinic to battle a cocaine addiction. She was later banned from spending her traditional summer cruise with William and Harry because Charles feared 'she might not be the best role model for them'.

Lord Frederick Windsor, the son of Prince and Princess Michael of Kent, was another member of Wills's circle to get into trouble with drugs. In the summer of 2001, he received treatment for an unspecified drug problem at a European clinic.

A source close to Camilla said: 'Naturally, as parents, both Charles and Camilla are concerned about the prevalence of drugs in the society their children are mixing in. This is when it is not about rank or title, but about being a mother and a father. Camilla has never tried to be a surrogate mother to William and Harry, but they do adore her and they have a shared history that goes back years. Both boys respect and love Camilla and their relationship has grown much stronger in the past couple of years. William very often has lunch alone with Camilla when they are both at Highgrove. They are very comfortable in each other's company. He calls her simply "Camilla". There was never any question she wanted to be called 'mother'. That was, and always will be, Diana's title.'

By the second anniversary of Diana's death in the summer of 1999, Camilla and Charles were regularly out and about, to the point where each new outing was relegated to just a few short paragraphs in the newspapers, rather than the blaring banner headlines of the earlier outings.

On one occasion, the couple drove to Birmingham in the Prince's green Bentley for a dinner to mark the retirement of a mutual friend, a hunt master. Unfortunately, the Prince's chauffeur Tim Williams fell sick and forgot to fill the car with enough petrol. At 1.30am, the trio was forced to stop at a motorway service station to fill the car. A witness said: 'The driver clearly looked peaky, so the Prince offered to take over at the wheel. It was quite a sight. Prince Charles behind the wheel, with Camilla beside him and the poor chauffeur in the back. It was one of those sights you just won't ever forget. It was like a comedy show sketch.'

While Camilla was still not officially 'recognised' by the Royal Family, she began attending 'Court' events. She played hostess at a dinner when Charles entertained a selection of Lord Lieutenants from England and Wales. She was later by his side at an official dinner for the Royal Shakespeare Company.

Even the Queen began mellowing in her initial disapproval of any plans for Camilla and Charles to 'come out.' An aide said: 'The Queen has always liked Camilla as a person, but she was adamantly against Camilla and Charles going public. But as Operation PB got underway, and was a resounding success, and there was no obvious backlash from the public, the Queen began to come around more and more to the idea of Charles and Camilla as a couple. She is a deeply religious woman and she prefers the idea of Charles making the relationship above board rather than sneaking around with his mistress. And she wants her grandsons to be happy. Their approval of Camilla weighed heavily in Camilla's favour with the Queen.'

The 'make-over' of Camilla continued apace. The woman whose flyaway hair and shabby country attire led to ridicule in the past, now began stocking her wardrobe with designer clothes. Prince Charles gave her a £25,000 'clothing allowance' which went on creations by favoured designers like Valentino and Amanda Wakeley. Her appearance was 'softened' with newly highlighted hair and regular facials undertaken by a beautician – again paid for by the Prince – at her home. She even had make-up lessons to show her how to put on a stylish 'face' for her increasing camera exposure. A friend of Camilla's who saw her for the first time in months in September 1999 said: 'I was stunned by the transformation in her. She was always a natural beauty in her youth, but she had allowed herself to slip during her marriage. Camilla has never been a vain person and she always seemed happiest wearing scruffy clothes covered in dog and horse hair. But once she and Charles started to go public, she really made an effort to shape up her appearance. She lost more than a stone in weight, and started learning about make-up and fashion.'

Camilla also became a regular 'lady who lunches' in London, popping into favourite restaurants like The Ivy, Wilton's and Mosimann's. She and Lady Carina Frost, the wife of broadcaster David Frost, were often seen lunching with Camilla's sister Annabel and her ex-husband's new wife, Rosemary.

The next stage of Operation PB was even more daring. Camilla joined Charles officially inside Buckingham Palace as he hosted a 'thank you' dinner party for 80 wealthy Americans who had helped raise millions for the Prince's favourite charities. While Palace aides informed me that Camilla was at the dinner as a 'friend' of Charles, rather than an official partner, it was yet another significant step forward. The dinner was recorded in the *Court Circular*, the official record of Court activities, although Camilla's name was not mentioned. But the Queen had clearly given her approval to Camilla sitting by the Prince's side *inside* her own home – a clear signal to the world that she no longer objected to Charles's illicit relationship. Charles even poked fun at the occasion, telling the assembled guests that his mother 'is not in residence tonight', adding cheekily: 'When the cat's away, the mice will play.' The couple returned to spend the night together at St James's Palace.

In August 1999, Camilla and her children joined Charles, William and Harry for their first 'family' holiday together, a cruise on the Aegean Sea. Intriguingly, it was William who suggested Camilla and her family be invited. A friend said: 'Charles was making plans for the annual summer cruise and William said, "Is Camilla coming?" Charles was genuinely taken aback by the question because Camilla and he had not even discussed it. He asked Wills: 'Do you think that is a good idea?' and William replied: 'Of course. She should come."'

Camilla and her family arrived at the yacht, the *Alexander* – owned by Greek tycoon John Latsis – a day before the royal party after leaving Britain on a private jet paid for by Charles. 'They wanted to avoid any big press scenes at the airport,' an aide said later.

Other friends on the cruise included Charles and Patti Palmer-Tomkinson and Princess Alexandra and her husband Sir Angus Ogilvy. Prince William invited his own friends, including Mark Dyer, who had accompanied him on a safari holiday, William Van Cutsem and a selection of young ladies, including Davina Duckworth-Chad, whose father Anthony was a former High Sheriff of Nottingham, and Laura Fellowes, the eldest daughter of Princess Diana's sister Lady Jane. The party spent a fortnight cruising through the Greek Islands.

When she returned, Camilla told her sister the holiday had been 'a terrific success'. Operation PB was about to launch its most daring plan yet – to introduce Camilla to America, a country that had taken Princess Diana to its heart. A senior aide said: 'If Camilla could conquer America, she could conquer anywhere. It was a risky plan. But it was a step both Charles and Camilla were anxious to take. In the words of the famous Sinatra song, if Camilla could make it there, she could make it anywhere. It was the next step along the road to introducing her to the world as Charles's partner in life.'

Acceptance

It had all the hallmarks of a royal tour. For weeks, Camilla and Charles had carefully gone over every detail of her trip to New York. The visit was only to last four days – but those four days were to be some of the most significant of Camilla's life. If she could woo the Americans, the people who had so warmly embraced Diana during her lifetime, it would be a massive step toward Prince Charles taking her as his bride. This was the city where Diana reigned supreme, from her first dazzling solo tour in 1989 to her last visit in June 1997, just weeks before her death.

From the start, Camilla's aides described the trip nonchalantly as 'a visit to see old friends'. But they fooled no one. The trip was paid for by Prince Charles, who used his own personal credit card to pay for Camilla's return Concorde flight. Two of his key advisers accompanied her. And Camilla sent regular 'reports' back to her lover waiting anxiously by the phone in Balmoral where he was on holiday with his grandmother, updating him of her progress on a special mobile phone hooked up to a scrambling device to prevent any repeat of the Camillagate fiasco.

She was accompanied by Mark Bolland, the master-mind of Operation PB and Charles's deputy private secretary and Michael Fawcett, Charles's former valet and a man who remains a major influence in his domestic circle. Bolland even flew out to New York three weeks before Camilla's arrival to 'recce' her trip. Said an aide: 'It was a royal tour in all but name. The same procedures as would be carried out for a real tour were carried out for Camilla. Her schedule was drawn up and overseen by St James's. Charles was involved every step of the way, down to approving the menu that would be served at various functions. It was a royal tour 'lite', if you will.'

Camilla's first stop – via a private jet from New York's Kennedy Airport – was the Hamptons, known as Manhattan's 'Millionaire's Row', an exclusive series of villages on Long Island where America's powerful, élite and downright filthy rich gather every summer to escape the stifling city heat. She was the guest of financier Scott Bessent, 38, a major supporter of the Prince's trust, at his beachfront mansion called Southern Dunes, in East Hampton. Bessent, a friend of Camilla's for two years since meeting her at a Prince's Trust function at Highgrove described his summer house guest as 'delightful'. The wealthy bachelor laid his private jet and helicopter at Camilla's disposal. It was the helicopter that took Camilla back into Manhattan the following day for a whirlwind tour of several New York galleries, under the watchful eye of heiress and philanthropist Eileen Guggenheim.

In the city, Camilla based herself at the £600-a-night, five-star Carlyle Hotel on the Upper East Side. Ironically, it had been Princess Diana's favourite hotel in New York. She and Bolland took in a production of *Cabaret* at Studio 54, once a debauched nightclub and now a theatre, with the *New York Post* gushing: 'Camilla looked glorious. Nothing like the Rottweiler of the past.'

Lunch the following day took place at the Park Avenue penthouse of legendary New York socialite Brooke Astor, known as the 'queen' of New York. Among the guests who tucked into a meal of eggplant with pesto sauce and red mullet were Welsh actress Catherine Zeta-Jones and new husband Michael Douglas, publisher Mort Zuckerman, United Nations head Kofi Annan and financier Michael Bloomberg. High society's favourite fashion designer Oscar de la Renta, who helped Jackie Kennedy become a fashion icon, sat beside Camilla and, during their conversation, offered to make her 'a wardrobe fit for a princess'. The offer was politely accepted.

The influential American broadcaster Barbara Walters was another guest. Walters, who would regularly 'squire' Diana around New York, and was said to have been preparing to conduct a 'warts and all' interview with the Princess shortly before her death, has been campaigning hard for Camilla to allow herself to be interviewed. A Palace aide said: 'It is not a matter of "if" Camilla does and interview, but "when?" She will do something tied into the National Osteoporosis Society and she may even choose to break her silence with someone like Barbara Walters in America because US interviewers are much more respectful of royalty than the British media. Don't be at all surprised if Camilla does a TV interview. She will, but it won't be anything like Diana's *Panorama* breakdown. This will be controlled, and any personal questions will be carefully vetted in advance.'

Said a guest at the Astor luncheon: 'Camilla met the

movers and the shakers and the powerful. And she also met the high-society figures and some glamour from the world of showbusiness. She handled everyone with charm and aplomb. People were genuinely surprised by how poised she was. We were all expecting some horsey woman from the shires but instead we discovered a sophisticate, who, it must be said, has rather more brains than Diana did. Diana always had the ultimate glamour pull for the New York crowd. But everyone knows Camilla has been the real power behind the throne for years. She was afforded the respect her position requires. Hell, Americans just love the royals. And we don't mind a bit of scandal and intrigue. In fact, we love it!'

According to another guest, Mrs Astor, whose husband's father died on the Titanic, proposed a wry toast to Camilla, alluding to the memory of Alice Keppel saying: 'You have done very well by your great-grandmother.'

The writer Dominick Dunne was invited to a cocktail party with Camilla. He said: 'I would have liked to have met her properly, but I only caught a glimpse. She was surrounded the whole time.' Jeweller Kenneth Lane added: 'She and I chatted for ten minutes. Camilla's a very nice, normal, attractive Englishwoman. She smiles, giggles, laughs – all the things we like.'

As she flew home on Concorde – to a dinner meeting with her Prince – Camilla and Bolland allowed themselves a celebratory drink. The 'royal' tour of New York had been a resounding success. The only problem? Camilla, a notorious chain-smoker, would later complain: 'I could not smoke anywhere. I tried lighting up in the car between functions but even that was frowned on. I was desperate for a smoke.'

While Operation PB was ticking along very smoothly, it

was also racking up some serious bills for the Prince. While Camilla was not 'broke' by any means – she took half of the £1.3 million from the sale of her marital home – she could not afford even to begin to compete with her lover's purchasing power. With her hunters, the upkeep of her house and now the additional expense of clothing, travel and beauty required in her new role as Charles's quasi-official partner, it was clear that the Prince was helping her financially. Indeed, a Palace source confirms that Charles spends an average of £200,000 a year on his mistress. While Diana was independently wealthy in her own right even before her marriage, Camilla was not. She also lost a considerable amount of money as a Lloyds name when the insurance market collapsed.

Shortly after Diana's death, Charles presented Camilla with a £8,000 leased Vauxhall Omega and he pays the £45,000 salary for her chauffeur. He also spends approximately £75,000 a year on her holidays and airfare and £100,000 on her domestic staff and office. Camilla now has a permanent personal assistant as well as a woman who answers her mail. He also funds the livery and stabling costs for her hunter horses. He has even started picking up several clothes' bills for her as her public role becomes more high profile.

Said a senior aide: 'Charles is determined that Camilla's lack of an official royal position will not affect the manner in which she lives.'

Charles's office put the tab on the successful New York tour at £20,000. To them, it was 'money well spent'.

By the end of 1999, Operation PB was beginning to pay dividends. A poll in the *Daily Mail* showed Charles was winning acceptance for his mistress. Almost half the public polled said they believed Charles and Camilla should marry – a three-fold increase since the dark days after Diana's death, and six out of ten said a marriage to Camilla should not prevent Charles from becoming King. But 78 per cent of those questioned by the reputable MORI agency were still against the idea of Camilla taking the title of 'Queen'.

The Queen was also warming to the idea. During one of her weekly meetings with her son, she gently suggested thatperhaps 'the time is nearing when I should meet your friend'. An aide said: 'Deep down, the Queen knows Charles and Camilla have stood the test of time. I don't think she gives it all that much thought. But the truth is, the Queen does not like loose ends.'

In December 1999, Camilla flew to Edinburgh to be a guest of Charles at the royal palace of Holyrood House. But when he led guests outside to watch the traditional 'beating retreat' on the castle walls, Camilla remained inside the main parlour, watching from behind half-closed curtains. 'She did not want to be photographed with him at a royal palace,' said a source. 'The time was still not appropriate. The thing you have to realise is that Operation PB is carefully crafted and no one is in any rush. There is no rush any more. Charles and Camilla have their life and they are committed to one another. With Diana gone, every step is carefully considered. Neither of them is in any hurry to rush things.'

The couple celebrated the millennium privately, with close friends at Highgrove. They avoided all public events, preferring instead to greet the new century holding hands in the garden of the country estate they both now called 'home.'

Camilla would later reflect: 'After all we had been through, we wanted to be alone together. There was no one else who could possibly have understood the feelings we had that night.'

Weeks later, Camilla played hostess at Sandringham, in the picturesque fourteenth century church on the Queen's estate. While Her Majesty was again away – this time in Australia – she was fully aware of Camilla's presence, even leaving her a small gift and note as a welcoming present.

Finally, in June 2000, the Queen ended decades of silence and agreed to meet Camilla. The final chapter in the War of the Windsors had been closed.

The historic meeting took place at Highgrove where Charles and Camilla hosted a sixtieth birthday lunch party for ex-King Constantine of Greece, a favourite of the British royals and a cousin of Prince Philip. The meeting between the Queen and her son's mistress was a closely guarded secret right up until the moment it happened. Not even Prime Minister Tony Blair was informed until after the meeting had taken place.

The Queen's softening over her previous decision never to meet Camilla came as the result of careful campaigning from those close to her. Ex-King Constantine himself, a godfather to Prince William and a close confidant of the monarch, had begged her to consider 'putting the rift' behind her. Sir Angus Ogilvy had also implored the Queen to consider meeting Camilla at a family rather than a State function.

Charles was told of his mother's decision to relent in a phone call from her three nights before the lunchtime barbeque. He said simply: ' Thank you, Mummy.'

On the day itself, Camilla dressed down in a simple beige dress, no jewellery and little make-up. She was already enjoying champagne and canapés in the garden of Highgrove with an illustrious guest list including ten crowned heads of Europe, when the Queen made her entrance. She went first to the former King Constantine and kissed him on the side of the cheek. Then she walked slowly across to Charles and kissed him. Camilla, who was by her lover's side, looked down to the ground and bobbed a deep curtsey. Then, in full view of the assembled guests, the two women exchanged a few pleasantries. The Queen, smiling broadly, nodded approvingly at Camilla.

The exchange lasted just 40 seconds. But it marked the healing of a rift that had torn apart the lives of both women for three decades.

A witness said: 'They both appeared very comfortable and relaxed. The Prince looked extremely happy. The two women who mean most to him in his life were finally face to face. It was a historic day for him.'

The meeting was made even more poignant by the fact that it was witnessed by both William and Harry. As the Queen moved to walk away from Camilla, William immediately walked to her side and reached out his hand to her. Said the source: 'It was a small gesture but a very significant one. William was smiling. He knew how much the encounter had meant to both his father and Camilla. Of all the things that had happened, the Queen's approval was the one thing Charles cared most about. Meeting Camilla is still a long way off her giving approval for a remarriage. But it is the first step in the right direction. Historically, that meeting will go down as one of the most pivotal moments in the lives of Charles and Camilla.'

Constitutional expert Lord St John of Fawsley said of the *rapprochement*: 'Life is too short for quarrelling,' adding: 'It was essentially a private meeting but the Queen is very well aware of the significance which will be attached to it. It is a long step from that to concluding that a marriage will take place between Mrs Parker Bowles and the Prince.'

A close friend of Camilla's said: 'She was very

pleased that the ice was broken. She is relieved for the Prince because more than anyone she knows what distress the matter has caused him, from complete rage to deep depression.'

It was enough for Camilla to allow herself to enjoy a celebratory mood. Two weeks later, looking stunning in a shimmering pink chiffon gown, she accompanied Charles to a Prince's Foundation dinner wearing her 'Alice Keppel' jewels. Walking side by side on the red carpet, the pair arrived at the entrance together, smiling happily for photographers the whole way. When one shouted out for the Prince to stop and pose for 'a happy snap', he grinned, saying: 'My feet have a nervous twitch. I can't stop moving.'

In private, Camilla's friends announced a new nickname for her – 'Queenie'. It struck one, who had also been friends with Diana, as particularly sad: 'Diana was always known to those who loved her as 'Duch'. Now people were openly calling Camilla 'Queenie' and 'Queen Camilla' in private. The Prince thought it was a hoot. Despite all that had gone on, a few of us found it less than appropriate. Diana has only been gone a relatively short while. It seems extraordinary that Charles and his mistress have taken so many significant steps in so short a time.'

It makes an interesting footnote that while Charles is not known for travelling light – he takes his own bed linen, pillows and towels, and even his own toilet seat – the one item he always packs is a framed photograph of William and Harry in a sterling silver Tiffany's photo frame. The picture was a gift from Camilla one Christmas.

Their new-found freedom allowed Charles and Camilla to enjoy increasingly more frequent holidays together. In September 2000 they stayed in a luxurious villa on the

French Riviera owned by Iraqi-born billionaire Namir Kirdar. Villa Serenada, near Cap d'Antibes, was loaned to the couple for a week, complete with an army of 25 staff, a Rolls-Royce and a luxurious yacht to whisk Camilla and Charles in style up the French coast.

By the end of 2000, both Charles and Camilla were 'thrilled' with the success of Operation PB. None of the expected public backlash had occurred. While polls regularly pronounced that Camilla should not be Queen, her personal popularity continued to soar and the pollsters regularly reported that the majority of the populace believed she and Charles should be allowed to marry.

It was time for the most audacious twist in the tale – for Camilla to appear in public with Prince William, the new 'jewel' in the Royal Family crown. But this was no ordinary event or charity dinner. The pair would 'come out' in the bravest and most public arena possible – at the tenth anniversary of the Press Complaints Commission (PCC).

The PCC was formed with the co-operation of every major British newspaper as a voluntary industry watchdog. On dozens of occasions over the years, the newspapers had been chastised by the PCC for intruding into the privacy of the Royal Family and its affiliates. But now Camilla was to come face to face with the editors and writers who had been so harshly critical of her.

The setting was glorious. On a chill February night in 2001, to a blaze of camera flashbulbs, Camilla, Charles and William stepped into the 'lion's den' at an evening reception at London's Somerset House.

Charles and William arrived first, to be greeted by Commission Chairman Lord Wakeham. Fourteen minutes later, Camilla with her loyal sister Annabel by her side, walked in. All three made their separate rounds of the room, Camilla pausing briefly to say 'Hello' to Stuart Higgins, the former Editor of the *Sun* and a man who had been the benefactor of several of Diana's 'tip-offs' to the press with negative stories about her husband. William, restricting himself to small-talk about university and his gap-year plans, mingled happily with the 550-strong crowd, which also included Sir Richard Branson, a collection of television and film stars and every major Fleet Street editor, columnist and editorial writer.

William, who sipped a single glass of chilled Chablis, told one editor: 'I am delighted to be here. I'm here to thank the newspapers for not giving me a hard time when I was at Eton and during the first part of my gap year. I hope they're going to continue like that.'

Camilla, in a blue cocktail dress, was steered through the potential minefield by her sister and private secretary, Amanda MacManus. A witness said: 'She looked relaxed but nervous. But who wouldn't be? It was the most extraordinary sight – Camilla, Charles and William all working a room full of the toughest and most cynical hacks in the world. It was a bold masterstroke. It was like throwing the Christians to the lions. But everyone came out relatively unscathed. And Camilla scored major points for the way she handled herself. The story got maximum coverage which it had to do – the whole of the British press was under one roof. Well, everyone who mattered was.'

As he left, William, attending his first official engagement, said: 'It was brilliant.' As Camilla left, she was overheard saying to her sister: 'Thank God that's over.'

The following day, the 'mission was accomplished'. Many newspapers referred to the 'sense of family' which existed between William, his father and Camilla.

Veteran royal-watcher James Whitaker said: 'They pulled off a major coup. Charles and Camilla established themselves as a couple who will be growing old – together. And they did it in front of two critical judges – the unblinking eye of a voracious press and Prince William.'

Camilla had been introduced to those who mattered as Charles's official escort. Inside St James's Palace that night, the champagne corks popped.

It was time to step up the campaign.

In the spring and summer of 2001, Operation PB went into overdrive. Camilla was photographed at one of the Queen's official residences for the first time – at a business reception at Edinburgh's Holyrood House.Wearing a light blue low-cut evening gown by Princess Diana's favourite designer Amanda Wakeley, Camilla seemed 'totally' at ease as she stood by the side of a kilt-wearing Charles, even gently allowing her hand to brush his at one stage, in full view of the assembled throng.

The two spent an evening at a charity fundraiser in Buckinghamshire for Macmillan Cancer Relief. Camilla spent the evening chatting to supermodels Naomi Campbell, Kate Moss, Sophie Dahl and Mick Jagger's daughter Jade. It was all a long way from the damp hunting fields where the 'old' Camilla once felt so at home. A guest said: 'She looked relaxed. She fitted in well. She seemed to be having a fine old time.'

Critically, at one dinner in Scotland, Camilla was seated next to the Earl of Airlie, the former Lord Chamberlain and one of the Queen's most trusted advisers. While it seemed a small gesture to royal observers, it was a clear signal that the Queen was, finally, accepting her son's choice of partner. Said an aide: 'The Queen said she would never accept Camilla while the majority of the public disliked her. But the campaign to win the acceptance of Camilla with the world was brilliant. Even the Queen softened. She understood that Camilla and Charles were now an item, and always would be. She had started to signal her approval.'

Prince Philip, however, still remained at odds with his first-born, whom he considered 'weak' and 'wimpish.' The rift between Philip and his son became glaringly clear in May 2001 when a new book by author Graham Turner was published to coincide with Philip's eightieth birthday. The biography, written with the full co-operation of Philip's most trusted friends, depicted Charles as a royal 'lightweight' who was dismissed by Philip as 'precious, extravagant and lacking in dedication'.

The rift was worsened, if that could be possible, by the failure of Philip to invite Camilla to his birthday party at Windsor Castle. A senior Palace aide said: 'The relationship was like a block of ice. Things had been getting frostier between them for years, but then they reached the Ice Age. Charles was bitter and very angry. Philip had nothing but contempt for his son. It was the new War of the Windsors.'

Charles's younger brother Prince Edward and his disgraced wife Sophie Rhys-Jones had also entered the row. Sophie, who is close to Philip, was publicly humiliated when a *News of the World* reporter, posing as an Arab sheikh, tape-recorded her bragging about her royal connections. The 'Sophiegate Tapes', as they were called, led to Sophie resigning her position as the head of her own PR firm. Philip felt that the 'sting' had been despicable and stood by her side. The rift between Charles and Edward worsened in September 2001 when, unbelievably, a television crew from Edward's Ardent Productions 'stalked' Prince William during his first week at St

Andrew's University in Scotland. The ensuing row left Edward and Charles not speaking.

In the summer of 2001, a behind-the-scenes war of words raged between the rival camps. Prince Edward and his wife accused Charles of having his aides 'brief against us' in the press. Charles denied the allegations, accusing his brother of being 'paranoid'. The resulting furore led to the Palace introducing new rules about permissible business activities for members of the Royal Family.

Even the Queen could not help heal the rift between father and son. The aide added: 'Charles couldn't speak to his mother about his feelings for Philip. On family matters, she always deferred totally to her husband. But she must have been painfully aware of how bad things were. You could not even get them in the same castle, let alone the same room.'

For Charles, the relationship with his father was an 'unnecessary unpleasantness' in a life which was, finally, beginning to settle down. Camilla had been by his side, she had been welcomed as part of the family by her children. Yet there was still one public display of affection left to enjoy – their first kiss. And the world did not have long to wait.

It was one tiny kiss – but a giant message to all. When Prince Charles finally gave a public kiss to the woman he had been kissing privately for more than three decades, he was certain the world was watching.

For weeks, his advisers had been briefing the press that 'a significant moment' was about to occur. One editor said: 'We had no idea what it would be. But we knew it was a "biggie". The rumours just kept building and building. When it came, it was not an earth-shattering, knee-trembling moment of abandonment, but it was a huge public statement, the most daring move yet in the plan to make Charles and Camilla husband and wife.'

The 'Big K' as it came to be known at St James's Palace was carefully choreographed down to the last second. It was to be one of the final pieces of the jigsaw puzzle.

It was to take place on 26 June 2001, the fifteenth anniversary of the National Osteoporosis Society. The £10,000 event was personally organised by Camilla at London's Somerset House, the same venue where she, Charles and William had met the press several months earlier.

In the event, Charles planted two tender, natural kisses on Camilla's cheeks, a carefully planned show of affection that seemed as natural and as honest as it was planned. The kiss lasted just seconds, but the resulting pictures were worth their weight in gold.

The *Daily Mail* pronounced: AT LAST, A PUBLIC KISS FOR CAMILLA FROM HER PRINCE. Public relations guru Mark Borkowski lauded it as a coup, saying: 'No *faux pas*, no lip-to-lip contact, no salacious tonsil tennis, no high drama, no media circus, just a loyal inner circle witnessing a very publicly engineered private moment.' The kiss generated just a handful of anti-Camilla letters. The mood of the country was clearly changing. It was time for Operation PB to step up.

The Long Road Home

For Charles and Camilla, the kiss marked the first stepping stone on the long road home to final acceptance as a couple. In private, Camilla strengthened her role as Charles's 'wife' at Highgrove. Publicly, she kept a low profile. As Mark Bolland handed over his role as Charles's private secretary to Sir Michael Peat, he admitted Operation PB had been a success, saying: 'There is no reason why Charles should not be able to marry Camilla.'

Privately, Camilla's relationship with William and Harry entered a new phase. She saw the boys regularly, even visiting Prince William at St Andrew's University. Harry, who still faced teasing from his friends over his father's mistress, was a harder nut to crack. Camilla went out of her way to befriend the troubled teen.

One friend said: 'Harry was much younger when Diana died and he had great difficulty in accepting Camilla as a future stepmother. But she slowly began to win him over. She arranged private teas and luncheons with him, and Harry's attitude began to soften. He saw how happy Camilla made his father and that her love for him was unswerving.'

The death of the Queen Mother in March 2002 at the age of 101 was a hugely significant event in paving the way for a Charles and Camilla wedding. The Queen Mother, the only member of the royal family to remember the 1936 abdication crisis of Edward and Mrs Simpson, was always adamantly opposed to Charles remarrying. 'It could spur another crisis,' she warned her grandson. With her passing, another barrier fell. Charles announced his intentions to move into the Queen Mother's old residence in London, Clarence House. Camilla was put in charge of the extensive £10.5 million refurbishment of the mansion.

In May 2002, Camilla attended an international conference on osteoporosis in Lisbon, where she made her first public speech. It was a polished performance. The following month, she attended a dinner at Buckingham Palace. For the first time, she sat directly beside the Monarch.

'The Queen turned to talk to Camilla,' described one witness. 'It was a clear signal that she had been fully accepted into the family. That night Camilla was normal and natural. She appeared completely relaxed in the company of the Queen. It was clear Camilla's rehabilitation was almost complete. She acted – and was viewed – that night as Charles's consort, rather than his mistress.'

Sir Michael Peat's role in the formalising of Camilla's relationship was vital. A dignified man in his mid-50s, Sir Michael went to Eton and Trinity College, Oxford, and spent 20 years in his family's accountancy firm KPMG before being approached by the Palace initially to take charge of the Queen's £20 million annual domestic budget. He was brilliant at his job, axing the royal train and halving the household's annual spending. He even persuaded Prince Philip to start turning off lights when he left rooms. Philip was heard to complain: 'He'll have me using cheap OAP tickets next.'

But the Queen was impressed. When Bolland left his job as Charles's private secretary, Peat was a natural choice as replacement. His first task was to review Charles's spending. Shortly after the conclusion of Sir Michael's 105-page report, Charles's favourite servant, Michael Fawcett resigned.

But supporters like MP Nicholas Soames, one of Charles's oldest friends says: 'The way Sir Michael has helped to move the royal household on is a credit to him and he has done much to scotch all the talk about the demise of the monarchy. Both Prince Charles and the Queen are thoroughly impressed by him.'

In July 2002, Camilla undertook her first formal royal engagement at the royal garden party at Holyrood Palace in Edinburgh. Prince William stood by her side as Camilla greeted guests. A month later, she was by her lover's side at the Highland Games close to the Castle of Mey in Scotland. Camilla's image was undergoing a rapid transformation. In her new role as Charles's consort, the smelly tweeds and dirty Wellington boots of the past were replaced with stylish outfits by her favourite designers like Antony Price, Robinson Valentine, Paddy Campbell and royal milliner Philip Treacy. She had her hair cut and tinted at the Mayfair studio of hairdresser Jo Hansford.

Prince Charles began to pay for Camilla's first full-time staff, including the husband and wife bodyguard team of Reg Spinney and Sheilagh Muston, a private secretary Amanda MacManus and personal assistant Joy Camm.

'The reasoning behind Operation PB was "slowly,

slowly"' said one source. 'Over the course of 2002 and 2003, Camilla's "coming out" was put on to a more formal footing. That Christmas, she joined Charles for a private celebration. She was still not permitted to attend the royal family's formal Christmas celebrations at Sandringham on the day itself, but she was there throughout the rest of the holiday.'

The year 2003 started poorly for the couple. First, Charles was rushed to hospital for surgery to treat a hernia injury. Camilla arrived at the hospital with him and spent the night by his bedside as he recovered from the minor surgery.

The couple then faced a backlash from the press and public over the cost of renovating the Queen Mother's old residence, Clarence House. The couple, who finally moved into the mansion in the summer of that year, was forced to issue a statement showing that the Prince had paid for Camilla's rooms – spending £ 2 million pounds of his own money.

Camilla and her father Major Shand, who also moved into Clarence House, were invited to attend a series of events to commemorate the 50th anniversary of the Queen's coronation, including the 'highlight' of the celebrations, a service of commemoration at Westminster Abbey. For the first time Camilla sat alongside other senior members of the royal family including Prince Philip, Princess Anne, Prince Andrew and the Earl and Countess of Wessex. A spokesman for the Queen confirmed: 'Mrs Parker Bowles was invited to the event at the personal request of Her Majesty.'

In June, Prince William celebrated his 21st birthday. Again, Camilla was invited to his party at the personal invitation of the Prince.

'William went out of his way that night to be seen laughing and joking with Camilla,' revealed one partygoer. 'She and Charles were by William's side for most of the evening, along with the Queen. They presented themselves as a happy and united family. I have never seen Camilla laugh so much.'

Yet despite the happiness, the dark clouds hovered. Princess Diana's former butler Paul Burrell released yet another tell-all book which included damning letters from Prince Philip to Diana, at the height of Charles and Diana's marriage difficulties: 'We never dreamed he might feel like leaving you for her,' wrote Prince Philip. 'I cannot imagine anyone in their right mind leaving you for Camilla. Such a prospect never even entered our heads.'

Yet, in another, Philip asked: 'Can you honestly look into your heart and say that Charles's relationship with Camilla had nothing to do with your behaviour towards him in your marriage?'

Other claims followed which caused Charles to be viewed as an object of ridicule. A servant painted Charles as a man obsessed with tiny details, saying that 'his daily breakfast tray has to contain a cup and saucer to the right with a silver spoon pointing outwards at an angle of 5 o'clock. Plates must be placed with the Prince of Wales crest pointing to 12 o'clock. Butter must come in three balls (no more) and be chilled. The royal toast is always in a silver rack, never on a plate.'

By the start of 2004, the long-awaited Scotland Yard inquest into the death of Diana was launched, with the findings expected to be published in the summer of 2005.

A source said: 'The inquest was vital to the future of Operation PB. Prince Charles knew the inquest had to absolve him from any blame in the crash. He was the one who personally pushed to have the inquest launched without any further delay.'

For the first time, Prince Charles also revealed his financial support of Camilla when he published his accounts. Sir Michael Peat said: 'This is the first time we have had the opportunity to outline his financial support of Mrs Parker Bowles. We never sought to hide it. Her staff have an office here to cope with the work that arises because of her connection with the Prince of Wales. There is sensitivity about public money and how it is used. Mrs Parker Bowles does not want anyone to suggest she is benefiting from public money.'

The 48-page accounts made fascinating reading. The Prince revealed an annual income of £16 million, largely made up from his income from the Duchy of Cornwall of £11.9 million. His expenditure totalled £14.5 million with just £4.4 million listed as tax and personal expenditure. The cost of 'running Camilla' was put at £300,000, twice what Charles spent on Princess Diana in the months before their divorce.

Charles would later reveal he gave Camilla a personal allowance of £130,000 a year to cover her living costs, paid quarterly by credit transfer from his bank account to hers. He also pays the £100,000 salaries for her two secretaries and provides her with two cars, an Audi estate and a Land Rover.

The Prince, anxious about Camilla's welfare should he die before her, also took out a £2 million-pound life-insurance policy of which Camilla was the sole beneficiary. A separate trust fund in her name provides her with an additional £150,000 a year.

One of her friends commented: 'Charles has always been more than generous to Camilla financially. Diana was always complaining he was a spendthrift, but with Camilla, he has always been very supportive. She has little money of her own and of course her expenditure has increased since her public role as his partner has grown. Once they are married, she will never have money worries again. As his widow, she will be entitled to a portion of his Duchy of Cornwall estate, which means she will get at least £5 million pounds on his death.'

By the end of 2004, Camilla's position in Charles's life was unassailable. The two were living together at Highgrove and Clarence House. William and Harry were fully supportive of the union. Public opinion polls showed more than 50 per cent of the British people now supported a marriage. The Church of England also backed a marriage. Camilla was set financially for life. Discussions over the marriage went into overdrive. The Queen and Sir Michael Peat, along with Charles and Camilla, held a series of meetings with top-ranking church leaders, politicians and courtiers to decide the timing of the announcement. Some wanted to wait until after the final inquest into Diana's death was announced in July 2005, but Charles was adamant the wedding would take place before then. The Queen supported her son. At 79, she was in robust health but feared a crisis if she were to die with Charles still unwed. 'That is a situation which cannot be allowed to happen,' she said.

Camilla's formal titles were worked out and the date of the wedding was set to fit in the royal engagement calendar. There was only one thing left to do – announce the plans to the world.

The Wedding

It was to be a small affair. Just 200 guests at a civil ceremony, followed by a blessing in St George's Chapel. After the flurry of headlines died down following the 10 February engagement announcement, Camilla was put in charge of the wedding plans. The gold bands the couple were to exchange were to be made from Cornish gold.

Of course, there were some last-minute – and very public – hitches. The original wedding announcement declared the marriage would take place in Windsor Castle, but a week later, red-faced Palace officials discovered that this would be impossible. An aide said: 'We discovered that registering the castle as a wedding venue meant we'd have had to make it readily available to ordinary couples and the Queen felt that would cause too much disruption in the castle.'

The couple switched their plans to the Guildhall, a red-brick building 400 yards away in Windsor High Street, used for local council meetings and other public gatherings. Coincidentally, the Guildhall was designed by Sir Christopher Wren, the architect of St Paul's Cathedral where Charles's glittering wedding to Diana took place.

While the wedding ceremony would not be televised, the blessing afterwards at the castle would be. Young designers Robinson Valentine would design a 'simple' dress, while royal milliner Philip Treacy would make Camilla's hat. Hairdresser Hugh Green of London-based Hugh and Stephen would attend to Camilla's locks. The couple revealed their intention to leave immediately afterwards for a ten-day honeymoon in Scotland.

For Camilla, the wedding marked the end of a long and turbulent journey. One of her friends said: 'She just wants a quiet wedding, with close family and friends. There will be none of the pomp and circumstance of Diana's wedding. Camilla is determined this will be a small, dignified affair, and then she and Charles will honeymoon at the Queen Mother's old estate at Birkhall in Scotland before Camilla formally steps out as his wife at official functions. Camilla has waited a long time for this moment. But she is someone who understands the sensitivity of not being seen to tarnish Diana's memory in the eyes of those who still think Diana was maligned.'

As a final gesture of appeasement, Diana's brother the Earl Spencer – who famously delivered the oratory lambasting the royal family at her funeral – would receive a wedding invitation, as would Diana's two sisters, Jane and Sarah. 'Camilla wanted to extend an olive branch to the Spencer family,' Camilla's friend went on to explain.

Even Diana's friends have admitted that the wedding was something she anticipated. One said: 'It is almost certain that Diana would have remarried by now. She made her peace with the Camilla and Charles situation long before she died. She knew Charles truly loved Camilla and she was even privately saying in the months before she died that she thought it was time for Charles to make an honest woman of Camilla. There was no bitterness at the end. Diana had moved on and she had accepted that Camilla was Charles's true love.'

And what of the future? For Camilla, being finally accepted as the wife of the man she has always loved has brought 'a sense of relief'. She and Charles are planning a formal trip to America, likely to take place in February 2006, where they will be guests of honour at a glittering gala hosted by President Bush.

A senior Foreign Office source said: 'In her new role as wife of the future King, Camilla can now be accepted as an equal. America has always been seen as traditional "Diana territory" but Camilla believes a successful royal tour of the States will help cement her in the world's eyes as the future Princess Consort.'

Friends say Camilla is 'happier than she has ever been in her life'. 'After all the years of turmoil and heartbreak, Camilla can finally rest easy,' said one. 'She has never wavered in her love and support of her Prince but, finally, she can come and take her rightful place at his side. She and Charles have never been happier or more in love. They are looking forward to growing old together. It truly is one of the greatest love stories of all times.'

It has been an extraordinary life and an extraordinary journey for Camilla Parker Bowles. From modest beginnings, Camilla became one of the most vilified women in the world because of her love for one man. The passage of time has served to soften her image until, finally, there were very few left who did not believe she and Charles should marry. Giddy with excitement, she confided in one friend: 'I cannot believe that we will finally be able to marry. Who would have thought it? I feel like the luckiest woman on earth.'

For Camilla, the wedding marks the end of the years of uncertainty. And it also promises a new beginning as the wife of the only man she has ever truly loved. As the bells ring out to celebrate the marriage of Camilla and Charles, the greatest love story of recent times will, finally, reach a conclusion.